CISA ®

Certified Information
Systems Auditor
Practice Exams

CISA®

Certified Information Systems Auditor Practice Exams

Peter H. Gregory

New York   Chicago   San Francisco
Athens   London   Madrid   Mexico City
Milan   New Delhi   Singapore   Sydney   Toronto

McGraw-Hill Education books are available at special quantity discounts to use as premiums and sales promotions, or for use in corporate training programs. To contact a representative, please visit the Contact Us pages at www.mhprofessional.com.

CISA® Certified Information Systems Auditor Practice Exams

1 2 3 4 5 6 7 8 9   LCR   24 23 22 21 20

ISBN   978-1-260-45984-5
MHID   1-260-45984-5

Sponsoring Editor Wendy Rinaldi	**Technical Editor** Bobby Rogers	**Composition** Cenveo Publisher Services
Editorial Supervisor Janet Walden	**Copy Editor** Bart Reed	**Illustration** Cenveo Publisher Services
Project Manager Anupriya Tyagi, Cenveo® Publisher Services	**Proofreader** Lisa McCoy	**Art Director, Cover** Jeff Weeks
Acquisitions Coordinator Emily Walters	**Production Supervisor** James Kussow	

To current and aspiring IT, security, and audit professionals who want to better understand the art and science of information systems auditing—in order to ensure effective protection of information systems and sensitive information. Increasing reliance on information systems for work and leisure calls for more of these professionals.

ABOUT THE AUTHOR

Peter H. Gregory, CISA, CISM, CRISC, CISSP, CIPM, CCISO, CCSK, PCI-QSA, is a 30-year career technologist and an executive director at Optiv Security, the world's leading security systems integrator (SSI). He has been developing and managing information security management programs since 2002 and has been leading the development and testing of secure IT environments since 1990. Also, Peter has spent many years as a software engineer and architect, systems engineer, network engineer, and security engineer. Throughout his career, he has written many articles, white papers, user manuals, processes, and procedures, and he has conducted numerous lectures, training classes, seminars, and university courses.

Peter is the author of more than 40 books about information security and technology, including *Solaris Security, CISSP Guide to Security Essentials, CISM Certified Information Security Manager All-In-One Exam Guide*, and *CISA Certified Information Systems Auditor All-In-One Exam Guide*. He has spoken at numerous industry conferences, including RSA, Interop, ISACA CACS, (ISC)² Congress, SecureWorld Expo, West Coast Security Forum, IP3, Society for Information Management, the Washington Technology Industry Association, the Victoria Privacy and Security Conference, and InfraGard.

Peter is an advisory board member at the University of Washington's certificate program in information security and risk management as well as the lead instructor (emeritus) and advisory board member for the University of Washington certificate program in cybersecurity. He is an advisory board member and instructor at the University of South Florida's Cybersecurity For Executives program, a former board member of the Washington State chapter of InfraGard, and a founding member of the Pacific CISO Forum. He is a 2008 graduate of the FBI Citizens Academy and a member of the FBI Citizens Academy Alumni Association.

Peter resides with his family in the Seattle, Washington, area and can be found at www.peterhgregory.com.

About the Technical Editor

Bobby E. Rogers is an information security engineer working as a contractor for Department of Defense agencies, helping to secure, certify, and accredit their information systems. His duties include information system security engineering, risk management, and certification and accreditation efforts. He retired after 21 years in the U.S. Air Force, serving as a network security engineer and instructor, and has secured networks all over the world. Bobby has a master's degree in information assurance (IA) and is pursuing a doctoral degree in cybersecurity from Capitol Technology University in Maryland. His many certifications include CISSP-ISSEP, CRISC, CEH, and MCSE: Security, as well as the CompTIA A+, CompTIA Network+, and CompTIA Security+ certifications. He is the author of *CRISC Certified in Risk and Information Systems Control All-In-One Exam Guide* (McGraw-Hill, 2016) and *CompTIA Mobility+ All-in-One Exam Guide* (McGraw-Hill, 2014). Bobby is also the technical editor for numerous books, including the eighth edition of *CISSP All-in-One Exam Guide* (McGraw-Hill, 2018).

CONTENTS AT A GLANCE

CONTENTS

ACKNOWLEDGMENTS

I am particularly grateful to Wendy Rinaldi for supporting the publication of this book. My readers, including current and future information systems auditors as well as auditees, deserve this resource.

Deepest thanks to Emily Walters for expertly managing this project, facilitating rapid turnaround, and ensuring I'm always getting the right tasks done at the right time.

I want to thank my colleague, Bobby Rogers, who took on the task of tech reviewing the manuscript. Bobby carefully and thoughtfully scrutinized the entire draft manuscript and made scores of valuable suggestions that have improved the book's quality and value for readers. Without Bobby's help, this book would be of considerably lower quality.

Many thanks to Janet Walden and Anupriya Tyagi for managing the editorial and production ends of the project and to Bart Reed for copyediting the book and further improving readability. Much appreciation to Cenveo Publisher Services for expertly laying out the pages.

Many thanks to my literary agent, Carole Jelen, for diligent assistance during this and other projects. Sincere thanks to Rebecca Steele, my business manager and publicist, for her long-term vision and for keeping me on track and my life in balance.

Despite having written more than 40 books, I have difficulty putting into words my gratitude for my wife Rebekah for tolerating my frequent absences (in the home office and away on business travel) while I developed the manuscript. This project could not have been completed without her loyal and unfailing support.

Writing a book is not a solo act but a team sport. Thank you, Wendy, for putting together a winning team yet again.

INTRODUCTION

Welcome to *CISA Certified Information Systems Auditor Practice Exams*.

Since you are reading this book, you're probably well-versed in the five CISA job practice areas and are refining your study through practicing taking exam questions. But if you are earlier in your journey and still accumulating knowledge and skill, I suggest you pick up a copy of the companion book, *CISA Certified Information Systems Auditor All-In-One Study Guide, Fourth Edition*. That book is filled with discussions, details, and real-life examples throughout the CISA domains and the world of professional auditing.

Let me make one thing clear: the CISA certification exam is difficult. The folks at ISACA do an outstanding job of developing certification exam questions for CISA—questions that rely on professional judgment and experience, not just questions that rely on your ability to memorize an incredible number of facts. The CISA certification does not rely on your ability to memorize a lot of stuff, but rather it's a reflection of years of audit and information security experience. No book can claim to be a substitute for that experience. I've taken the CISA exam myself (almost 20 years ago, and the CISM and others more recently), and like many who take exams for advanced certifications, I was not sure whether I had passed it or not. Back to ISACA for a moment: I've participated in their certification exam "item writing workshops" for the CRISC certification, so I can attest to the level of rigor and the attention to quality for every certification exam question. Long story short: if you are expecting that this book will make it "easy" for you to pass the CISA exam, let me influence you just a little bit: this book can make the very difficult task of passing the CISA exam easier for you, through practice answering difficult questions that are not unlike those you'll encounter in the actual exam.

Let me crush another myth if I may. Earning advanced certifications does not mean you will soon land that dream security or auditing job. Organizations are—for the most part—smart enough to know that someone with a single certification, or even an impressive list of them, is not necessarily *the right person* for a specific job. But what I can tell you is this: earning and maintaining advanced certifications such as CISA will open doors for you, provided you also work just as hard on your soft skills such as oral and written communications.

If you're still with me, then you are one of the more motivated CISA candidates who is focusing on an important milestone in your career. If you already have at least some security or audit experience, or have worked on a team where you've been observing IS auditors for a while, then this book can help you from the perspective of experiencing a long series of difficult security and audit brain-twisting questions.

Best of luck on your exam! And I hope that this proves to be one of those milestones that propels your career further along.

Purpose of This Book

Practice makes perfect. This adage applies to many things in life, and that includes those brutal security certification exams. For many of you, preparing for the big day includes answering practice exam questions. This book provides 450 practice questions throughout all of the CISA domains to help you feel more confident that you will pass the actual exam.

Rather than just tell you "correct" and "wrong!", I explain why the right answers are correct and why the wrong answers are incorrect. This feedback loop helps you add to your knowledge, even when you answer a practice exam question incorrectly. Operating in Practice Mode or Exam Mode, the web-based practice exam provides this feedback differently. Practice Mode provides chapter references and explanations, while Exam Mode is designed to closely resemble the actual certification exam (which does not tell you whether each question is correct or incorrect, or the reason).

How This Book Is Organized

Aside from this "front matter" section and Chapter 1, "Becoming a CISA," this book is organized into chapters that correspond to the five principal domains in the CISA job practice: Information System Auditing Process; Governance and Management of IT; Information Systems Acquisition, Development, and Implementation; Information Systems Operations and Business Resilience; and Protection of Information Assets. The number of study questions for each domain is in proportion to the weight of each domain on the certification exam.

In addition to the 300 exam questions in this book, there are another 150 exam questions found online. Instructions for accessing these web-based exam questions can be found in the appendix.

Becoming a CISA

This chapter discusses the following topics:

- What it means to be a CISA-certified professional
- Getting to know ISACA, its code of ethics, and its standards
- Undergoing the certification process
- Applying for the exam
- Maintaining your certification
- Getting the most from your CISA journey

Congratulations on choosing to become a Certified Information Systems Auditor (CISA). Whether you have worked for several years in the field of information systems auditing or have just recently been introduced to the world of controls, assurance, and security, don't underestimate the hard work and dedication required to obtain and maintain CISA certification. Although ambition and motivation are essential, the rewards of being CISA certified can far exceed the effort.

You probably never imagined you would find yourself working in the world of information system (IS) or information technology (IT) auditing or looking to obtain a professional auditing certification. Perhaps the increase in legislative or regulatory requirements for information system security led to your introduction to this field. Or possibly you noticed that CISA-related career options are increasing exponentially, and you have decided to get ahead of the curve. You aren't alone—consider the following quick facts:

- Since the inception of CISA certification in 1978, more than 140,000 professionals worldwide reached the same conclusion and have earned this well-respected certification.

- In 2009 and again in 2017, *SC Magazine* named CISA certification the winner of the Best Professional Certification Program, and in 2014 and 2019 it was a finalist for the same award.

- The "2016 Global Knowledge IT Skills and Salary Report" and a recent "IT Skills and Certifications Pay Index" (ITSCPI) from Foote Partners both show the CISA certification among the highest-paying IT certifications.

- The "2020 Robert Half Salary Guide" lists the CISA as one of the top certifications across all of technology.
- The Infosec Institute shows the CISA as one of the top seven IT certifications (ISACA's CISM is also on this list).
- *CIO Magazine* listed the CISA as one of the top-paying IT certifications (ISACA's CRISC and CISM were also on the list).

Welcome to the journey and the amazing opportunities that await you! I have put together this information to help you understand the commitment needed, prepare for the exam, and maintain your certification. Not only is it my wish that you prepare for and pass the exam with flying colors, but I also provide you with the information and resources to maintain your certification and to represent yourself and the professional world of IS auditing proudly with your new credentials.

ISACA (formerly known as the Information Systems Audit and Control Association) is a recognized leader in the areas of control, assurance, and IT governance. Formed in 1967, this nonprofit organization represents more than 140,000 professionals in more than 200 countries. ISACA administers several exam certifications, including the CISA, the Certified Information Security Manager (CISM), the Certified in Risk and Information Systems Control (CRISC), the Certified in the Governance of Enterprise IT (CGEIT), and the CSX Practitioner certifications. The certification program itself has been accredited by the American National Standards Institute (ANSI) under International Organization for Standardization and International Electrotechnical Commission standard ISO/IEC 17024:2012, which means that ISACA's procedures for accreditation meet international requirements for quality, continuous improvement, and accountability.

If you're new to ISACA, I recommend that you tour the organization's web site (www.isaca .org) and become familiar with the guides and resources available. Also, if you're near one of the 200-plus local ISACA chapters in more than 80 countries worldwide, consider taking part in the activities and even reaching out to the chapter board for information on local meetings, training days, conferences, or study sessions. You may be able to meet other IS auditors who can give you additional insight into the CISA certification and the audit profession.

Established in 1978, the CISA certification primarily focuses on audit, controls, assurance, and security. It certifies the individual's knowledge of testing and documenting IS controls and his or her ability to conduct formal IS audits. Organizations seek out qualified personnel for assistance with developing and maintaining robust control environments. A CISA-certified individual is a great candidate for this.

Through the phenomenon of digital transformation, organizations in every industry sector around the world are becoming increasingly reliant on information systems for daily business operations. Further, the upward trend in IT outsourcing in the form of Software-as-a-Service (SaaS), Platform-as-a-Service (PaaS), and Infrastructure-as-a-Service (IaaS) offerings means organizations are put in a position of having to trust those service providers that their SaaS, PaaS, and IaaS platforms are secure. This reliance compels organizations to rely heavily on IS auditors to provide assurances that IT environments have the necessary security, integrity, and resilience that today's organizations require.

Benefits of CISA Certification

Obtaining the CISA certification offers several significant benefits:

- **Expands knowledge and skills, builds confidence** Developing knowledge and skills in the areas of audit, controls, assurance, and security can prepare you for advancement or expand your scope of responsibilities. The personal and professional achievement can boost confidence, which encourages you to move forward and seek new career opportunities.

- **Increases marketability and career options** Because of various legal and regulatory requirements, such as the Health Insurance Portability and Accountability Act (HIPAA), the Payment Card Industry Data Security Standard (PCI-DSS), Sarbanes-Oxley (SOX), the Gramm-Leach-Bliley Act (GLBA), the Food and Drug Administration (FDA), the Federal Energy Regulatory Commission/North American Electric Reliability Corporation (FERC/NERC), the European General Data Protection Regulation (GDPR), and the California Consumer Privacy Act (CCPA), along with the growing need for information systems and automation, controls, assurance, and audit experience, demand is growing for individuals with experience in developing, documenting, and testing controls. Further, obtaining your CISA certification demonstrates to current and potential employers your willingness and commitment to improve your knowledge and skills in information systems auditing. Having a CISA can provide a competitive advantage and open up many doors of opportunity in various industries and countries.

- **Helps you meet other certification requirements** The Payment Card Industry Qualified Security Assessor (PCI-QSA) certification requires that all certificate holders have a current security audit certification, either CISA or ISO 27001 Lead Auditor.

- **Helps you meet employment requirements** Many government agencies and organizations, such as the United States Department of Defense (DoD), require CISA certifications for positions involving IS audit activities. DoD Directive 8140.01 (formerly DoD Directive 8570.01-M) mandates that those personnel performing information assurance activities within the agency are certified with a commercial accreditation approved by the DoD. The DoD has approved the ANSI-accredited CISA certificate program because it meets ISO/IEC 17024:2012 requirements. All Information Assurance Technical (IAT) Level III personnel are mandated to obtain CISA certification, as are those who are contracted to perform similar activities.

- **Builds customer confidence and international credibility** Prospective customers needing control or audit work will have faith that the quality of the audits and controls documented or tested are in line with internationally recognized standards.

Regardless of your current position, demonstrating knowledge and experience in the areas of IT controls, audit, assurance, and security can expand your career options. The certification does not limit you to auditing; it can provide additional value and insight to those in or seeking the following positions:

- Executives such as chief executive officers (CEOs), chief financial officers (CFOs), and chief information officers (CIOs)
- Chief audit executives, audit partners, and audit directors
- Security and IT operations executives (chief technology officers [CTOs], chief information security officers [CISOs], chief information risk officers [CIROs], chief security officers [CSOs]), directors, managers, and staff
- Compliance executives and management
- Security and audit consultants
- Audit committee members

The CISA Certification Process

To become a CISA, you are required to pay the exam fee, pass the exam, prove that you have the required experience and education, and agree to uphold ethics and standards. To keep your CISA certification, you are required to take at least 20 continuing education hours each year (120 hours in three years) and pay annual maintenance fees. This is depicted in Figure 1-1.

The following list outlines the primary requirements for becoming certified:

- **Experience** A CISA candidate must be able to submit verifiable evidence of at least five years' experience, with a minimum of two years' professional work experience in IS auditing, control, assurance, or security. Experience can be in any of the job content areas, but it must be verified. For those with less than five years' experience, substitution and waiver options for up to three years' experience are available.

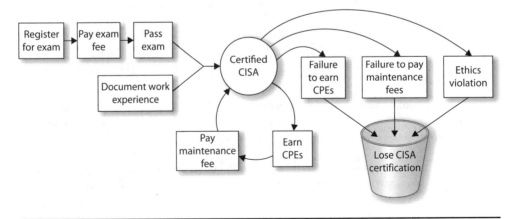

Figure 1-1 The CISA certification life cycle

- **Ethics**   Candidates must commit to adhere to ISACA's Code of Professional Ethics, which guides the personal and professional conduct of those certified.

- **Standards**   Those certified agree to abide by IS auditing standards and minimum guidelines for performing IS audits.

- **Exam**   Candidates must receive a passing score on the CISA exam. A passing score is valid for up to five years, after which the score is void. This means that a CISA candidate who passes the exam has a *maximum* of five years to apply for CISA certification; candidates who pass the exam but fail to act after five years will have to retake the exam if they want to become CISA certified.

- **Application**   After successfully passing the exam, meeting the experience requirements, and having read through ISACA's Code of Professional Ethics and Information Systems Auditing Standards, a candidate is ready to apply for certification. An application must be received within five years of passing the exam.

- **Education**   Those certified must adhere to the CISA Continuing Education Policy, which requires a minimum of 20 continuing professional education (CPE) hours each year, with a total requirement of 120 CPEs over the course of the certification period (three years).

Experience Requirements

To qualify for CISA certification, you must have completed the equivalent of five years' total work experience. These five years can take many forms, with several substitutions available. Additional details on the minimum certification requirements, substitution options, and various examples are discussed next.

 NOTE   Although it is not recommended, a CISA candidate can take the exam before completing any work experience directly related to IS auditing. As long as the candidate passes the exam and the work experience requirements are fulfilled within five years of the exam date, and within ten years from application for certification, the candidate is eligible for certification.

Direct Work Experience

As of this book's printing, you are required to have a minimum of five years' work experience in the field of IS audit, controls, or security. This is equivalent to approximately 10,000 actual work hours, which must be related to one or more of the five following CISA job practice areas:

- **Information Systems Auditing Process**   Planning and conducting information systems audits in accordance with IS standards and best practices, communicating results, and advising on risk management and control practices.

- **Governance and Management of IT**   Ensuring that adequate organizational structures and processes are in place to align and support the organization's strategies and objectives.

- **Information Systems Acquisition, Development, and Implementation**   Ensuring that appropriate processes and controls are in place for the acquisition, development, testing, and implementation of information systems in order to provide reasonable assurance that the organization's strategies and objectives will be met.

- **Information Systems Operations and Business Resilience**   Ensuring that systems and infrastructure have appropriate operations, maintenance, and service management processes and controls in place to support meeting the organization's strategies and objectives.

- **Protection of Information Assets**   Ensuring that the organization's security policies, standards, procedures, and controls protect the confidentiality, integrity, and availability of information assets.

All work experience must be completed within the ten-year period before completing the certification application or within five years from the date of initially passing the CISA exam. You will need to complete a separate Verification of Work Experience form for each segment of experience.

There is only one exception to this minimum two-year direct work experience requirement: if you are a full-time instructor. This option is discussed in the next section.

Substitution of Experience

Up to a maximum of three years' direct work experience can be substituted with the following to meet the five-year experience requirement:

- One year of information systems or one year of non-IS auditing experience can be substituted for up to one year of direct work experience.

- Completion of a two- or four-year degree (60 to 120 completed university semester credit hours), regardless of when completed, can be substituted for one or two years of direct work experience, respectively. Transcripts or a letter confirming degree status must be sent from the university attended to obtain the experience waiver.

- If you have completed a bachelor's or master's degree from a university that enforces an ISACA-sponsored curriculum, it can be substituted for one or two years of direct work experience, respectively (for information on ISACA-sponsored Model Curricula and participating universities, see www.isaca.org/modeluniversities). Transcripts or a letter confirming degree status must be sent from the university to obtain an experience waiver. This option cannot be used if you have already substituted or waived three years of direct work experience.

- Association of Chartered Certified Accountants (ACCA) members and Chartered Institute of Management Accountants (CIMA) members with full certification can apply for a two-year educational waiver.

- Those applying with a master's degree in information systems or information technology (IT) from an accredited university can apply for a one-year experience waiver.

As noted, there is only one exception to the experience requirements. Should you have experience as a full-time university instructor in a related field (that is, information security, computer science, or accounting), each two years of your experience can be substituted for one year of required direct work experience, without limitation.

Here is an example CISA candidate whose experience and education are considered for CISA certification:

Jane Doe graduated in 2004 with a bachelor's degree in accounting. She spent five years working for an accounting firm conducting non-IS audits, and in January 2009, she began conducting IS audits full time. In January 2011, she took some time off work for personal reasons. She rejoined the workforce in December 2017, working for a public company in its internal audit department, documenting and testing financial controls. Jane passed the CISA exam in June 2018 and applied for CISA certification in January 2019. Does Jane have all of the experience required? What evidence will she need to submit?

- **Two-year substitution** Jane obtained a bachelor's degree in accounting, which equates to two years' experience substitution.

- **Two years' direct experience** She can count her two full years of IS audit experience (in 2009 and 2010).

- **One-year substitution** She cannot take into account one year of non-IS audit experience completed between January 2008 to January 2009, as it was not completed within ten years of application.

- **One-year substitution** Jane would want to utilize her new internal audit financial controls experience for experience substitution rather than her earlier non-IS audit experience.

Jane would need to send the following with her application to prove experience requirements are met:

- Verification of Work Experience forms filled out and signed by her supervisors (or any superior) at the accounting firm, verifying both the IS and non-IS audit work conducted.

- Transcripts or letter confirming degree status sent from the university.

 NOTE I recommend you also read the CISA certification qualifications on the ISACA web site. From time to time, ISACA changes the qualification rules, and I want you to have the most up-to-date information available.

ISACA Code of Professional Ethics

Becoming a CISA means that you agree to adhere to the ISACA Code of Professional Ethics, a formal document outlining those things you will do to ensure the utmost integrity and that best support and represent the organization and certification.

The ISACA Code of Professional Ethics requires ISACA members and certification holders to do the following (taken directly from www.isaca.org/Certification/Code-of-Professional-Ethics/Pages/default.aspx):

1. Support the implementation of, and encourage compliance with, appropriate standards and procedures for the effective governance and management of enterprise information systems and technology, including audit, control, security and risk management.

2. Perform their duties with objectivity, due diligence and professional care, in accordance with professional standards.

3. Serve in the interest of stakeholders in a lawful manner, while maintaining high standards of conduct and character, and not discrediting their profession or the Association.

4. Maintain the privacy and confidentiality of information obtained in the course of their activities unless disclosure is required by legal authority. Such information shall not be used for personal benefit or released to inappropriate parties.

5. Maintain competency in their respective fields and agree to undertake only those activities they can reasonably expect to complete with the necessary skills, knowledge and competence.

6. Inform appropriate parties of the results of work performed including the disclosure of all significant facts known to them that, if not disclosed, may distort the reporting of the results.

7. Support the professional education of stakeholders in enhancing their understanding of the governance and management of enterprise information systems and technology, including audit, control, security and risk management.

Failure to follow the Code of Professional Ethics can result in an investigation of the person's actions; potential disciplinary measures range from a written warning to the loss of certification and/or membership.

You'll find the full text and terms of enforcement of the ISACA Code of Professional Ethics at www.isaca.org/ethics.

ISACA IS Standards

An auditor can gather information from several credible resources to conduct an audit with integrity and confidence. ISACA has developed its own set of standards of mandatory requirements for IS auditing and reporting, known as the ITAF: Information Technology Assurance Framework.

ITAF offers multiple levels of IS audit and assurance guidance: standards, guidelines, and tools and techniques. Standards are higher-level *mandatory* requirements that inform IS audit and assurance professionals of minimal performance expectations. Guidelines provide additional guidance in applying the standards, while tools and techniques provide examples of procedures that audit and assurance professionals may follow.

As a CISA, you are required to abide by and promote the IS standards where applicable, encouraging compliance, and supporting their implementation. As you prepare for certification and beyond, you will need to read through and become familiar with these standards. These standards were created to define the minimum level of acceptable performance necessary to meet the professional requirements as defined by ISACA and to help set expectations. They have been established, vetted, and approved by ISACA.

For more about ITAF, visit www.isaca.org/itaf.

 NOTE I recommend that you check the ISACA web site periodically for updates to these standards. As an ISACA member, you will automatically be notified when changes have been submitted and the documents are open for review (www.isaca.org/standards).

The Certification Exam

The certification exam is offered almost continuously throughout the year in periods known as *testing windows* that are generally several months in length. The ISACA web site will have information about current testing windows and sometimes about future testing windows. When you begin planning for your CISA examination, you'll want to consult the ISACA web site to see what scheduling options are available in your testing window. Other terms and conditions change from time to time, from one testing window to the next.

Here is the schedule of exam fees in U.S. dollars for 2019:

- CISA application fee: $50
- Regular registration: $575 member/$760 nonmember

The exam is administered by an ISACA-approved testing vendor, PSI Services, at numerous locations. For additional details on the locations nearest you, go to www.isaca.org/examlocations.

Once registration is complete, you will immediately receive an e-mail acknowledging your registration. Within four weeks of processing, you will receive a hard copy of the letter and a registration receipt in the mail. Two to three weeks before the test date, you will receive an exam admission letter via e-mail and regular mail. You will need the admission letter to enter the test site—be sure to keep it unmarked and in a safe place until test time.

Each registrant has four hours to take the multiple-choice-question exam. There are 150 questions on the computerized exam representing the five job practice areas. Each question has four answer choices; test-takers can select only one best answer by clicking it. You will be scored for each job practice area and then provided one final score. Before you close out the computerized exam, you will be notified of your tentative pass/fail status. All exam scores are scaled. Scores range from 200 to 800; however, a final score of 450 is required to pass.

Exam questions are derived from a job practice analysis study conducted by ISACA. The areas selected represent those tasks performed in a CISA's day-to-day activities and represent the background knowledge required to perform IS audit, control, assurance, and security tasks. More detailed descriptions of the task and knowledge statements can be found at www.isaca.org/cisajobpractice.

The CISA exam is quite broad in its scope. The exam covers five job practice areas, as shown in Table 1-1.

Domain	CISA Job Practice Area	Percentage of Exam
1	Information Systems Auditing Process	21
2	Governance and Management of IT	17
3	Information Systems Acquisition, Development, and Implementation	12
4	Information Systems Operations and Business Resilience	23
5	Protection of Information Assets	27

Table 1-1 CISA Exam Practice Areas

Independent committees have been developed to determine the best questions, review exam results, and statistically analyze the results for continuous improvement. Should you come across a horrifically difficult or strange question, do not panic. This question may have been written for another purpose. A few questions on the exam are included for research and analysis purposes and will not be counted against your score.

Exam Preparation

The CISA certification requires a great deal of knowledge and experience from the CISA candidate. You need to map out a long-term study strategy to pass the exam. The following sections offer some tips and are intended to help guide you to, through, and beyond exam day.

Before the Exam

Consider the following list of tips on tasks and resources for exam preparation. They are listed in sequential order.

- **Read the ISACA Exam Candidate Information Guide**   For information on the certification exam and requirements for the current year, see www.isaca.org/Certification/Pages/Candidates-Guide-for-Exams.aspx. Be sure to download the correct (usually the most recent) version of the guide.

- **Register**   Register to solidify your commitment to moving forward with this professional achievement.

- **Become familiar with the CISA job practice areas**   The job practice areas serve as the basis for the exam and requirements. Beginning with the June 2019 exam, the job practice areas have changed. Ensure that your study materials align with the current list at www.isaca.org/cisajobpractice. This book, and the companion book, *CISA Certified Information Systems Auditor All-In-One Exam Guide, Fourth Edition*, are aligned to the new 2019 CISA job practice areas.

- **Self-assess**   Work through the questions in this book and online. You may also go to the ISACA web site for a free 50-question CISA self-assessment.

- **Iterative study**   Depending on how much work experience in IS auditing you have already, I suggest you plan your study program to take at least two months but as long as six months. During this time, periodically take practice exams and note your areas of strength and weakness. Once you have identified your weak areas, focus on those areas weekly by rereading the related sections in this book and retaking practice exams, and note your progress.

- **Avoid cramming**   We've all seen the books on the shelves with titles that involve last-minute cramming. Just one look on the Internet reveals a variety of web sites that cater to teaching individuals how to cram for exams most effectively. There are also research sites claiming that exam cramming can lead to susceptibility to colds and flu, sleep disruptions, overeating, and digestive problems. One thing is certain: many people find that good, steady study habits result in less stress and greater clarity and focus during the exam. Because of the complexity of this exam, I highly recommend the long-term, steady-study option. Study the job practice areas thoroughly. There are many study options. If time permits, investigate the many resources available to you.

- **Find a study group**   Many ISACA chapters have formed specific study groups or offer less expensive exam review courses. Contact your local chapter to see if these options are available to you. Also be sure to keep your eye on the ISACA web site and your local chapter's web site.

- **Admission letter**   Approximately two to three weeks before the exam, you will receive your admission letter. Do not write on or lose this letter. Put it in a safe place, and take note of what time you will need to arrive at the site. Note this on your calendar.

- **Logistics check**   Check the Candidate Information Guide and your admission letter for the exact time you are required to report to the test site. Check the site a few days before the exam—become familiar with the location and tricks to getting there. If you are taking public transportation, be sure that you are looking at the schedule for the day of the exam. If you are driving, know the route and know where to park your vehicle.

- **Pack**   Place your admissions letter and a photo ID in a safe place, ready to go. Your ID must be a current, government-issued photo ID that matches the name on the admission letter and must not be handwritten. Examples of acceptable forms of ID are passports, driver's licenses, state IDs, green cards, and national IDs. Make sure you leave food, drinks, laptops, cell phones, and other electronic devices behind, as they are not permitted at the test site. For information on what can and cannot be brought to the exam site, see www.isaca.org/cisabelongings.

- **Notification decision**   Decide whether you want your exam results e-mailed to you. You will have the opportunity to consent to e-mail notification of the exam results. If you are fully paid (zero balance on exam fee) and have consented to the e-mail notification, you should receive a single e-mail a few weeks from the date of the exam with your exam results.

- **Sleep**   Get a sound night's sleep before the exam. Research suggests that you should avoid caffeine at least four hours before bedtime, keep a notepad and pen next to the bed to capture late-night thoughts that might keep you awake, eliminate as much noise and light as possible, and keep your room a good temperature for sleeping. In the morning, arise early so as not to rush and subject yourself to additional stress.

Day of the Exam

Consider the following list of tips that can help you on exam day:

- **Arrive early**   Check the Candidate Information Guide and your admission letter for the exact time you are required to report to the test site. The letter and the Candidate Information Guide explain that you must be at the test site *no later* than approximately 30 minutes *before* testing time. If you are late, you may miss your opportunity to take the exam on that day, and you'll have to reschedule your exam.

- **Observe test center rules**   There may be rules about taking breaks. This will be discussed by the examiner along with exam instructions. If at any time during the exam you need something and are unsure as to the rules, be sure to ask first. For information on conduct during the exam, see www.isaca.org/cisabelongings.

- **Answering exam questions**   Read questions carefully, but do not try to overanalyze. Remember to select the *best* solution. There may be several reasonable answers, but one is *better* than the others.

After the Exam

Although you'll be shown your preliminary pass/fail results when you have completed and closed your exam, you will receive your official exam results by e-mail or regular mail within a few weeks from the date of the exam. Each job practice area score will be noted in addition to the overall final score. Should you receive a passing score, you will also receive the application for certification.

Those unsuccessful in passing will also be notified. These individuals will want to take a close look at the job practice area scores to determine areas for further study. They may retake the exam as many times as needed on future exam dates, as long as they have registered and paid the applicable fees. Regardless of pass or fail, exam results will not be disclosed via telephone, fax, or e-mail (with the exception of the consented one-time e-mail notification).

CAUTION   You are not yet permitted to use the CISA moniker after passing the exam. You must first apply for CISA certification, which is described in the next section.

Applying for CISA Certification

To apply for certification, you must be able to submit evidence of a passing score and related work experience. Keep in mind that once you receive a passing score, you have five years to use this score on a CISA application. After this time, you will need to retake the exam. Also, all work experience submitted must have been within ten years of your new certification application.

To complete the application process, you need to submit the following information:

- **CISA application**   Note the exam ID number located in your exam results letter; list the information systems audit, control, security experience, and/or any experience substitutions; and identify which ISACA job practice area(s) the experience pertains to.
- **Verification of Work Experience form(s)**   These must be filled out and signed by your immediate supervisor or a person of higher rank in the organization to verify work experience noted on the application. You must fill out a complete set of Work Experience forms for each separate employer.
- **Transcript or letter**   If you are using an educational experience waiver, you must submit an original transcript or a letter from the college or university confirming degree status.

As with the exam, after you've successfully mailed the application, you must wait approximately eight weeks for processing. If your application is approved, you will receive a package in the mail containing your letter of certification, a certificate, and a copy of the Continuing Education Policy. You can then proudly display your certificate and use the designation ("CISA") on your CV, résumé, e-mail profile, or business cards.

Retaining Your CISA Certification

There is more to becoming a CISA than merely passing an exam, submitting an application, and receiving a paper certificate. Being a CISA is an ongoing lifestyle. Those with the CISA certification not only agree to abide by the ISACA Code of Professional Ethics and adhere to the IS standards, but they must also meet ongoing education requirements and pay certification maintenance fees. I describe the continuing education requirements, maintenance fees, and revocation of your certification in the companion book, *CISA Certified Information Systems Auditor All-In-One Exam Guide, Fourth Edition.* You can also get this information from ISACA at www.isaca.org.

CISA Exam Preparation Pointers

Following are a few general pointers for exam prep:

- Register for the exam early to ensure that you can take the exam at a location and date of your choosing.
- When studying for the exam, take as many practice exams as possible.
- Memorization will not work—for this exam, you must understand the concepts.
- If you have time while studying for the exam, begin gathering relevant Work Experience Verification forms from past employers and original transcripts from your college or university (if using the education experience waiver).

- Do not arrive late to the exam site. Latecomers are immediately disqualified, and they forfeit exam fees.

- Begin keeping track of CPEs as soon as you obtain certification.

- Mark your calendar for CPE renewal time, which begins in October/November each year and ends January 15. Don't wait for the e-mail; set your own reminder.

- Become familiar with the ISACA Code of Professional Ethics and IS standards.

- Become involved in your local ISACA chapter for networking and educational opportunities.

Summary

Becoming and being a CISA is a lifestyle, not just a one-time event. It takes motivation, skill, good judgment, and proficiency to be a strong leader in the world of information systems auditing. The CISA was designed to help you navigate the IS auditing world with greater ease and confidence.

This book will help you study for the exam in the form of answering practice questions that are similar to the actual certification exam questions. If you find that you're consistently getting low scores in any of the CISA practice areas, you'll want to pick up a copy of the companion book, *CISA Certified Information Systems Auditor All-In-One Exam Guide, Fourth Edition.*

CHAPTER 2

IT Governance and Management

This chapter covers CISA Domain 2, "Governance and Management of IT," and includes questions from the following topics:

- Business alignment
- Security strategy development
- Security governance
- Information security strategy development
- Resources needed to develop and execute a security strategy
- Information security metrics

The topics in this chapter represent 17 percent of the CISA examination.

ISACA defines this domain as follows: "Establish and/or maintain an information security governance framework and supporting processes to ensure that the information security strategy is aligned with organizational goals and objectives."

When properly implemented, security governance is management's visibility of, and control of, the entire information security management system. Governance is a process whereby senior management exerts strategic control over business functions through policies, objectives, delegation of authority, and monitoring. Governance is management's oversight for all other business processes to ensure that business processes continue to effectively meet the organization's business vision and objectives.

Organizations usually establish governance through a steering committee that is responsible for setting long-term business strategy and by making changes to ensure that business processes continue to support business strategy and the organization's overall needs. This is accomplished through the development and enforcement of documented policies, standards, requirements, and various reporting metrics.

1. Management's control of information technology processes is best described as:

   A. Information technology policies

   B. Information technology policies along with audits of those policies

   C. Information technology governance

   D. Metrics as compared to similar organizations

2. What is the best method for ensuring that an organization's IT department achieves adequate business alignment?

   A. Find and read the organization's articles of incorporation.

   B. Understand the organization's vision, mission statement, and objectives.

   C. Determine who the CIO reports to in the organization.

   D. Study the organization's application portfolio.

3. Roberta has located her organization's mission statement and a list of strategic objectives. What steps should Roberta take to ensure that the IT department aligns with the business?

   A. Discuss strategic objectives with business leaders to better understand what they wish to accomplish and what steps are being taken to achieve them.

   B. Develop a list of activities that will support the organization's strategic objectives, and determine the cost of each.

   C. Select those controls from the organization's control framework that align to each objective, and then ensure that those controls are effective.

   D. Select the policies from the organization's information security policy that are relevant to each objective, and ensure that those policies are current.

4. Michael wants to improve the risk management process in his organization by creating content that will help management understand when certain risks should be accepted and when certain risks should be mitigated. The policy that Michael needs to create is known as:

   A. A security policy

   B. A control framework

   C. A risk appetite statement

   D. A control testing procedure

5. In a typical risk management process, the best person(s) to make a risk treatment decision is:

   A. The chief risk officer (CRO)

   B. The chief information officer (CIO)

   C. The department head associated with the risk

   D. The chief information security officer (CISO)

6. The ultimate responsibility for an organization's cybersecurity program lies with:

   A. The board of directors

   B. The chief executive officer (CEO)

   C. The chief information officer (CIO)

   D. The chief information security officer (CISO)

7. In a U.S. public company, a CIO will generally report the state of the organization's IT function to:

   A. The Treadway Commission

   B. Independent auditors

   C. The U.S. Securities and Exchange Commission

   D. The board of directors

8. A new CIO in an organization is building its formal IT department from the ground up. In order to ensure collaboration among business leaders and department heads in the organization, the CIO should form and manage:

   A. A technology committee of the board of directors

   B. An IT steering committee

   C. An audit committee of the board of directors

   D. A business-aligned IT policy

9. The best person or group to make risk treatment decisions is:

   A. The chief information security officer (CISO)

   B. The audit committee of the board of directors

   C. The cybersecurity steering committee

   D. External auditors

10. Which is the best party to conduct access reviews?

    A. Users' managers

    B. Information security manager

    C. IT service desk

    D. Department head

11. Which is the best party to make decisions about the configuration and function of business applications?

    A. Business department head

    B. IT business analyst

    C. Application developer

    D. End user

12. Which of the following is the best definition of custodial responsibility?

   A. The custodian protects assets based on the customer's defined interests.

   B. The custodian protects assets based on its own defined interests.

   C. The custodian makes decisions based on its own defined interests.

   D. The custodian makes decisions based on the customer's defined interests.

13. What is the primary risk of IT acting as custodian for a business owner?

   A. IT may not have enough interest to provide quality care for business applications.

   B. IT may not have sufficient staffing to properly care for business applications.

   C. IT may have insufficient knowledge of business operations to make good decisions.

   D. Business departments might not give IT sufficient access to properly manage applications.

14. An organization needs to hire an executive who will build a management program that considers threats and vulnerabilities. The best job title for this position is:

   A. CSO

   B. CRO

   C. CISO

   D. CIRO

15. An organization needs to hire an executive who will be responsible for ensuring that the organization's policies, business processes, and information systems are compliant with laws and regulations concerning the proper collection, use, and protection of personally identifiable information. What is the best job title for the organization to use for this position?

   A. CSO

   B. CIRO

   C. CISO

   D. CPO

16. The Big Data Company is adjusting several position titles in its IT department to reflect industry standards. Included in the consideration are two individuals: The first is responsible for the overall relationships and data flows among the company's internal and external information systems. The second is responsible for the overall health and management of systems containing information. Which two job titles are most appropriate for these two roles?

   A. Systems architect and database administrator

   B. Data architect and data scientist

   C. Data scientist and database administrator

   D. Data architect and database administrator

17. What is the primary distinction between a network engineer and a telecom engineer?

    A. A network engineer is primarily involved with networks and internal network media, whereas a telecom engineer is primarily involved with networks and external (carrier) network media.

    B. A network engineer is primarily involved with networks and external (carrier) network media, whereas a telecom engineer is primarily involved with networks and internal network media.

    C. A network engineer is primarily involved with layer 3 protocols and above, whereas a telecom engineer is primarily involved with layer 1 and layer 2 protocols.

    D. There is no distinction, as both are involved in all aspects of an organization's networks.

18. An organization that is a U.S. public company is redesigning its access management and access review controls. What is the best role for Internal Audit in this redesign effort?

    A. Develop procedures.

    B. Design controls.

    C. Provide feedback on control design.

    D. Develop controls and procedures.

19. A security operations manager is proposing that engineers who design and manage information systems play a role in the monitoring of those systems. Is design and management compatible with monitoring? Why or why not?

    A. No. Personnel who design and manage systems should not perform a monitoring role, as this is a conflict of interest.

    B. Yes. Personnel who design and manage systems will be more familiar with the steps to take, as well as the reasons to take them, when alerts are generated.

    C. No. Personnel who design and manage systems will not be familiar with response procedures when alerts are generated.

    D. No. Personnel who design and manage systems are not permitted access to production environments and should not perform monitoring.

20. The purpose of metrics in an IT department is to:

    A. Measure the performance and effectiveness of controls.

    B. Measure the likelihood of an attack on the organization.

    C. Predict the likelihood of an attack on an organization.

    D. Predict the next IT service outage.

21. Which security metric is best considered a leading indicator of an attack?

    A. Number of firewall rules triggered

    B. Number of security awareness training sessions completed

    C. Percentage of systems scanned

    D. Mean time to apply security patches

22. Steve, a CISO, has vulnerability management metrics and needs to build business-level metrics. Which of the following is the best business-level, leading indicator metric suitable for his organization's board of directors?

   A. Average time to patch servers supporting manufacturing processes

   B. Frequency of security scans of servers supporting manufacturing processes

   C. Percentage of servers supporting manufacturing processes that are scanned by vulnerability scanning tools

   D. Number of vulnerabilities remediated on servers supporting manufacturing processes

23. The metric "percentage of systems with completed installation of advanced anti-malware" is best described as:

   A. A key operational indicator (KOI)

   B. A key performance indicator (KPI)

   C. A key goal indicator (KGI)

   D. A key risk indicator (KRI)

24. A member of the board of directors has asked Ravila, a CIRO, to produce a metric showing the reduction of risk as a result of the organization making key improvements to its security information and event management system. Which type of metric is most suitable for this purpose?

   A. KGI

   B. RACI

   C. KRI

   D. ROSI

25. A common way to determine the effectiveness of IT metrics is the SMART method. SMART stands for:

   A. Security Metrics Are Risk Treatment

   B. Specific, Measurable, Attainable, Relevant, Timely

   C. Specific, Measurable, Actionable, Relevant, Timely

   D. Specific, Manageable, Actionable, Relevant, Timely

26. The statement "Complete migration of flagship system to latest version of vendor-supplied software" is an example of:

   A. A mission statement

   B. A vision statement

   C. A purpose statement

   D. An objective statement

27. Ernie, a CIO who manages a large IT team, wants to create a mission statement for the team. What is the best approach for creating this mission statement?

   A. Start with the organization's mission statement.

   B. Start with Ernie's most recent performance review.

   C. Start with the results of the most recent risk assessment.

   D. Start with the body of open items in the project portfolio.

28. Which of the following statements is the best description for the purpose of performing risk management?

   A. Identify and manage vulnerabilities that may permit security events to occur.

   B. Identify and manage threats that are relevant to the organization.

   C. Assess the risks associated with third-party service providers.

   D. Assess and manage risks associated with doing business online.

29. Key metrics showing the effectiveness of a risk management program would *not* include:

   A. Reduction in the number of security events

   B. Reduction in the impact of security events

   C. Reduction in the time to remediate vulnerabilities

   D. Reduction in the number of patches applied

30. Examples of security program performance metrics include all of the following *except*:

   A. Time to detect security incidents

   B. Time to remediate security incidents

   C. Time to perform security scans

   D. Time to discover vulnerabilities

31. Two similar-sized organizations are merging. Paul will be the CIO of the new, combined organization. What is the greatest risk that may occur as a result of the merger?

   A. Differences in practices that may not be understood

   B. Duplication of effort

   C. Gaps in coverage of key processes

   D. Higher tooling costs

32. The purpose of value delivery metrics is:

   A. Long-term reduction in costs

   B. Reduction in ROSI

   C. Increase in ROSI

   D. Increase in net profit

33. Joseph, a CIO, is collecting statistics on several operational areas and needs to find a standard way of measuring and publishing information about the effectiveness of his program. Which of the following is the best approach to follow?

    A. Scaled score

    B. NIST Cybersecurity Framework (CSF)

    C. Business Model for Information Security (BMIS)

    D. Balanced scorecard (BSC)

34. Which of the following is the best description of the Business Model for Information Security (BMIS)?

    A. Describes the relationships (as dynamic interconnections) between policy, people, process, and technology.

    B. Describes the relationships (as dynamic interconnections) between people, process, technology, and the organization.

    C. Describes the primary elements (people, process, and technology) in an organization.

    D. Describes the dynamic interconnections (people, process, and technology) in an organization.

35. What is the correct name for the model shown here?

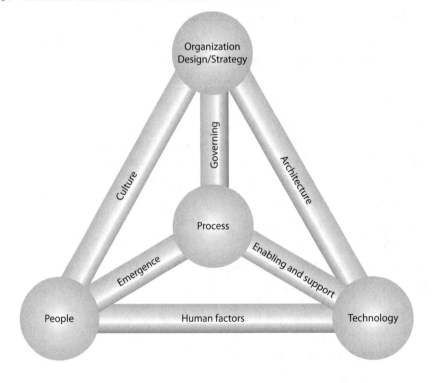

    A. COBIT Model for Information Technology

    B. COBIT Model for Information Security

    C. Business Model for Information Security

    D. Business Model for Information Technology

36. Jacqueline, an experienced CISO, is reading the findings in a recent risk assessment that describes deficiencies in the organization's vulnerability management process. How would Jacqueline use the Business Model for Information Security (BMIS) to analyze the deficiency?

    A. Identify the elements connected to the process DI.

    B. Identify the dynamic interconnections (DIs) connected to the process element.

    C. Identify the dynamic elements connected to human factors.

    D. Identify the dynamic elements connected to technology.

37. Which of the following would constitute an appropriate use of the Zachman enterprise framework?

    A. An IT service management model as an alternative to ITIL

    B. Identifying system components, followed by high-level design and business functions

    C. Development of business requirements translated top-down into technical architecture

    D. IT systems described at a high level and then in increasing levels of detail

38. An IT architect needs to document the flow of data from one system to another, including external systems operated by third-party service providers. What kind of documentation does the IT architect need to develop?

    A. Data flow diagrams (DFDs)

    B. Entity relationship diagrams (EFDs)

    C. A Zachman architecture framework

    D. Visio diagrams showing information systems and data flows

39. Carole is a CISO in a new organization with a fledgling security program. Carole needs to identify and develop mechanisms to ensure desired outcomes in selected business processes. What is a common term used to define these mechanisms?

    A. Checkpoints

    B. Detective controls

    C. Controls

    D. Preventive controls

40. What is the best approach to developing security controls in a new organization?

    A. Start with a standard control framework and make risk-based adjustments as needed.

    B. Start from scratch and develop controls based on risk as needed.

    C. Start with NIST CSF and move up to ISO 27001, then NIST 800-53 as the organization matures.

    D. Develop controls in response to an initial risk assessment.

41. Which of the following is the best description of the COBIT framework?

    A. A security process and controls framework that can be integrated with ITIL or ISO 20000.

    B. An IT controls and process framework, on which IT controls and processes can be added at an organization's discretion.

    C. An IT process framework with optional security processes when Extended COBIT is implemented.

    D. An IT process framework that includes security processes that are interspersed throughout the framework.

42. One distinct disadvantage of the ISO 27001 standard is:

    A. The standard is costly (over one hundred U.S. dollars per copy).

    B. The standard is costly (a few thousand U.S. dollars per copy).

    C. The standard is available only for use in the United States.

    D. The standard is suitable only in large organizations.

43. Which of the following statements about ISO 27001 is correct?

    A. ISO 27001 consists primarily of a framework of security controls, followed by an appendix of security requirements for running a security management program.

    B. ISO 27001 consists primarily of a body of requirements for running a security management program, along with an appendix of security controls.

    C. ISO 27001 consists of a framework of information security controls.

    D. ISO 27001 consists of a framework of requirements for running a security management program.

44. The U.S. law that regulates the protection of data related to medical care is:

    A. PIPEDA

    B. HIPAA

    C. GLBA

    D. GDPR

45. The regulation "Security and Privacy Controls for Federal Information Systems and Organizations" is better known as:

   A. ISO/IEC 27001

   B. ISO/IEC 27002

   C. NIST CSF

   D. NIST SP800-53

46. What is the best explanation for the Implementation Tiers in the NIST Cybersecurity Framework?

   A. Implementation Tiers are levels of risk as determined by the organization.

   B. Implementation Tiers are stages of implementation of controls in the framework.

   C. Implementation Tiers are likened to maturity levels.

   D. Implementation Tiers are levels of risk as determined by an external auditor or regulator.

47. Jeffrey is a CIO in an organization that performs financial services for private organizations as well as government agencies and U.S. federal agencies. Which is the best information security controls framework for this organization?

   A. CIS

   B. ISO 27001

   C. NIST CSF

   D. NIST 800-53

48. The scope of requirements of PCI-DSS is:

   A. All systems that store, process, and transmit credit card numbers, as well as all other systems that can communicate with these systems

   B. All systems that store, process, and transmit credit card numbers

   C. All systems that store, process, and transmit unencrypted credit card numbers

   D. All systems in an organization where credit card numbers are stored, processed, and transmitted

49. Which of the following statements is true about controls in the Payment Card Industry Data Security Standard?

   A. Many controls are required, while some are "addressable," or optional, based on risk.

   B. All controls are required, regardless of actual risk.

   C. Controls that are required are determined for each organization by the acquiring bank.

   D. In addition to core controls, each credit card brand has its own unique controls.

50. The PCI-DSS is an example of:

    A. An industry regulation that is enforced with fines

    B. A private industry standard that is enforced with contracts

    C. A voluntary standard that, if used, can reduce cyber insurance premiums

    D. An international law enforced through treaties with member nations

51. What are three factors that a risk manager might consider when developing an information security strategy?

    A. Threats, risks, and solutions

    B. Prevention, detection, and response

    C. Risk levels, staff qualifications, and security tooling

    D. Risk levels, operating costs, and compliance levels

52. The responsibility for facilitation of an organization's cybersecurity program lies with:

    A. The board of directors

    B. The chief executive officer (CEO)

    C. The chief information officer (CIO)

    D. The chief information security officer (CISO)

1. C	19. B	37. D
2. B	20. A	38. A
3. A	21. D	39. C
4. C	22. A	40. A
5. C	23. C	41. D
6. A	24. C	42. A
7. D	25. B	43. B
8. B	26. D	44. B
9. C	27. A	45. D
10. D	28. B	46. C
11. A	29. D	47. D
12. D	30. C	48. A
13. C	31. A	49. B
14. B	32. A	50. B
15. D	33. D	51. D
16. D	34. B	52. D
17. A	35. C	
18. C	36. B	

1. Management's control of information technology processes is best described as:

   A. Information technology policies

   B. Information technology policies along with audits of those policies

   C. Information technology governance

   D. Metrics as compared to similar organizations

   ☑ **C.** ISACA defines governance as a set of processes that "Ensures that stakeholder needs, conditions and options are evaluated to determine balanced, agreed-on enterprise objectives to be achieved; setting direction through prioritization and decision making; and monitoring performance and compliance against agreed-on direction and objectives."

   ☒ **A** is incorrect. Although information technology policies are an essential part of an information technology program, they do not by themselves control IT processes.

   ☒ **B** is incorrect because IT policies and activities (such as audits) to measure their effectiveness are only one component of management's observation and control of an organization.

   ☒ **D** is incorrect because the comparison of metrics to other organizations is not a significant part of a governance program. Indeed, many organizations forego benchmarking entirely.

2. What is the best method for ensuring that an organization's IT department achieves adequate business alignment?

   A. Find and read the organization's articles of incorporation.

   B. Understand the organization's vision, mission statement, and objectives.

   C. Determine who the CIO reports to in the organization.

   D. Study the organization's application portfolio.

   ☑ **B.** The best way to align an IT department to the business is to find and understand the organization's vision statement, mission statement, goals, and objectives. Many organizations develop and publish one or more of these statements. Others take a simpler approach and develop strategic objectives for a calendar or fiscal year. Whatever can be found is valuable: once an IT manager understands these statements, he or she can prioritize resources and activities in the IT department to support the vision, mission, goals, or other strategic statements.

   ☒ **A** is incorrect because an organization's articles of incorporation do not provide sufficient information about an organization's mission or objectives.

   ☒ **C** is incorrect because the org chart reveals little about what the organization wants to accomplish.

☒ **D** is incorrect because the organization's application portfolio reveals little or nothing about the organization's strategic objectives and will provide little or no aid in aligning the program to the business.

3. Roberta has located her organization's mission statement and a list of strategic objectives. What steps should Roberta take to ensure that the IT department aligns with the business?

   A. Discuss strategic objectives with business leaders to better understand what they wish to accomplish and what steps are being taken to achieve them.

   B. Develop a list of activities that will support the organization's strategic objectives, and determine the cost of each.

   C. Select those controls from the organization's control framework that align to each objective, and then ensure that those controls are effective.

   D. Select the policies from the organization's information security policy that are relevant to each objective, and ensure that those policies are current.

   ☑ **A.** The best first step in aligning an IT department to the organization's strategic objectives is to better understand those objectives, including the resources and activities that will be employed to achieve them.

   ☒ **B** is incorrect because without a dialogue with business leaders, simply identifying supporting activities is more likely to miss important details.

   ☒ **C** is incorrect because proper alignment of an IT department does not generally begin with the selection or implementation of controls. In fact, the implementation of controls may play only a minor part (if any) in support of strategic objectives.

   ☒ **D** is incorrect because proper alignment of an IT department does not generally involve identifying relevant security policies. This may be a minor, supporting activity, but would not be a primary activity when aligning an IT department to the business.

4. Michael wants to improve the risk management process in his organization by creating content that will help management understand when certain risks should be accepted and when certain risks should be mitigated. The policy that Michael needs to create is known as:

   A. A security policy

   B. A control framework

   C. A risk appetite statement

   D. A control testing procedure

   ☑ **C.** A risk appetite statement (sometimes known as a risk tolerance statement or risk capacity statement) provides guidance on the types of risk and the amount of risk an organization may be willing to accept versus what risks an organization may instead prefer to mitigate, avoid, or transfer. Risk appetite statements are most often created in financial services organizations, although they are seen in other types of organizations as well. They help management seek a more consistent approach to risk treatment decisions. In part, this can help management avoid the appearance of being biased or preferential through the use of objective or measurable means for risk treatment decisions.

☒ **A** is incorrect because security policy is not a primary means for making risk treatment decisions.

☒ **B** is incorrect because an organization's control framework is not typically used for making risk treatment decisions.

☒ **D** is incorrect because control testing procedures are not related to risk treatment decisions.

5. In a typical risk management process, the best person(s) to make a risk treatment decision is:

   A. The chief risk officer (CRO)

   B. The chief information officer (CIO)

   C. The department head associated with the risk

   D. The chief information security officer (CISO)

   ☑ **C.** The department head (or division head or business owner, as appropriate) associated with the business activity regarding the risk treatment decision should be the person making the risk treatment decision. This is because a risk treatment decision is a business decision that should be made by the person who is responsible for the business function. Many organizations employ a cybersecurity steering committee to discuss such matters, but the final decision often rests with the business unit head.

   ☒ **A** is incorrect because the chief risk officer (CRO) should not be making business function risk decisions on behalf of department heads or business owners. At best, the CRO should be facilitating discussions leading to risk treatment decisions.

   ☒ **B** is incorrect because the CIO should not be making business function risk decisions on behalf of department heads or business owners.

   ☒ **D** is incorrect because the CISO should not be making risk treatment decisions. Instead, the CISO should, at best, be facilitating discussions that lead to risk treatment decisions made by department heads or business owners.

6. The ultimate responsibility for an organization's cybersecurity program lies with:

   A. The board of directors

   B. The chief executive officer (CEO)

   C. The chief information officer (CIO)

   D. The chief information security officer (CISO)

☑ **A.** The ultimate responsibility for everything in an organization, including its cybersecurity program, lies with its board of directors. Various laws and regulations define board member responsibilities, particularly in publicly traded organizations in the United States and in other countries.

☒ **B** is incorrect because the board of directors is the party responsible for cybersecurity.

☒ **C** is incorrect because the board of directors is the party responsible for cybersecurity.

☒ **D** is incorrect because the CISO's role should be one of a facilitator wherein other members of executive management, as well as board members, make business decisions (including cybersecurity-related decisions) on behalf of the organization.

7. In a U.S. public company, a CIO will generally report the state of the organization's IT function to:

A. The Treadway Commission

B. Independent auditors

C. The U.S. Securities and Exchange Commission

D. The board of directors

☑ **D.** In most U.S. publicly traded companies, the CIO will report the state of the organization's IT function to members of the board of directors. While this is the best answer, in some organizations, the CIO or COO may instead report on the IT function.

☒ **A** is incorrect because an organization would not report anything to the Treadway Commission.

☒ **B** is incorrect because the CIO would typically not report the state of the IT function to independent auditors. In public companies, however, the CIO and independent auditors will periodically meet to discuss IT and the cybersecurity program and to cooperate with auditors on the audit process.

☒ **C** is incorrect because the CIO would not be reporting to the U.S. Securities and Exchange Commission (SEC). However, an organization's internal auditor or CFO will submit reports about the organization's financial results to the SEC, although these filings will rarely include information about IT, unless there has been an incident that had material impact on the organization.

8. A new CIO in an organization is building its formal IT department from the ground up. In order to ensure collaboration among business leaders and department heads in the organization, the CIO should form and manage:

A. A technology committee of the board of directors

B. An IT steering committee

C. An audit committee of the board of directors

D. A business-aligned IT policy

☑ **B.** An IT steering committee, consisting of senior executives, business unit leaders, and department heads, when properly facilitated by the CIO, can discuss organization-wide issues related to IT and make strategic decisions about the allocation of resources.

☒ **A** is incorrect because the CIO will not be involved in the formation and management of a board of directors technology committee.

☒ **C** is incorrect because a CIO would not be involved in the formation or management of a board of directors audit committee.

☒ **D** is incorrect because a business-aligned IT policy, while important, would not significantly foster collaboration among business leaders.

9. The best person or group to make risk treatment decisions is:

   A. The chief information security officer (CISO)

   B. The audit committee of the board of directors

   C. The cybersecurity steering committee

   D. External auditors

   ☑ **C.** The cybersecurity steering committee, which should consist of senior executives, business unit leaders, and department heads, should openly discuss, collaborate, and decide on most risk treatment issues in an organization. If decisions are made by individuals such as the CISO or CRO, then business leaders may be less likely to support those decisions, as they may not have had as large a part in decision making.

   ☒ **A** is incorrect because the CISO unilaterally making risk treatment decisions for the organization is less likely to get buy-in from other business leaders, who may feel they did not have a voice in the making of these decisions.

   ☒ **B** is incorrect because audit committee members rarely get involved in risk treatment decision making.

   ☒ **D** is incorrect because external auditors should not be making any decisions on behalf of the organizations they audit.

10. Which is the best party to conduct access reviews?

    A. Users' managers

    B. Information security manager

    C. IT service desk

    D. Department head

    ☑ **D.** The persons who are responsible for business activities should be the ones who review users' access to applications that support their business activities. All too often, however, access reviews are performed by persons less qualified to make decisions about which persons should have access (and at what levels or capabilities) to systems and applications critical to their business processes. Commonly, IT personnel perform these reviews as a proxy for business owners, but often IT personnel do not have as much knowledge about relevant business operations and are therefore less qualified to make quality decisions about user access.

☒ **A** is incorrect because the managers of users with access to systems and applications are not the best parties to review access.

☒ **B** is incorrect because information security managers have insufficient knowledge about business operations and the persons using them.

☒ **C** is incorrect because IT service desk personnel have insufficient knowledge about business operations and the persons using them. More often, IT service personnel are the ones who carry out access changes. Since they are the ones carrying out changes (in most cases), they should not also be the party reviewing who has access, because they would be reviewing their own work.

11. Which is the best party to make decisions about the configuration and function of business applications?

   A. Business department head

   B. IT business analyst

   C. Application developer

   D. End user

   ☑ **A.** As the parties who are responsible for the ongoing operations and success of business operations and business processes, business department heads are best suited to determine the behavior of business applications supporting business processes.

   ☒ **B** is incorrect because IT business analysts are not responsible for decisions about business unit operations. That said, IT business analysts' role may include facilitation of discussions concerning the configuration and function of business applications, and in some cases may be the persons who make configuration changes.

   ☒ **C** is incorrect because application developers are not responsible for decisions about business unit operations. In some cases, however, application developers may have intimate knowledge of the internal workings of business applications and may provide insight into the function of applications. Thus, they may provide information in support of decisions made by business department heads.

   ☒ **D** is incorrect because end users are generally not responsible for decisions about business unit operations.

12. Which of the following is the best definition of custodial responsibility?

   A. The custodian protects assets based on the customer's defined interests.

   B. The custodian protects assets based on its own defined interests.

   C. The custodian makes decisions based on its own defined interests.

   D. The custodian makes decisions based on the customer's defined interests.

☑ **D.** A custodian is charged with a potentially wide range of decisions regarding the care of an asset. Decisions are based upon the customer's defined interests. A germane example is an IT department that builds and maintains information systems on behalf of internal customers; the IT department will make various decisions about the design and operation of an information system so that the system will best meet customers' needs.

☒ **A** is incorrect because protection of an asset is only a part of the scope of responsibility of a custodian.

☒ **B** is incorrect because a custodian does not protect assets based on its own interests, but instead on its customers' interests.

☒ **C** is incorrect because a custodian does not make decisions based on its own interests, but instead on its customers' interests.

13. What is the primary risk of IT acting as custodian for a business owner?

    A. IT may not have enough interest to provide quality care for business applications.

    B. IT may not have sufficient staffing to properly care for business applications.

    C. IT may have insufficient knowledge of business operations to make good decisions.

    D. Business departments might not give IT sufficient access to properly manage applications.

☑ **C.** IT personnel tend to focus their thoughts on the technology supporting business departments and do not focus enough on the business operations occurring in the business departments they support. Often, IT departments are observed to make too many assumptions about the needs of their customers and do not work hard enough to understand their users' needs to ensure that business applications will support them properly.

☒ **A** is incorrect because level of interest is not a compelling factor.

☒ **B** is incorrect because sufficient staffing is not a compelling factor.

☒ **D** is incorrect because business units are not generally in a position to restrict IT departments from administrative access to business applications.

14. An organization needs to hire an executive who will build a management program that considers threats and vulnerabilities. The best job title for this position is:

    A. CSO

    B. CRO

    C. CISO

    D. CIRO

☑ **B.** The CRO (chief risk officer) is responsible for managing risk for multiple types of assets, commonly information assets, as well as physical assets and/or workplace safety. In financial services organizations, the CRO will also manage risks associated with financial transactions or financial asset portfolios.

☒ **A** is incorrect because the CSO (chief security officer) is not necessarily responsible for risk management, but instead with the design, deployment, and operation of protective controls, commonly for information systems, as well as other assets such as equipment or work centers.

☒ **C** is incorrect because the CISO (chief information security officer) is typically responsible for protection of only information assets and not other types of assets, such as property, plant, and equipment.

☒ **D** is incorrect because the CIRO (chief information risk officer) is typically responsible for risk management and protection of information assets, but not other types of assets, such as property, plant, and equipment.

15. An organization needs to hire an executive who will be responsible for ensuring that the organization's policies, business processes, and information systems are compliant with laws and regulations concerning the proper collection, use, and protection of personally identifiable information. What is the best job title for the organization to use for this position?

A. CSO

B. CIRO

C. CISO

D. CPO

☑ **D.** The chief privacy officer (CPO) is the best title for a position in which the executive ensures that the organization's policies, practices, controls, and systems ensure the proper collection, use, and protection of personally identifiable information (PII).

☒ **A** is incorrect because the chief security officer (CSO) is typically not responsible for privacy-related activities concerning the collection and use of personally identifiable information (PII).

☒ **B** is incorrect because the chief information risk officer (CIRO) is typically not responsible for privacy-related activities concerning the collection and use of personally identifiable information (PII).

☒ **C** is incorrect because the chief information security officer (CISO) is typically not responsible for privacy-related activities concerning the collection and use of personally identifiable information (PII).

16. The Big Data Company is adjusting several position titles in its IT department to reflect industry standards. Included in the consideration are two individuals: The first is responsible for the overall relationships and data flows among the company's internal and external information systems. The second is responsible for the overall health and management of systems containing information. Which two job titles are most appropriate for these two roles?

    A. Systems architect and database administrator

    B. Data architect and data scientist

    C. Data scientist and database administrator

    D. Data architect and database administrator

    ☑ **D.** Data architect is the best position title for someone who is responsible for the overall relationships and data flows among its information systems. Database administrator (DBA) is the best position title for someone who is responsible for maintaining the database management systems (DBMSs) throughout the organization.

    ☒ **A** is incorrect because systems architect is not the best title for someone who is responsible for the overall relationships and data flows among its information systems.

    ☒ **B** is incorrect because data scientist is not the best title for someone who is responsible for the overall health and management of systems containing information.

    ☒ **C** is incorrect because data scientist is not the best title for someone who is responsible for the overall relationships and data flows among its internal and external information systems.

17. What is the primary distinction between a network engineer and a telecom engineer?

    A. A network engineer is primarily involved with networks and internal network media, whereas a telecom engineer is primarily involved with networks and external (carrier) network media.

    B. A network engineer is primarily involved with networks and external (carrier) network media, whereas a telecom engineer is primarily involved with networks and internal network media.

    C. A network engineer is primarily involved with layer 3 protocols and above, whereas a telecom engineer is primarily involved with layer 1 and layer 2 protocols.

    D. There is no distinction, as both are involved in all aspects of an organization's networks.

    ☑ **A.** A network engineer is primarily involved with networks and internal network media (including cabling and internal wireless networks such as Wi-Fi), whereas a telecom engineer is primarily involved with networks and external (carrier) network media such as MPLS, Frame Relay, and dark fiber.

☒ **B** is incorrect because the definitions in this answer are swapped.

☒ **C** is incorrect because the distinction between a network engineer and a telecom engineer are not strictly among protocol layers.

☒ **D** is incorrect because there *is* a distinction between the network engineer and telecom engineer position titles.

18. An organization that is a U.S. public company is redesigning its access management and access review controls. What is the best role for Internal Audit in this redesign effort?

   A. Develop procedures.

   B. Design controls.

   C. Provide feedback on control design.

   D. Develop controls and procedures.

   ☑ **C.** Any Internal Audit function should not design or implement controls or procedures, other than those in its own department. Internal Audit may, however, opine on the design of controls for their suitability to achieve control objectives and auditability. Internal Audit cannot play a design role in any process or control that it may later be required to audit.

   ☒ **A** is incorrect because Internal Audit should not develop procedures that it may later be required to audit. Instead, Internal Audit can provide feedback on procedures developed by others. Internal Audit can never be in a position to audit its own work.

   ☒ **B** is incorrect because Internal Audit should not develop controls that it may later be required to audit. Internal Audit can provide feedback on controls designed by others. Internal Audit can never be in a position to audit its own work.

   ☒ **D** is incorrect because Internal Audit should not develop controls or procedures. This is because Internal Audit may be required to audit these controls and/or procedures. Internal Audit can never be in a position to audit its own work.

19. A security operations manager is proposing that engineers who design and manage information systems play a role in the monitoring of those systems. Is design and management compatible with monitoring? Why or why not?

   A. No. Personnel who design and manage systems should not perform a monitoring role, as this is a conflict of interest.

   B. Yes. Personnel who design and manage systems will be more familiar with the steps to take, as well as the reasons to take them, when alerts are generated.

   C. No. Personnel who design and manage systems will not be familiar with response procedures when alerts are generated.

   D. No. Personnel who design and manage systems are not permitted access to production environments and should not perform monitoring.

   ☑ **B.** Personnel who design and manage information systems are more likely to be familiar with the nature of alerts, as well as procedures for responding to them.

☒ **A** is incorrect because there would normally not be any conflict of interest between design, management, and monitoring.

☒ **C** is incorrect because personnel who design and manage information systems are in a position to understand how those systems work and would be more likely to know how to respond to alerts.

☒ **D** is incorrect because personnel who manage information systems would be permitted to access them in production environments.

20. The purpose of metrics in an IT department is to:

    A. Measure the performance and effectiveness of controls.

    B. Measure the likelihood of an attack on the organization.

    C. Predict the likelihood of an attack on an organization.

    D. Predict the next IT service outage.

    ☑ **A.** The purpose of metrics is to manage the performance and effectiveness of security controls. The meaning and usefulness of specific metrics will depend upon the context and measurement method of specific controls.

    ☒ **B** is incorrect because metrics do not necessarily foretell an attack on an organization.

    ☒ **C** is incorrect because metrics are not always used to predict an attack on an organization.

    ☒ **D** is incorrect because metrics do not necessarily foretell future outages.

21. Which security metric is best considered a leading indicator of an attack?

    A. Number of firewall rules triggered

    B. Number of security awareness training sessions completed

    C. Percentage of systems scanned

    D. Mean time to apply security patches

    ☑ **D.** There is a strong correlation between the absence of security patches and the likelihood and success of attacks on systems. Information systems patched soon after patches are available are far less likely to be successfully attacked, whereas systems without security patches (and those where the organization takes many months to apply patches) are easy targets for intruders.

    ☒ **A** is incorrect because this is not the best answer. While the number of firewall rules triggered may signal the level of unwanted network activity, there is not necessarily a strong correlation between this and the likelihood of an attack. This is because the likelihood of a successful attack is more dependent on other conditions such as patch levels and login credentials.

    ☒ **B** is incorrect because this is not the best answer. While a higher percentage of completion of security awareness training may be an indication of a workforce that is more aware of social engineering techniques, other factors such as patch levels are usually more accurate indicators.

    ☒ **C** is incorrect because the number of systems scanned is not a reliable attack indicator. This is still a valuable metric, as it contributes to an overall picture of vulnerability management process effectiveness.

22. Steve, a CISO, has vulnerability management metrics and needs to build business-level metrics. Which of the following is the best business-level, leading indicator metric suitable for his organization's board of directors?

    A. Average time to patch servers supporting manufacturing processes

    B. Frequency of security scans of servers supporting manufacturing processes

    C. Percentage of servers supporting manufacturing processes that are scanned by vulnerability scanning tools

    D. Number of vulnerabilities remediated on servers supporting manufacturing processes

    ☑ **A.** This is the best metric that serves as a leading indicator. This metric portrays the average time that critical servers are potentially exposed to new security threats. A metric is considered a leading indicator if it foretells future events.

    ☒ **B** is incorrect because the number of scans provides no information about vulnerabilities and, therefore, risk of successful attack. Frequency of security scans is a good operational metric, although a better one would be percentage of critical servers scanned.

    ☒ **C** is incorrect because the percentage of critical systems scanned reveals little about vulnerabilities and their remediation. This is, however, a good operational metric that helps the CISO understand the effectiveness of the vulnerability management process.

    ☒ **D** is incorrect because a raw number, such as number of vulnerabilities remediated, tells board members little or nothing useful to them.

23. The metric "percentage of systems with completed installation of advanced anti-malware" is best described as:

    A. A key operational indicator (KOI)

    B. A key performance indicator (KPI)

    C. A key goal indicator (KGI)

    D. A key risk indicator (KRI)

    ☑ **C.** An "installation completion" metric is most likely associated with a strategic goal, in this case, the installation of advanced anti-malware on systems. This metric could arguably be a KRI as well since this may also indicate risk reduction on account of an improved capability.

    ☒ **A** is incorrect because "key operational indicator" is not an industry standard term. Still, this type of metric is not operational in nature, but more associated with the completion of a strategic objective.

☒ **B** is incorrect because KPI is not the best description of this type of metric, and this activity of completion of software installations is not typically associated with performance (except, possibly, the performance of the team performing the installations).

☒ **D** is incorrect because this metric is a better KGI than it is a KRI. However, this metric could also be considered a KRI if the installation of advanced anti-malware can be shown to help reduce risk.

24. A member of the board of directors has asked Ravila, a CIRO, to produce a metric showing the reduction of risk as a result of the organization making key improvements to its security information and event management system. Which type of metric is most suitable for this purpose?

    A. KGI

    B. RACI

    C. KRI

    D. ROSI

    ☑ **C.** The most suitable metric is a key risk indicator (KRI). Still, this will be a challenge since high-impact events usually occur rarely.

    ☒ **A** is incorrect because a key goal indicator is not the best indicator of risk.

    ☒ **B** is incorrect because RACI is not a metric indicator. RACI stands for Responsible, Accountable, Consulted, and Informed, and is used to assign roles and responsibilities.

    ☒ **D** is incorrect because return on security investment (ROSI) is not a suitable metric since significant events occur rarely.

25. A common way to determine the effectiveness of IT metrics is the SMART method. SMART stands for:

    A. Security Metrics Are Risk Treatment

    B. Specific, Measurable, Attainable, Relevant, Timely

    C. Specific, Measurable, Actionable, Relevant, Timely

    D. Specific, Manageable, Actionable, Relevant, Timely

    ☑ **B.** SMART, in the context of metrics, stands for Specific, Measurable, Attainable, Relevant, and Timely.

    ☒ **A** is incorrect because this is not the definition of SMART in the context of metrics.

    ☒ **C** is incorrect because this is not the definition of SMART in the context of metrics.

    ☒ **D** is incorrect because this is not the definition of SMART in the context of metrics.

26. The statement "Complete migration of flagship system to latest version of vendor-supplied software" is an example of:

A. A mission statement

B. A vision statement

C. A purpose statement

D. An objective statement

   ☑ **D.** This is a statement of a strategic objective.

   ☒ **A** is incorrect because the statement is too specific to be a mission statement.

   ☒ **B** is incorrect because the statement is not typical of a vision statement.

   ☒ **C** is incorrect because the statement is not typical of a purpose statement.

27. Ernie, a CIO who manages a large IT team, wants to create a mission statement for the team. What is the best approach for creating this mission statement?

A. Start with the organization's mission statement.

B. Start with Ernie's most recent performance review.

C. Start with the results of the most recent risk assessment.

D. Start with the body of open items in the project portfolio.

   ☑ **A.** The best way to manage an IT department is to align it with the business it is supporting. When creating an IT department mission statement, a good start is to look at the overall organization's mission statement; this way, the IT department's mission is more likely to align with the overall organization. If the overall organization lacks a mission statement, the CIO can use what he knows about the organization's purpose to build an IT department mission statement that is sure to support the organization.

   ☒ **B** is incorrect because it is not the best answer. Still, it is possible that the CIO's performance review may be well aligned with the overall business and a useful reference for creating an IT team mission statement.

   ☒ **C** is incorrect because a risk assessment report, while it may be an indicator of the nature of the work that the IT department may be undertaking in the future, by itself will not provide much information about the overall business's purpose.

   ☒ **D** is incorrect because the project portfolio's open items will not provide much information about the organization's overall purpose. While the project portfolio's open items may be an indicator of the types of work that the IT department will be working on, this does not provide sufficient information to develop the IT department's mission statement. This is because the CIO's mission is more than just solving short-term problems.

28. Which of the following statements is the best description for the purpose of performing risk management?

A. Identify and manage vulnerabilities that may permit security events to occur.

B. Identify and manage threats that are relevant to the organization.

C. Assess the risks associated with third-party service providers.

D. Assess and manage risks associated with doing business online.

☑ **B.** The purpose of risk management is to identify threats that, if they occurred, would cause some sort of harm to the organization.

☒ **A** is incorrect because the management of vulnerabilities is only a single facet of risk management. A sound risk management program will, however, consider vulnerabilities within each risk assessment and risk analysis to help in the identification of risk treatment options.

☒ **C** is incorrect because the scope of risk management encompasses the entire organization, not only its third-party service providers. That said, it is important for an organization's overall risk management program to identify and manage risks associated with third-party service providers.

☒ **D** is incorrect because the scope of risk management is far broader than just an organization's online business, even if the organization's entire business operation consists of doing business online. Even then, there will be other business activities that should be a part of its risk management program.

29. Key metrics showing the effectiveness of a risk management program would *not* include:

A. Reduction in the number of security events

B. Reduction in the impact of security events

C. Reduction in the time to remediate vulnerabilities

D. Reduction in the number of patches applied

☑ **D.** The number of patches applied is not a metric that indicates risk management program effectiveness, or even of the effectiveness of a vulnerability management program.

☒ **A** is incorrect because the reduction in the number of security events *is* potentially a useful risk management program metric.

☒ **B** is incorrect because the reduction in the impact of security events *is* potentially a useful risk management program metric.

☒ **C** is incorrect because the time to remediate vulnerabilities *is* potentially a useful risk management program metric.

30. Examples of security program performance metrics include all of the following *except*:

A. Time to detect security incidents

B. Time to remediate security incidents

C. Time to perform security scans

D. Time to discover vulnerabilities

☑ **C.** The time required to perform security scans is *not* a good example of a security program performance metric.

☒ **A** is incorrect because time to detect security incidents *is* a good example of a security program performance metric.

☒ **B** is incorrect because time to remediate security incidents *is* a good example of a security program performance metric.

☒ **D** is incorrect because time to discover vulnerabilities *is* a good example of a security program performance metric.

31. Two similar-sized organizations are merging. Paul will be the CIO of the new, combined organization. What is the greatest risk that may occur as a result of the merger?

A. Differences in practices that may not be understood

B. Duplication of effort

C. Gaps in coverage of key processes

D. Higher tooling costs

☑ **A.** A merger of two organizations typically results in the introduction of new practices that are not always understood. The CIO may specify directives to the new, combined IT department that could result in an increase in one or more risks. For example, the combining of two different organizations' device configuration standards could result in a new standard that leads to new, unforeseen problems.

☒ **B** is incorrect because duplication of effort is not the greatest risk.

☒ **C** is incorrect because coverage gaps, while a potential risk, is not the greatest risk.

☒ **D** is incorrect because higher tooling costs, if managed properly, is a short-term spending matter that should not result in increased risk.

32. The purpose of value delivery metrics is:

A. Long-term reduction in costs

B. Reduction in ROSI

C. Increase in ROSI

D. Increase in net profit

☑ **A.** Value delivery metrics are most often associated with long-term reduction in costs in proportion to other measures, such as the number of employees and assets.

☒ **B** is incorrect because value delivery metrics are not usually associated with return on security investment (ROSI).

⊠ **C** is incorrect because value delivery metrics are not usually associated with return on security investment (ROSI).

⊠ **D** is incorrect because value delivery metrics are not associated with profit.

33. Joseph, a CIO, is collecting statistics on several operational areas and needs to find a standard way of measuring and publishing information about the effectiveness of his program. Which of the following is the best approach to follow?

   A. Scaled score

   B. NIST Cybersecurity Framework (CSF)

   C. Business Model for Information Security (BMIS)

   D. Balanced scorecard (BSC)

   ☑ **D.** The balanced scorecard is a well-known framework that is used to measure the performance and effectiveness of an organization. The balanced scorecard is used to determine how well an organization can fulfill its mission and strategic objectives and how well it is aligned with overall organizational objectives.

   ⊠ **A** is incorrect, as a scaled score is not a method used to publish metrics.

   ⊠ **B** is incorrect because the NIST CSF is not typically used as a framework for publishing security program metrics.

   ⊠ **C** is incorrect, as the Business Model for Information Security (BMIS), while valuable for understanding the relationships between people, process, technology, and the organization, is not used for publishing metrics.

34. Which of the following is the best description of the Business Model for Information Security (BMIS)?

   A. Describes the relationships (as dynamic interconnections) between policy, people, process, and technology.

   B. Describes the relationships (as dynamic interconnections) between people, process, technology, and the organization.

   C. Describes the primary elements (people, process, and technology) in an organization.

   D. Describes the dynamic interconnections (people, process, and technology) in an organization.

   ☑ **B.** The Business Model for Information Security (BMIS) describes the dynamic interconnections between the four elements of an organization: people, process, technology, and the organization itself. The dynamic interconnections describe the relationship between each of the relationship pairs. For example, the dynamic interconnection between people and technology, known as "human factors," describes the relationship between people and technology.

   ⊠ **A** is incorrect because "organization" is one of the elements of BMIS that is missing in this answer.

   ⊠ **C** is incorrect because there are four primary elements in an organization: people, process, technology, and the organization itself.

☒ **D** is incorrect because people, process, and technology are not the labels for the dynamic interconnections. Instead, the dynamic interconnections are human factors (between people and technology), emergence (between people and process), enabling and support (between process and technology), culture (between people and organization), architecture (between technology and organization), and governing (between process and organization).

35. What is the correct name for the model shown here?

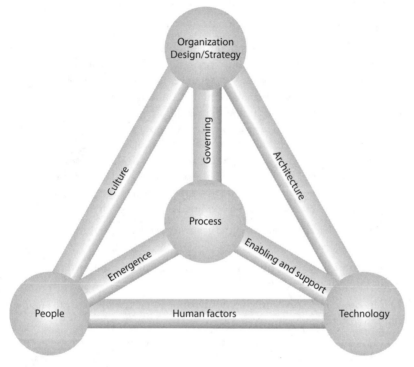

A. COBIT Model for Information Technology

B. COBIT Model for Information Security

C. Business Model for Information Security

D. Business Model for Information Technology

☑ **C.** This is a depiction of the Business Model for Information Security (BMIS), which was developed by ISACA to help individuals better understand the nature of the relationships between people, process, technology, and the organization itself.

☒ **A** is incorrect because this does not depict the COBIT model.

☒ **B** is incorrect because this does not depict the COBIT model.

☒ **D** is incorrect, as this does not depict the Business Model for Information Technology.

36. Jacqueline, an experienced CISO, is reading the findings in a recent risk assessment that describes deficiencies in the organization's vulnerability management process. How would Jacqueline use the Business Model for Information Security (BMIS) to analyze the deficiency?

A. Identify the elements connected to the process DI.

B. Identify the dynamic interconnections (DIs) connected to the process element.

C. Identify the dynamic elements connected to human factors.

D. Identify the dynamic elements connected to technology.

☑ **B.** The deficiency was identified in the vulnerability management process. The CISO would see what dynamic interconnections (DIs) are connected to the process element. They are emergence (connecting to people), enabling and support (connecting to technology), and governing (connecting to organization). A description of the deficiency in the vulnerability management process should lead Jacqueline to one of the dynamic interconnections: emergence, enabling and support, or governing. In this case, the process deficiency is related to the frequency of scans, which is most likely the governing DI. Further investigation reveals that policy permits vulnerability scans only during small service windows, which are not enough time for scans to be completed. The solution to this deficiency is likely a process or policy change so that scans will be permitted to run through to completion.

☒ **A** is incorrect because identifying the elements connected to the process DI is not the correct approach.

☒ **C** is incorrect because identifying the dynamic elements connected to human factors is not the correct approach.

☒ **D** is incorrect because identifying the dynamic elements connected to technology is not the correct approach.

37. Which of the following would constitute an appropriate use of the Zachman enterprise framework?

A. An IT service management model as an alternative to ITIL

B. Identifying system components, followed by high-level design and business functions

C. Development of business requirements translated top-down into technical architecture

D. IT systems described at a high level and then in increasing levels of detail

☑ **D.** Zachman is an IT enterprise framework that describes IT systems at a high level and in increasing levels of detail, down to individual components.

☒ **A** is incorrect because Zachman is not an IT service management framework.

☒ **B** is incorrect because Zachman is a top-down framework, not a bottom-up framework as described.

☒ **C** is incorrect because Zachman does not start with business requirements, but describes only the IT architecture itself.

38. An IT architect needs to document the flow of data from one system to another, including external systems operated by third-party service providers. What kind of documentation does the IT architect need to develop?

    A. Data flow diagrams (DFDs)

    B. Entity relationship diagrams (EFDs)

    C. A Zachman architecture framework

    D. Visio diagrams showing information systems and data flows

    ☑ **A.** The IT architect needs to develop data flow diagrams, which are visual depictions showing information systems (and information system components, optionally) and the detailed nature of data flowing among them. DFDs are sometimes accompanied by documents that describe metadata, such as system specifications and descriptions.

    ☒ **B** is incorrect because an entity relationship diagram (ERD) does not depict data flows among and between information systems. Instead, ERDs describe entities (for instance, information systems) and the relationships between them. ERDs are often depicted visually.

    ☒ **C** is incorrect because a Zachman framework describes the architecture of an IT environment in detail, but not necessarily the flows of data between systems in an environment.

    ☒ **D** is incorrect because this is a vague description. While it is true that a DFD may be composed in Visio (or other graphical drawing tool), this is not the best answer, as it is unspecific.

39. Carole is a CISO in a new organization with a fledgling security program. Carole needs to identify and develop mechanisms to ensure desired outcomes in selected business processes. What is a common term used to define these mechanisms?

    A. Checkpoints

    B. Detective controls

    C. Controls

    D. Preventive controls

    ☑ **C.** "Controls" is the best term describing the mechanisms designed to ensure desired outcomes in business processes.

    ☒ **A** is incorrect because "checkpoints" is not the term that describes these mechanisms.

    ☒ **B** is incorrect because there will not only be detective controls but also preventive controls, administrative controls, and perhaps even compensating and recovery controls.

    ☒ **D** is incorrect because there will not only be preventive controls but also corrective controls, detective controls, and perhaps even compensating and recovery controls.

40. What is the best approach to developing security controls in a new organization?

   A. Start with a standard control framework and make risk-based adjustments as needed.

   B. Start from scratch and develop controls based on risk as needed.

   C. Start with NIST CSF and move up to ISO 27001, then NIST 800-53 as the organization matures.

   D. Develop controls in response to an initial risk assessment.

   ☑ **A.** Starting with a standard control framework is the best approach, particularly if an appropriate, business-relevant framework is selected. In a proper risk management framework, risk assessment and risk treatment will result in adjustments to the framework (removing, improving, and adding controls) over time.

   ☒ **B** is incorrect. While technically this approach will work, too much time may elapse while waiting for the initial set of controls to be developed. In most organizations, over several years, the resulting control framework will not be that different from a standard, industry-relevant framework.

   ☒ **C** is incorrect because there is little to be gained by changing from one control framework to another. Because this approach is not risk-based, there is a chance that some risks will result in never having appropriate controls developed to compensate for those risks.

   ☒ **D** is incorrect. This approach implies that only an initial risk assessment takes place. Instead, the accepted approach is one where risk assessments are performed periodically, resulting in periodic adjustments to the control framework in response to newly discovered risks.

41. Which of the following is the best description of the COBIT framework?

   A. A security process and controls framework that can be integrated with ITIL or ISO 20000.

   B. An IT controls and process framework, on which IT controls and processes can be added at an organization's discretion.

   C. An IT process framework with optional security processes when Extended COBIT is implemented.

   D. An IT process framework that includes security processes that are interspersed throughout the framework.

   ☑ **D.** COBIT is an IT process framework with security processes that appear throughout the framework. Developed by ISACA and now in its fifth major release, COBIT's four domains are Plan and Organize, Acquire and Implement, Deliver and Support, and Monitor and Evaluate. IT and security processes are contained in each of these domains.

   ☒ **A** is incorrect because COBIT is not strictly a security controls framework.

☒ **B** is incorrect because the security processes are not considered optional in COBIT.

☒ **C** is incorrect because there is no such thing as Extended COBIT.

42. One distinct disadvantage of the ISO 27001 standard is:

    A. The standard is costly (over one hundred U.S. dollars per copy).

    B. The standard is costly (a few thousand U.S. dollars per copy).

    C. The standard is available only for use in the United States.

    D. The standard is suitable only in large organizations.

    ☑ **A.** Single copies of the ISO 27001 standard (as well as virtually all other ISO standards) cost over one hundred U.S. dollars each. This prevents widespread adoption of the standard, as organizations are somewhat less likely to implement it since the standard costs hundreds of dollars to download and understand. Further, students are unlikely to learn about the standard in school because of its cost. Contrast this with most other standards, such as NIST 800-53 or CIS, which are free to download and use.

    ☒ **B** is incorrect because the ISO 27001 standard does not cost thousands of dollars per copy.

    ☒ **C** is incorrect because there are no restrictions on where ISO 27001 (and virtually all other standards) can be used.

    ☒ **D** is incorrect because ISO 27001 is suitable for organizations of all sizes, from very large to very small, and everything in between.

43. Which of the following statements about ISO 27001 is correct?

    A. ISO 27001 consists primarily of a framework of security controls, followed by an appendix of security requirements for running a security management program.

    B. ISO 27001 consists primarily of a body of requirements for running a security management program, along with an appendix of security controls.

    C. ISO 27001 consists of a framework of information security controls.

    D. ISO 27001 consists of a framework of requirements for running a security management program.

    ☑ **B.** ISO 27001's main focus is the body of requirements that describe all of the required activities and business records needed to run an information security program. ISO 27001 also includes an appendix containing a framework of information security controls. The controls here are described briefly; the ISO 27002 standard contains the same control framework, but with extensive descriptions for each control.

    ☒ **A** is incorrect because the main focus of ISO 27001 is the requirements for running a security management program, not the security controls.

☒ **C** is incorrect because ISO 27001's main focus is the requirements for running a security management program.

☒ **D** is incorrect because ISO 27001 does not contain *only* the requirements for running a security management program, but also an appendix of security controls that are fully explained in ISO 27002.

44. The U.S. law that regulates the protection of data related to medical care is:

   A. PIPEDA

   B. HIPAA

   C. GLBA

   D. GDPR

   ☑ **B.** HIPAA is the Health Insurance Portability and Accountability Act, which is composed of a "Privacy Rule" and a "Security Rule."

   ☒ **A** is incorrect. PIPEDA is the Canadian data privacy law.

   ☒ **C** is incorrect. GLBA is the Gramm Leach Bliley Act, which established requirements for the protection of personal information in the U.S. financial services industry. Generally, organizations subject to GLBA are banks, credit unions, insurance companies, and securities trading firms.

   ☒ **D** is incorrect. GDPR is the European Union General Data Protection Regulation, the law that regulates the protection and use of personally identifiable information for European residents.

45. The regulation "Security and Privacy Controls for Federal Information Systems and Organizations" is better known as:

   A. ISO/IEC 27001

   B. ISO/IEC 27002

   C. NIST CSF

   D. NIST SP800-53

   ☑ **D.** NIST SP800-53, also known as NIST 800-53, is the security controls framework developed by the U.S. National Institute for Standards and Technology and published in its 800-series Special Publication library. NIST 800-53 is required of all branches of the U.S. federal government and has also been widely adopted by other government agencies and private industry in the United States and around the world.

   ☒ **A** is incorrect. ISO/IEC 27001 is known as "Information technology – Security techniques – Information security management systems – Requirements."

   ☒ **B** is incorrect. ISO/IEC 27002 is known as "Information technology – Security techniques – Code of practice for information security controls."

   ☒ **C** is incorrect. NIST CSF is known as the U.S. National Institute of Standards and Technology: Cybersecurity Framework.

46. What is the best explanation for the Implementation Tiers in the NIST Cybersecurity Framework?

    A. Implementation Tiers are levels of risk as determined by the organization.

    B. Implementation Tiers are stages of implementation of controls in the framework.

    C. Implementation Tiers are likened to maturity levels.

    D. Implementation Tiers are levels of risk as determined by an external auditor or regulator.

    ☑ **C.** While the CSF states that Implementation Tiers are not strictly maturity levels, they are very similar to maturity levels.

    ☒ **A** is incorrect because Implementation Tiers are not risk levels.

    ☒ **B** is incorrect because Implementation Tiers are not related to the progress of the implementation of controls.

    ☒ **D** is incorrect because Implementation Tiers are not risk levels.

47. Jeffrey is a CIO in an organization that performs financial services for private organizations as well as government agencies and U.S. federal agencies. Which is the best information security controls framework for this organization?

    A. CIS

    B. ISO 27001

    C. NIST CSF

    D. NIST 800-53

    ☑ **D.** As a service provider for the U.S. federal government, Jeffrey's organization is required to adopt the NIST SP800-53 controls framework.

    ☒ **A** is incorrect. While CIS is a high-quality controls framework, service providers that perform information-related services to the U.S. federal government are required to adopt the NIST SP800-53 controls framework.

    ☒ **B** is incorrect. While ISO 27001 is a high-quality information security controls framework, it is not required for service providers that provide services to agencies of the U.S. federal government.

    ☒ **C** is incorrect. While the NIST CSF (Cybersecurity Framework) is a good methodology for building an information security program, it is not a controls framework.

48. The scope of requirements of PCI-DSS is:

    A. All systems that store, process, and transmit credit card numbers, as well as all other systems that can communicate with these systems

    B. All systems that store, process, and transmit credit card numbers

    C. All systems that store, process, and transmit unencrypted credit card numbers

D. All systems in an organization where credit card numbers are stored, processed, and transmitted

☑ **A.** The systems that are in scope for PCI-DSS are all those that store, process, or transmit credit card numbers, as well as all other systems that can communicate with those systems.

☒ **B** is incorrect. The scope of PCI-DSS is not limited to just those systems that store, process, or transmit credit card numbers, but also all other systems that can communicate with those systems.

☒ **C** is incorrect. The scope of PCI-DSS includes those systems that store, process, or transmit credit card numbers, even if encrypted.

☒ **D** is incorrect. The scope of PCI-DSS is not necessarily all systems in an organization where credit card numbers are stored, processed, or transmitted. If the organization has implemented effective network segmentation (that is, if systems that store, process, or transmit credit card numbers are isolated on subnets or VLANs where firewalls or ACLs have severely restricted communications to and from in-scope systems), then the systems not in the subnetworks or VLANs where credit card data resides are not in scope.

49. Which of the following statements is true about controls in the Payment Card Industry Data Security Standard?

   A. Many controls are required, while some are "addressable," or optional, based on risk.

   B. All controls are required, regardless of actual risk.

   C. Controls that are required are determined for each organization by the acquiring bank.

   D. In addition to core controls, each credit card brand has its own unique controls.

   ☑ **B.** All controls are required for all organizations. There are additional controls required for service providers.

   ☒ **A** is incorrect because no controls are optional.

   ☒ **C** is incorrect because acquiring banks do not make determinations of applicability of controls.

   ☒ **D** is incorrect because individual card brands do not impose additional controls. Individual card brands do, however, impose specific requirements for compliance reporting.

50. The PCI-DSS is an example of:

   A. An industry regulation that is enforced with fines

   B. A private industry standard that is enforced with contracts

   C. A voluntary standard that, if used, can reduce cyber insurance premiums

   D. An international law enforced through treaties with member nations

☑ **B.** PCI-DSS was developed by a consortium of the major credit card brands in the world: Visa, MasterCard, American Express, Discover, and JCB. PCI is enforced through credit card brands' operating rules, as well as by acquiring banks.

☒ **A** is incorrect because PCI-DSS is not a law or regulation.

☒ **C** is incorrect because PCI-DSS is not voluntary for merchants and service providers that store, process, or transmit credit card numbers. Compliance with PCI-DSS may influence the cost of premiums for cyber-insurance premiums.

☒ **D** is incorrect because PCI-DSS is not an international law.

51. What are three factors that a risk manager might consider when developing an information security strategy?

A. Threats, risks, and solutions

B. Prevention, detection, and response

C. Risk levels, staff qualifications, and security tooling

D. Risk levels, operating costs, and compliance levels

☑ **D.** When a risk manager is developing a long-term strategy for an information security program, the best three factors are risk levels, operating costs, and compliance levels. One of these factors may be more important than others in any given organization and for a variety of reasons. Generally, a long-term strategy is being developed to improve the state of one of these: reduction of risk, reduction of cost, or improvement of compliance.

☒ **A** is incorrect because this is not the best answer. These are factors that may be considered in some circumstances.

☒ **B** is incorrect because these are information security program capabilities.

☒ **C** is incorrect because these are not the best available factors.

52. The responsibility for facilitation of an organization's cybersecurity program lies with:

A. The board of directors

B. The chief executive officer (CEO)

C. The chief information officer (CIO)

D. The chief information security officer (CISO)

☑ **D.** A primary role of the CISO is the facilitation of an organization's cybersecurity program and with the risk management process. With few exceptions, the CISO should facilitate discussions and decisions on risk treatment, but should not be the final decision maker on such matters.

☒ **A, B,** and **C** are incorrect because the facilitation of an organization's cybersecurity program lies with the CISO, not with the board of directors, CEO, or CIO. That said, the board of directors has ultimate responsibility for cybersecurity in the organization, but the CISO is responsible for facilitating the cybersecurity program.

The Audit Process

This chapter covers CISA Domain 1, "Information Systems Auditing Process," and includes questions from the following topics:

- Audit management
- ISACA auditing standards and guidelines
- Audit and risk analysis
- Internal controls
- Performing an audit
- Control self-assessments
- Audit recommendations

The topics in this chapter represent 21 percent of the CISA examination.

ISACA defines this domain as follows: "Establish and/or maintain an information security governance framework and supporting processes to ensure that the information security strategy is aligned with organizational goals and objectives."

The IS audit process is the procedural and ethical structure used by auditors to assess and evaluate the effectiveness of the IT organization and how well it supports the organization's overall goals and objectives. The audit process is backed up by the Information Technology Assurance Framework (ITAF) and the ISACA Code of Professional Ethics. The ITAF is used to ensure that auditors will take a consistent approach from one audit to the next throughout the entire industry. This will help to advance the entire audit profession and facilitate its gradual improvement over time.

1. The IT Assurance Framework consists of all of the following *except:*

   A. ISACA Code of Professional Ethics

   B. IS audit and assurance standards

   C. ISACA Audit Job Practice

   D. IS audit and assurance guidelines

2. An auditor is examining an IT organization's change control process. The auditor has determined that change advisory board (CAB) meetings take place on Tuesdays and Fridays, where planned changes are discussed and approved. The CAB does not discuss emergency changes that are not approved in advance. What opinion should the auditor reach concerning emergency changes?

   A. The CAB should not be discussing changes made in the past.

   B. The CAB should be discussing recent emergency changes.

   C. Personnel should not be making emergency changes without CAB permission.

   D. Change control is concerned only with planned changes, not emergency changes.

3. A conspicuous video surveillance system would be characterized as what type(s) of control?

   A. Detective and deterrent

   B. Detective only

   C. Deterrent only

   D. Preventive and deterrent

4. Michael is developing an audit plan for an organization's data center operations. Which of the following will help Michael determine which controls require potentially more scrutiny than others?

   A. Security incident log

   B. Last year's data center audit results

   C. Risk assessment of the data center

   D. Data center performance metrics

5. An organization processes payroll and expense reports in an SaaS-based environment to thousands of corporate customers. Those customers want assurance that the organization's processes are effective. What kind of an audit should the organization undertake?

   A. Compliance audit

   B. Operational audit

   C. Service provider audit

   D. IS audit

6. An audit project has been taking far too long, and management is beginning to ask questions about its schedule and completion. This audit may be lacking:

   A. Effective project management

   B. Cooperation from individual auditees

   C. Enough skilled auditors

   D. Clearly stated scope and objectives

7. An auditor is auditing the user account request and fulfillment process. The event population consists of hundreds of transactions, so the auditor cannot view them all. The auditor wants to view a random selection of transactions. This type of sampling is known as:

   A. Judgmental sampling

   B. Random sampling

   C. Stratified sampling

   D. Statistical sampling

8. An auditor is auditing an organization's user account request and fulfillment process. What is the first type of evidence collection the auditor will likely want to examine?

   A. Observation

   B. Document review

   C. Walkthrough

   D. Corroborative inquiry

9. A lead auditor is building an audit plan for a client's financial accounting system. The plan calls for periodic testing of a large number of transactions throughout the audit project. What is the best approach for accomplishing this?

   A. Reperform randomly selected transactions.

   B. Periodically submit test transactions to the audit client.

   C. Develop one or more CAATs.

   D. Request a list of all transactions to analyze.

10. A lead auditor is building an audit plan for a client's financial transaction processing system. The audit will take approximately three months. Which of the following is the best approach for reporting audit exceptions to the audit client?

    A. Report the exceptions to the audit committee.

    B. List the exceptions in the final audit report.

    C. Include the exceptions in a weekly status report.

    D. Advise the client of exceptions as they are discovered and confirmed.

11. Which of the following is true about the ISACA Audit Standards and Audit Guidelines?

   A. ISACA Audit Standards are mandatory.

   B. ISACA Audit Standards are optional.

   C. ISACA Audit Guidelines are mandatory.

   D. ISACA Audit Standards are only mandatory for SOX audits.

12. An auditor is auditing an organization's identity and access management program. The auditor has found that automated workflows are used to receive and track access requests and approvals. However, the auditor has identified a number of exceptions where subjects were granted access without the necessary requests and approvals. What remedy should the auditor recommend?

   A. Monthly review of access approvers

   B. Annual review of access approvers

   C. Annual user access reviews

   D. Monthly user access reviews

13. Why are preventive controls preferred over detective controls?

   A. Preventive controls are easier to justify and implement than detective controls.

   B. Preventive controls are less expensive to implement than detective controls.

   C. Preventive controls stop unwanted events from occurring, while detective controls only record them.

   D. Detective controls stop unwanted events from occurring, while preventive controls only record them.

14. For the purposes of audit planning, can an auditor rely upon the audit client's risk assessment?

   A. Yes, in all cases.

   B. Yes, if the risk assessment was performed by a qualified external entity.

   C. No. The auditor must perform a risk assessment himself or herself.

   D. No. The auditor does not require a risk assessment to develop an audit plan.

15. An organization processes payroll and expense reports in an SaaS-based environment to thousands of corporate customers. Those customers want assurance that the organization's processes are effective. What kind of an audit should the organization undertake?

   A. AUP

   B. PA-DSS

   C. PCI-DSS

   D. SSAE18

16. An auditor is auditing an organization's system-hardening policy within its vulnerability management process. The auditor has examined the organization's system-hardening standards and wants to examine the configuration of some of the production servers. What is the best method for the auditor to obtain evidence?

   A. Capture screenshots from servers selected by the systems engineer during a walkthrough.

   B. Request screenshots from servers selected by the systems engineer.

   C. Request screenshots from randomly selected servers from the systems engineer.

   D. Capture screenshots from randomly selected servers during a walkthrough with the systems engineer.

17. An auditor is auditing the user account request and fulfillment process. The event population consists of hundreds of transactions, so the auditor cannot view them all. The auditor wants to view a random selection of transactions, as well as some of the transactions for privileged access requests. This type of sampling is known as:

   A. Judgmental sampling

   B. Random sampling

   C. Stratified sampling

   D. Statistical sampling

18. An auditor is auditing an organization's user account request and fulfillment process. An auditor has requested that the control owner describe the process to the auditor. What type of auditing is taking place?

   A. Observation

   B. Document review

   C. Walkthrough

   D. Corroborative inquiry

19. An external audit firm is performing an audit of a customer's financial accounting processes and IT systems. While examining a data storage system's user access permissions, the staff auditor has discovered the presence of illegal content. What should the staff auditor do next?

   A. Notify law enforcement.

   B. Inform his or her supervisor.

   C. Notify the auditee.

   D. Notify the auditee's audit committee.

20. A QSA auditor in an audit firm has completed a PCI-DSS audit of a client and has found the client to be noncompliant with one or more PCI-DSS controls. Management in the audit firm has asked the QSA auditor to sign off on the audit as compliant, arguing that the client's level of compliance has improved from prior years. What should the QSA auditor do?

A. Refuse to sign the audit report as compliant.

B. Sign the audit report as compliant, but under duress.

C. Sign the audit report as compliant.

D. Notify the audit client of the matter.

21. An organization wants to drive accountability for the performance of security controls to their respective control owners. Which activity is the best to undertake to accomplish this objective?

A. Direct control owners to sign a document of accountability.

B. Have the internal audit department audit the controls.

C. Have an external audit firm audit the controls.

D. Undergo control self-assessments (CSAs).

22. An auditor is evaluating a control related to a key card mechanism protecting a data center from unauthorized visitors. The auditor has determined that the key card control is ineffective because visitors often "piggyback" their way into the data center. What detective control should be implemented to compensate for this control deficiency?

A. A video surveillance system with 90-day content retention that records all entrances and exits from the data center

B. A visitors log inside the data center that all visitors would be required to sign

C. A man trap

D. A policy requiring all visitors to be escorted

23. A U.S.-based organization processes payroll and expense reports in an SaaS-based environment to thousands of corporate customers. Customers outside the United States want assurance that the organization's processes are effective. What kind of an audit should the organization undertake?

A. ISO/IEC 27001

B. SOC2

C. ISAE3402

D. SSAE18

24. A QSA (PCI) audit firm has been commissioned by a large merchant organization to perform a PCI-DSS report on compliance (ROC). The audit firm has noted that the merchant's compliance deadline is less than one month away. What should the audit firm do next?

A. File a compliance extension with the PCI Standards Council on behalf of the merchant.

B. Inform the merchant that the ROC can be completed on time.

C. Inform the merchant that the ROC cannot be completed on time and that an extension should be requested.

D. File a compliance extension with the merchant's acquiring bank.

25. An auditor is developing an audit plan for an accounts payable function. Rather than randomly selecting transactions to examine, the auditor wants to select transactions from low, medium, and large payment amounts. Which sample methodology is appropriate for this approach?

A. Judgmental sampling

B. Stratified sampling

C. Non-random sampling

D. Statistical sampling

26. A cybersecurity audit firm has completed a penetration test of an organization's web application. The final report contains two findings that indicate the presence of two critical vulnerabilities. The organization disputes the findings because of the presence of compensating controls outside of the web application interface. How should the audit proceed?

A. The audit firm should remove the findings from the final report.

B. The organization should select another firm to conduct the penetration test.

C. Organization's management should protest the findings and include a letter that accompanies the pen test report.

D. The audit firm should permit the customer to have some management comments included in the final report.

27. What is the objective of the ISACA audit standard on organizational independence?

A. The auditor's placement in the organization should ensure the auditor can act independently.

B. The auditor should not work in the same organization as the auditee.

C. To ensure that the auditor has the appearance of independence.

D. To ensure that the auditor has a separate operating budget.

28. An auditor is auditing an organization's risk management process. During the walkthrough, the auditor asked the auditee to list all of the sources of information that contribute to the process. The auditee cited penetration tests, vendor advisories, non-vendor advisories, and security incidents as all of the inputs. What conclusion should the auditor draw from this?

A. The process is effective because risks are obtained from several disparate sources.

B. The process is ineffective, as risk assessments apparently do not occur or contribute to the process.

C. The process is effective because both internal and external sources are used.

D. The process is ineffective because an anonymous tip line was not among the sources.

29. The capability wherein a server is constituted from backup media is known as which type of control?

    A. Primary control

    B. Manual control

    C. Compensating control

    D. Recovery control

30. Prior to planning an audit, an auditor would need to conduct a risk assessment to identify high-risk areas in all of the following situations *except* for:

    A. When a client's most recent risk assessment is two years old

    B. When a client's risk assessment does not appear to be adequately rigorous

    C. A PCI "report on compliance" audit

    D. A SOC2 audit

31. Which of the following audit types is appropriate for a financial services provider such as a payroll service?

    A. SSAE18

    B. SAS70

    C. AUP

    D. Sarbanes-Oxley

32. Which of the following is the best method for ensuring that an audit project can be completed on time?

    A. Distribute a "provided by client" evidence request list at the start of the audit.

    B. Pre-populate the issues list with findings likely to occur.

    C. Increase the number of auditors on the audit team.

    D. Reduce the frequency of status meetings from weekly to monthly.

33. An auditor is about to start an audit of a user account access request and fulfillment process. The audit covers a six-month period from January through June. The population contains 1,800 transactions. Which of the following sampling methodologies is best suited for this audit?

    A. Examine the results of the client's control self-assessment (CSA).

    B. Submit some user account access requests and observe how they are performed.

    C. Request the first 30 transactions from the auditee.

    D. Request the first five transactions from each month in the audit period.

34. An auditor is auditing an organization's personnel onboarding process and is examining the background check process. The auditor is mainly interested in whether background checks are performed for all personnel and whether background check results lead to

no-hire decisions. Which of the following evidence collection techniques will support this audit objective?

    A. Request the full contents of background checks along with hire/no-hire decisions.

    B. Request the background check ledger that includes the candidates' names, results of background checks, and hire/no-hire decisions.

    C. Request the hire/no-hire decisions from the auditee.

    D. Examine the background check process and note which characteristics for each candidate are included.

35. An auditor wants to audit the changes made to the DBMS configuration of a financial accounting system. What should the auditor use as the transaction population?

    A. All of the transactions in the database

    B. All of the requested changes in the change management process

    C. All of the changes made to the database

    D. All of the approved changes in the change management business process

36. A credit card payment processor undergoes an annual PCI report on compliance (ROC) audit. What evidence of a passing audit should the payment processor provide to merchant organizations and others?

    A. The signed report on compliance (ROC)

    B. The signed attestation of compliance (AOC)

    C. The signed report of validation (ROV)

    D. The signed self-assessment questionnaire (SAQ)

37. Which of the following statements about the ISACA Audit Guidelines is correct?

    A. ISACA Audit Guidelines apply only to audit firms and not to internal audit departments.

    B. ISACA Audit Guidelines are required. Violations may result in fines for violators.

    C. ISACA Audit Guidelines are required. Violations may result in loss of certifications.

    D. ISACA Audit Guidelines are not required.

38. An external auditor is auditing an organization's third-party risk management (TPRM) process. The auditor has observed that the organization has developed an ISO-based questionnaire that is sent to all third-party service providers annually. What value-added remarks can the auditor provide?

    A. The process can be more efficient if the organization develops risk-based tiers to save time auditing low-risk vendors.

    B. The organization should not be sending questionnaires to vendors every year.

    C. The organization should structure its questionnaires based on CSA Star.

    D. The organization should outsource its third-party management process.

39. What is the difference between an SSAE18 Type I audit and an SSA18 Type II audit?

    A. A Type I audit is an audit of process effectiveness, whereas a Type II audit is an audit of process effectiveness and process design.

    B. A Type I audit is an audit of process design and process effectiveness, whereas a Type II audit is an audit of process design.

    C. A Type I audit is an audit of process design, whereas a Type II audit is an audit of process design and process effectiveness.

    D. A Type I audit is an audit of process design and effectiveness, whereas a Type II audit is an audit of process effectiveness.

40. An auditor is auditing the payment systems for a retail store chain that has 80 stores in the region. The auditor needs to observe and take samples from some of the stores' systems. The audit client has selected two stores that are located in the same city as the store chain headquarters and two stores in a nearby town. How should the audit of the store locations proceed?

    A. The auditor should learn more about the stores' systems and practices before deciding what to do.

    B. The auditor should audit the selected stores and proceed accordingly.

    C. The auditor should accept the sampling but select additional stores.

    D. The auditor should select which stores to examine and proceed accordingly.

41. As a part of an audit of a business process, the auditor has had a discussion with the control owner, as well as the control operators, and has collected procedure documents and records. The auditor is asking internal customers of the business process to describe in their own words how the business process is operated. What kind of evidence collection are these discussions with internal customers?

    A. Reconciliation

    B. Reperformance

    C. Walkthrough

    D. Corroborative inquiry

42. Three months after the completion of an audit, the auditor has contacted the auditee to inquire about the auditee's activities since the audit and whether the auditee has made any progress related to audit findings. What sort of a communication is this outreach from the auditor?

    A. The auditor is being a good audit partner and wants to ensure the auditee is successful.

    B. The auditor is acting improperly by contacting the auditee outside of an audit and should be censored for unethical behavior.

    C. The auditee should assume that the auditor's outreach is personal in nature since this kind of communication is forbidden.

D. The auditor is clearly making sure that the auditee is happy with the auditor's work so that the auditor gets the next year's audit assignment.

43. According to ISACA Audit Standard 1202, which types of risks should be considered when planning an audit?

    A. Fraud risk

    B. Business risk

    C. Cybersecurity risk

    D. Financial risk

44. An IT service desk department that provisions user accounts performs a monthly activity whereby all user account changes that occurred in the prior month are checked against the list of corresponding requests in the ticketing system. This activity is known as:

    A. An audit

    B. A monthly provisioning review

    C. A control threat-assessment (CTA)

    D. A risk assessment

45. An organization with video surveillance at a work center has placed visible notices on building entrances that inform people that video surveillance systems are in use. The notices are an example of:

    A. Administrative controls

    B. Preventive controls

    C. Detective controls

    D. Deterrent controls

46. An auditor is planning an audit of a financial planning application. Can the auditor rely on a recent penetration test of the application as a risk-based audit?

    A. No, because a penetration test does not reveal risks.

    B. No, because a penetration test is not a risk assessment.

    C. Yes, the auditor can make use of the pen test, but a risk assessment is still needed.

    D. Yes, the penetration test serves as a risk assessment in this case.

47. Which of the following is the best example of a control self-assessment of a user account provisioning process?

    A. An examination of Active Directory to ensure that only domain administrators can make user account permission changes

    B. Checks to see that only authorized personnel made user account changes

    C. Confirmation that all user account changes were approved by appropriate personnel

    D. Reconciliation of all user account changes against approved requests in the ticketing system

48. The proper sequence of an audit of an accounts payable process is:

   A. Identify control owners, make evidence requests, perform walkthroughs, do corroborative interviews.

   B. Make evidence requests, identify control owners, do corroborative interviews.

   C. Identify control owners, do corroborative interviews, make evidence requests, perform walkthroughs.

   D. Do corroborative interviews, identify control owners, make evidence requests, and perform walkthroughs.

49. An auditor is auditing an accounts payable process and has found no exceptions. The auditor has decided to select additional samples to see whether any exceptions may be found. Which type of sampling is the auditor performing?

   A. Stop-or-go sampling

   B. Discovery sampling

   C. Judgmental sampling

   D. Exception sampling

50. Which of the following methods is best suited for an auditee to deliver evidence to an auditor during the audit of a background check process?

   A. FTP server

   B. Secure file transfer portal

   C. E-mail with SMTP over TLS

   D. Courier

51. An auditor has completed an audit, and the deliverable is ready to give to the audit client. What is the best method for delivering the audit report to the client?

   A. Courier

   B. Secure file transfer portal

   C. E-mail using SMTP over TLS

   D. In person, in a close-out meeting

52. What are the potential consequences if an IS auditor is a member of ISACA and is CISA certified and violates the ISACA Code of Professional Ethics?

   A. Fines

   B. Imprisonment

   C. Termination of employment

   D. Loss of ISACA certifications

53. An auditor is auditing an accounts payable process and has discovered that a single individual has requested and also approved several payments to vendors. What kind of an issue has the auditor found?

A. A separation of duties issue.

B. A split custody issue.

C. A dual custodian issue.

D. No issue has been identified.

54. An organization uses an automated workflow process for request, review, approval, and provisioning of user accounts. Anyone in the organization can request access. Specific persons are assigned to the review and approval steps. Provisioning is automated. What kind of control is the separation of duties between the review and approval steps?

A. Compensating control

B. Manual control

C. Preventive control

D. Administrative control

55. An auditor is planning an audit of a monthly terminated users review procedure. The auditor is planning to ask the auditee for a list of current user accounts in Active Directory, as well as a list of current employees and a list of terminated employees from Human Resources, so that the auditor can compare the lists. What kind of an audit is the auditor planning to perform?

A. Reperformance

B. Observation

C. Corroboration

D. Walk-back

56. An IT service desk manager is the control owner for the IT department change control process. In an audit of the change control process, the auditor has asked the IT service desk manager to provide all change control tickets whose request numbers end with the digit "6." What sampling methodology has the auditor used?

A. Judgmental sampling

B. Statistical sampling

C. Stratified sampling

D. Stop-or-go sampling

57. An audit firm is planning an audit of an organization's asset management records. For what reason would the auditor request a copy of the entire asset database from the DBA versus a report of assets from the owner of the asset process?

    A. Honesty of the evidence provider

    B. Objectivity of the evidence provider

    C. Independence of the evidence provider

    D. Qualification of the evidence provider

58. An auditor has delivered a Sarbanes-Oxley audit report containing 12 exceptions to the audit client, who disagrees with the findings. The audit client is upset and is asking the auditor to remove any six findings from the report. A review of the audit findings resulted in the confirmation that all 12 findings are valid. How should the auditor proceed?

    A. Remove the three lowest-risk findings from the report.

    B. Remote the six lowest-risk findings from the report.

    C. Report the auditee to the Securities and Exchange Commission.

    D. Explain to the auditee that the audit report cannot be changed.

59. An auditor has delivered a Sarbanes-Oxley audit report containing 12 exceptions to the audit client, who disagrees with the findings. The audit client is upset and is asking the auditor to remove any six findings from the report in exchange for a payment of $25,000. A review of the audit findings resulted in the confirmation that all 12 findings are valid. How should the auditor proceed?

    A. The auditor should report the matter to his or her manager.

    B. The auditor should reject the payment and meet the auditee halfway by removing three of the findings.

    C. The auditor should reject the payment and remove six of the findings.

    D. The auditor should report the incident to the audit client's audit committee.

60. An auditor is auditing a change control process. During a walkthrough, the control owner described the process as follows: "Engineers plan their changes and send an e-mail about their changes to the IT manager before 5 P.M. on Wednesday. The engineers then proceed with their changes during the change window on Friday evening." What, if any, findings should the auditor identify?

    A. The change control process is fine as is, but could be improved by creating a ledger of changes.

    B. The change control process is fine as is.

    C. The change control process lacks a review step.

    D. The change control process lacks review and approval steps.

61. An organization utilizes a video surveillance system on all ingress and egress points in its work facility; surveillance cameras are concealed from view, and there are no visible notices. What type of control is this?

A. Administrative control

B. Secret control

C. Detective control

D. Deterrent control

62. An auditor is selecting samples from records in the user access request process. While privileged access requests account for approximately 5 percent of all access requests, the auditor wants 20 percent of the samples to be requests for administrative access. What sampling technique has the auditor selected?

A. Judgmental sampling

B. Stratified sampling

C. Statistical sampling

D. Variable sampling

63. An auditor is auditing a change control process by examining change logs in a database management system and requesting change control records to show that those changes were approved. The auditor plans to proceed until the first exception is found. What sampling technique is being used here?

A. Discovery sampling

B. Stop-or-go sampling

C. Attribute sampling

D. Exception sampling

1. C	22. A	43. B
2. B	23. C	44. B
3. A	24. C	45. D
4. C	25. B	46. C
5. C	26. D	47. D
6. A	27. A	48. A
7. D	28. B	49. B
8. B	29. D	50. B
9. C	30. C	51. D
10. D	31. A	52. D
11. A	32. A	53. A
12. D	33. D	54. C
13. C	34. B	55. A
14. B	35. C	56. B
15. D	36. B	57. C
16. D	37. D	58. D
17. A	38. A	59. A
18. C	39. C	60. D
19. B	40. A	61. C
20. A	41. D	62. B
21. D	42. A	63. A

1. The IT Assurance Framework consists of all of the following *except:*

    A. ISACA Code of Professional Ethics

    B. IS audit and assurance standards

    C. ISACA Audit Job Practice

    D. IS audit and assurance guidelines

    ☑ **C.** The IT Assurance Framework is an ISACA publication that includes the ISACA Code of Professional Ethics, IS audit and assurance standards, IS audit and assurance guidelines, and IS audit and assurance tools and techniques. It does not contain the ISACA Audit Job Practice.

    ☒ **A** is incorrect because the ITAF does include the ISACA Code of Professional Ethics.

    ☒ **B** is incorrect because the ITAF does include IS audit and assurance standards.

    ☒ **D** is incorrect because the ITAF does include IS audit and assurance guidelines.

2. An auditor is examining an IT organization's change control process. The auditor has determined that change advisory board (CAB) meetings take place on Tuesdays and Fridays, where planned changes are discussed and approved. The CAB does not discuss emergency changes that are not approved in advance. What opinion should the auditor reach concerning emergency changes?

    A. The CAB should not be discussing changes made in the past.

    B. The CAB should be discussing recent emergency changes.

    C. Personnel should not be making emergency changes without CAB permission.

    D. Change control is concerned only with planned changes, not emergency changes.

    ☑ **B.** The CAB should be discussing emergency changes that were made since the last CAB meeting. While the changes were already made, they should go through a similar approval process to ensure that all stakeholders are aware of the changes and that they agree that the changes made were appropriate.

    ☒ **A** is incorrect because a change control process needs to address all changes, including planned changes and emergency changes.

    ☒ **C** is incorrect because emergency changes are often necessary to counteract the effects of unexpected downtime, capacity issues, and other matters.

    ☒ **D** is incorrect because the change control process should address all changes, both planned future changes and recent emergency changes.

3. A conspicuous video surveillance system would be characterized as what type(s) of control?

    A. Detective and deterrent

    B. Detective only

    C. Deterrent only

    D. Preventive and deterrent

☑ **A.** A video surveillance system is considered a detective control because it only records events without actually preventing events such as controls like locked doors and other barriers. A video surveillance system, when its components are conspicuous, is also considered a deterrent control, because its obvious presence serves as a visible deterrent to persons who may be considering an intrusion into a building.

☒ **B** is incorrect because a visible video surveillance system is not considered *only* as a detective control but also as a deterrent control. If the video surveillance system's components are hidden from view, then it would be considered only a detective control.

☒ **C** is incorrect because a visible working video surveillance system is not considered *only* a deterrent control but also a detective control since it would record wanted and unwanted events. If the video surveillance system was fake or inoperative, only then would it be considered solely a deterrent control.

☒ **D** is incorrect because a video surveillance system is never considered a preventive control since it does not actually prevent unwanted events, as does a locked entrance.

4. Michael is developing an audit plan for an organization's data center operations. Which of the following will help Michael determine which controls require potentially more scrutiny than others?

A. Security incident log

B. Last year's data center audit results

C. Risk assessment of the data center

D. Data center performance metrics

☑ **C.** A risk assessment is the primary means for determining which controls may represent greater risk to the organization.

☒ **A** is incorrect because an incident log will not reveal all types of risks. Further, if the incident detection and response processes are ineffective, then the incident log could provide a false sense of security.

☒ **B** is incorrect because there may have been changes in operations since the prior audit that only a risk assessment would reveal.

☒ **D** is incorrect because performance metrics would probably not reveal enough information about risks in controls.

5. An organization processes payroll and expense reports in an SaaS-based environment to thousands of corporate customers. Those customers want assurance that the organization's processes are effective. What kind of an audit should the organization undertake?

A. Compliance audit

B. Operational audit

C. Service provider audit

D. IS audit

☑ **C.** A service provider audit, such as an SSAE18, SOC2, ISO 27001 certification, or AUP audit, is designed for service providers that want to provide objective assurance of the integrity of their control environment.

☒ **A** is incorrect because a compliance audit is used to ensure that an organization is in compliance with specific laws, regulations, or standards.

☒ **B** is incorrect because an operational audit is an audit that is performed for internal use. This is a potential answer, but not the best answer.

☒ **D** is incorrect because an IS audit is an audit that is performed for internal use. This is a potential answer, but not the best answer.

6. An audit project has been taking far too long, and management is beginning to ask questions about its schedule and completion. This audit may be lacking:

A. Effective project management

B. Cooperation from individual auditees

C. Enough skilled auditors

D. Clearly stated scope and objectives

☑ **A.** While any of these answers is plausible, the first thing that should be examined is whether the audit is being effectively project managed, so that all parties understand the audit's objectives, schedule, resources required, and regular status reporting.

☒ **B** is incorrect. While plausible, there isn't enough information here to draw this conclusion.

☒ **C** is incorrect. While plausible, there isn't enough information here to draw this conclusion.

☒ **D** is incorrect. While plausible, there isn't enough information here to draw this conclusion.

7. An auditor is auditing the user account request and fulfillment process. The event population consists of hundreds of transactions, so the auditor cannot view them all. The auditor wants to view a random selection of transactions. This type of sampling is known as:

A. Judgmental sampling

B. Random sampling

C. Stratified sampling

D. Statistical sampling

☑ **D.** In an audit where an auditor needs to select a portion of events to test, statistical sampling is the best approach.

☒ **A** is incorrect because the auditor is not examining individual transactions to determine whether each should be included in the sampling.

☒ **B** is incorrect because "random sampling" may be a common vernacular for this approach, but this is not the official ISACA term for it.

☒ **C** is incorrect because stratified sampling involves selecting samples from various portions of the population.

8. An auditor is auditing an organization's user account request and fulfillment process. What is the first type of evidence collection the auditor will likely want to examine?

   A. Observation

   B. Document review

   C. Walkthrough

   D. Corroborative inquiry

   ☑ **B.** An auditor generally will examine process documentation first to understand how a process is supposed to be performed. This will be followed by a walkthrough, observation, examination of records, and corroborative inquiry (and often in that sequence).

   ☒ **A** is incorrect because an auditor will generally first want to read process documentation before watching personnel perform tasks.

   ☒ **C** is incorrect because an auditor will generally first want to read process documentation before performing a walkthrough.

   ☒ **D** is incorrect because an auditor will generally want to examine a process thoroughly before performing a corroborative inquiry.

9. A lead auditor is building an audit plan for a client's financial accounting system. The plan calls for periodic testing of a large number of transactions throughout the audit project. What is the best approach for accomplishing this?

   A. Reperform randomly selected transactions.

   B. Periodically submit test transactions to the audit client.

   C. Develop one or more CAATs.

   D. Request a list of all transactions to analyze.

   ☑ **C.** The task of auditing a large number of transactions needs to be automated with one or more computer-assisted audit techniques (CAATs). Manually testing a large number of transactions would be onerous and costly.

   ☒ **A** is incorrect because the volume of transactions is too high to consider reperforming them manually.

   ☒ **B** is incorrect because this approach would require excessive manual effort.

   ☒ **D** is incorrect because it is not the best answer. This approach might be the best alternative, however, but the auditor would have to develop techniques to analyze the data.

10. A lead auditor is building an audit plan for a client's financial transaction processing system. The audit will take approximately three months. Which of the following is the best approach for reporting audit exceptions to the audit client?

    A. Report the exceptions to the audit committee.

    B. List the exceptions in the final audit report.

    C. Include the exceptions in a weekly status report.

    D. Advise the client of exceptions as they are discovered and confirmed.

    ☑ **D.** There is rarely a valid reason why the audit client should not be notified right away of an audit exception. That said, often the auditor will need to reserve the final audit opinion until all of the testing has been completed and all of the audit exceptions analyzed. Still, notifying the audit client of individual exceptions during the audit provides the audit client with opportunities to begin remediation.

    ☒ **A** is incorrect because an audit committee is not always the audit client.

    ☒ **B** is incorrect because there is rarely a valid reason for waiting until the final audit report to inform an audit client of audit exceptions.

    ☒ **C** is incorrect because this is not the best answer; this is a valid alternative, however.

11. Which of the following is true about the ISACA Audit Standards and Audit Guidelines?

    A. ISACA Audit Standards are mandatory.

    B. ISACA Audit Standards are optional.

    C. ISACA Audit Guidelines are mandatory.

    D. ISACA Audit Standards are only mandatory for SOX audits.

    ☑ **A.** ISACA Audit Standards are mandatory for all audit professionals—compliance with ISACA Audit Standards is a condition for earning and retaining the CISA certification.

    ☒ **B** is incorrect because ISACA Audit Standards are not optional for CISA certification holders.

    ☒ **C** is incorrect because ISACA Audit Guidelines are not mandatory, but instead serve as helpful guidelines for the implementation of ISACA Audit Standards.

    ☒ **D** is incorrect because ISACA Audit Standards are mandatory for all audits. That said, often there are additional audit standards for specific types of audits, such as Sarbanes-Oxley (SOX), PCI-DSS, SSAE18, and others.

12. An auditor is auditing an organization's identity and access management program. The auditor has found that automated workflows are used to receive and track access requests and approvals. However, the auditor has identified a number of exceptions where subjects were granted access without the necessary requests and approvals. What remedy should the auditor recommend?

   A. Monthly review of access approvers

   B. Annual review of access approvers

   C. Annual user access reviews

   D. Monthly user access reviews

   ☑ **D.** The problem with the existing business process can be partly remedied by a frequent user access review, which will partly compensate for the control failures. However, the organization should seek to identify and correct the root cause(s) of the control failures so that there are fewer exceptions identified in the monthly user access reviews as well as in subsequent audits.

   ☒ **A** is incorrect because the problem with this process is not whether the right approvers are involved, but that user accesses are being granted through bypassing the request process altogether.

   ☒ **B** is incorrect because the problem with this process is not whether the right approvers are involved, but that user accesses are being granted through bypassing the request process altogether.

   ☒ **C** is incorrect because an annual user access review is too infrequent for this situation.

13. Why are preventive controls preferred over detective controls?

   A. Preventive controls are easier to justify and implement than detective controls.

   B. Preventive controls are less expensive to implement than detective controls.

   C. Preventive controls stop unwanted events from occurring, while detective controls only record them.

   D. Detective controls stop unwanted events from occurring, while preventive controls only record them.

   ☑ **C.** The best and first approach to unwanted events is prevention. Where prevention is difficult or expensive, detection is the next best approach.

   ☒ **A** is incorrect because preventive controls are not necessarily easier to justify or implement.

   ☒ **B** is incorrect because preventive controls are not necessarily less expensive to implement.

   ☒ **D** is incorrect because detective controls do not prevent events.

14. For the purposes of audit planning, can an auditor rely upon the audit client's risk assessment?

   A. Yes, in all cases.

   B. Yes, if the risk assessment was performed by a qualified external entity.

C. No. The auditor must perform a risk assessment himself or herself.

D. No. The auditor does not require a risk assessment to develop an audit plan.

☑ **B.** An auditor can use a risk assessment performed by a qualified external party to develop a risk-based audit plan. This will result in areas of higher risk being examined more closely than areas of lower risk.

☒ **A** is incorrect because there are certainly cases where an auditor cannot use a client's risk assessment—for example, if the client's risk assessment was performed by unqualified persons or if there were signs of bias.

☒ **C** is incorrect because it is not always necessary for an auditor to perform the audit himself or herself. Often an external risk assessment can be used, provided it is sound.

☒ **D** is incorrect because a risk assessment will result in a better audit plan that is risk-aligned.

15. An organization processes payroll and expense reports in an SaaS-based environment to thousands of corporate customers. Those customers want assurance that the organization's processes are effective. What kind of an audit should the organization undertake?

    A. AUP

    B. PA-DSS

    C. PCI-DSS

    D. SSAE18

    ☑ **D.** The payroll services organization should undertake an SSAE18 audit. This type of audit is designed for financial services providers so that the auditors of the customers of the payroll services organization can rely on the payroll services organization's SSAE18 audit report in the course of auditing financial controls.

    ☒ **A** is incorrect because an AUP audit is not the best choice. This is a viable alternative, however, in the event the organization decides not to undertake an SSAE18 audit.

    ☒ **B** is incorrect because a PA-DSS audit is an audit of a commercial credit card payment application.

    ☒ **C** is incorrect because a PCI-DSS audit is an audit of an organization's credit card data processing environment.

16. An auditor is auditing an organization's system-hardening policy within its vulnerability management process. The auditor has examined the organization's system-hardening standards and wants to examine the configuration of some of the production servers. What is the best method for the auditor to obtain evidence?

    A. Capture screenshots from servers selected by the systems engineer during a walkthrough.

    B. Request screenshots from servers selected by the systems engineer.

    C. Request screenshots from randomly selected servers from the systems engineer.

    D. Capture screenshots from randomly selected servers during a walkthrough with the systems engineer.

☑ **D.** The auditor should select which servers are to be sampled (by whatever sampling methodology) and view the configurations during a walkthrough with a systems engineer. This is the most reliable method for ensuring the integrity of the evidence.

☒ **A** is incorrect because the systems engineer should not be permitted to select the servers to be sampled; the systems engineer could deliberately avoid servers known to violate the policy.

☒ **B** and **C** are incorrect because the auditor cannot be sure that the requested screenshots actually correspond to the servers selected.

17. An auditor is auditing the user account request and fulfillment process. The event population consists of hundreds of transactions, so the auditor cannot view them all. The auditor wants to view a random selection of transactions, as well as some of the transactions for privileged access requests. This type of sampling is known as:

   A. Judgmental sampling

   B. Random sampling

   C. Stratified sampling

   D. Statistical sampling

   ☑ **A.** The auditor wants to examine the population and select specific high-risk transactions.

   ☒ **B** is incorrect because some of the transactions are not being randomly selected, and because "random sampling" is not the official term for this technique.

   ☒ **C** is incorrect because this is not an example of stratified sampling.

   ☒ **D** is incorrect because some of the transactions are not being randomly selected.

18. An auditor is auditing an organization's user account request and fulfillment process. An auditor has requested that the control owner describe the process to the auditor. What type of auditing is taking place?

   A. Observation

   B. Document review

   C. Walkthrough

   D. Corroborative inquiry

   ☑ **C.** A control owner describing a process is known as a walkthrough. Here, each step of a process is described in detail to the auditor.

   ☒ **A** is incorrect because observation refers to an auditor watching personnel perform the process.

⊠ **B** is incorrect because document review generally consists of the auditor reading the document on his or her own, away from the presence of the control owner. Document review usually precedes a walkthrough.

⊠ **D** is incorrect because corroborative inquiry usually takes place after a walkthrough and after examining records.

19. An external audit firm is performing an audit of a customer's financial accounting processes and IT systems. While examining a data storage system's user access permissions, the staff auditor has discovered the presence of illegal content. What should the staff auditor do next?

  A. Notify law enforcement.

  B. Inform his or her supervisor.

  C. Notify the auditee.

  D. Notify the auditee's audit committee.

  ☑ **B.** The staff auditor should first notify his or her supervisor, who in turn may notify others in the audit firm. Depending upon the nature of the illegal content, it may be appropriate for the audit firm to notify law enforcement, the auditee, or senior officials in the auditee organization, such as audit committee members. Local laws and regulations may influence this decision.

  ⊠ **A** is incorrect because this may not be the best next step, depending on local laws and regulations. In most cases, it's best to notify one's supervisor, who in turn will discuss the matter with others in the audit firm.

  ⊠ **C** is incorrect because the auditee could be the person responsible for placing the illegal content on the storage system. Notifying this person could give them an opportunity to quickly remove the content before law enforcement is able to examine the storage system.

  ⊠ **D** is incorrect because the audit committee is not necessarily the appropriate party to notify first. Depending upon local laws and regulations, law enforcement may need to be notified. The best course of action is for the auditor to notify his or her supervisor, who can then assemble individuals in the audit firm who can decide the appropriate course of action.

20. A QSA auditor in an audit firm has completed a PCI-DSS audit of a client and has found the client to be noncompliant with one or more PCI-DSS controls. Management in the audit firm has asked the QSA auditor to sign off on the audit as compliant, arguing that the client's level of compliance has improved from prior years. What should the QSA auditor do?

  A. Refuse to sign the audit report as compliant.

  B. Sign the audit report as compliant, but under duress.

  C. Sign the audit report as compliant.

  D. Notify the audit client of the matter.

☑ **A.** The QSA auditor signing the audit report as compliant would be a violation of the ISACA Code of Professional Ethics. Were ISACA to learn about this matter, the auditor could lose his or her ISACA certifications.

☒ **B** is incorrect because this may still jeopardize the auditor's standing with the ISACA Code of Professional Ethics.

☒ **C** is incorrect because this would be a clear violation of the ISACA Code of Professional Ethics, and the auditor could lose his or her ISACA certifications.

☒ **D** is incorrect because this may cause confusion or anger on the part of the auditee organization.

21. An organization wants to drive accountability for the performance of security controls to their respective control owners. Which activity is the best to undertake to accomplish this objective?

    A. Direct control owners to sign a document of accountability.

    B. Have the internal audit department audit the controls.

    C. Have an external audit firm audit the controls.

    D. Undergo control self-assessments (CSAs).

    ☑ **D.** Control self-assessments (CSAs) force control owners to focus on the effectiveness of their controls. For the most part, control owners will self-regulate and make improvements to their control procedures in order to ensure that their controls are more effective.

    ☒ **A** is incorrect because signing a document will not necessarily compel control owners to take ownership of their controls in the same way a CSA would.

    ☒ **B** and **C** are incorrect. While an audit would highlight control deficiencies, a CSA is a more effective means for control owners to pay attention to the effectiveness of their controls by forcing them to evaluate them.

22. An auditor is evaluating a control related to a key card mechanism protecting a data center from unauthorized visitors. The auditor has determined that the key card control is ineffective because visitors often "piggyback" their way into the data center. What detective control should be implemented to compensate for this control deficiency?

    A. A video surveillance system with 90-day content retention that records all entrances and exits from the data center

    B. A visitors log inside the data center that all visitors would be required to sign

    C. A man trap

    D. A policy requiring all visitors to be escorted

☑ **A.** A video surveillance system would record all persons entering and leaving the data center. A security manager could examine the video contents from time to time to understand whether there are specific persons who violate the policy.

☒ **B** is incorrect because visitors who know they are not authorized to enter the data center are unlikely to sign the visitor log.

☒ **C** is incorrect because a man trap, while effective, is a costly control. It may ultimately prove necessary if review of video surveillance and disciplinary action do not resolve the matter.

☒ **D** is incorrect because visitors who know they are not authorized to enter the data center are not likely to conform to the policy; further, if they are outsiders, they may not be aware of the policy.

23. A U.S.-based organization processes payroll and expense reports in an SaaS-based environment to thousands of corporate customers. Customers outside the United States want assurance that the organization's processes are effective. What kind of an audit should the organization undertake?

    A. ISO/IEC 27001

    B. SOC2

    C. ISAE3402

    D. SSAE18

    ☑ **C.** An ISAE3402 audit is the international version of the SSAE18 audit.

    ☒ **A** is incorrect because, while valuable, an ISO/IEC 27001 audit is not the best choice. An ISO audit would cover a broad spectrum of security controls but no financially specific controls.

    ☒ **B** is incorrect because a SOC2 audit is a general-purpose audit of a service provider, but it lacks financially specific controls.

    ☒ **D** is incorrect because an SSAE18 audit is technically valid only within the United States.

24. A QSA (PCI) audit firm has been commissioned by a large merchant organization to perform a PCI-DSS report on compliance (ROC). The audit firm has noted that the merchant's compliance deadline is less than one month away. What should the audit firm do next?

    A. File a compliance extension with the PCI Standards Council on behalf of the merchant.

    B. Inform the merchant that the ROC can be completed on time.

    C. Inform the merchant that the ROC cannot be completed on time and that an extension should be requested.

    D. File a compliance extension with the merchant's acquiring bank.

☑ **C.** There is little hope that the ROC can be completed in four weeks. After being notified by the audit firm, the merchant organization should request an extension of its acquiring bank.

☒ **A** is incorrect because a QSA firm does not file extensions on behalf of its audit clients.

☒ **B** is incorrect because it is unlikely that the ROC can be completed in four weeks. A PCI-DSS audit of a large merchant organization is sure to take several weeks from start to finish.

☒ **D** is incorrect because QSA firms do not file extensions of behalf of their audit clients.

25. An auditor is developing an audit plan for an accounts payable function. Rather than randomly selecting transactions to examine, the auditor wants to select transactions from low, medium, and large payment amounts. Which sample methodology is appropriate for this approach?

    A. Judgmental sampling

    B. Stratified sampling

    C. Non-random sampling

    D. Statistical sampling

☑ **B.** Stratified sampling involves selecting samples based on some quantified value in each sample (in this case, the payment amount). Stratified sampling is useful for situations like this where auditors want to be sure to examine very high- or very low-value samples that might not be selected in random sampling.

☒ **A** is incorrect because judgmental sampling is, by definition, not random. However, this would be the next best choice.

☒ **C** is incorrect because non-random sampling is not a sampling methodology.

☒ **D** is incorrect because statistical sampling might not capture enough of the high- or low-value transactions if there are too few of these.

26. A cybersecurity audit firm has completed a penetration test of an organization's web application. The final report contains two findings that indicate the presence of two critical vulnerabilities. The organization disputes the findings because of the presence of compensating controls outside of the web application interface. How should the audit proceed?

    A. The audit firm should remove the findings from the final report.

    B. The organization should select another firm to conduct the penetration test.

    C. Organization's management should protest the findings and include a letter that accompanies the pen test report.

    D. The audit firm should permit the customer to have some management comments included in the final report.

☑ **D.** Management's comments will appear in the report where the specific findings are discussed.

☒ **A** is incorrect because the audit firm should not remove a finding simply because the audit client disagrees with it.

☒ **B** is incorrect because this may not be a viable option for cost and scheduling reasons.

☒ **C** is incorrect because a separate management letter would be seen in a more negative light. However, this may be the organization's best option if the audit firm is unwilling to include management comments in the final report.

27. What is the objective of the ISACA audit standard on organizational independence?

  A. The auditor's placement in the organization should ensure the auditor can act independently.

  B. The auditor should not work in the same organization as the auditee.

  C. To ensure that the auditor has the appearance of independence.

  D. To ensure that the auditor has a separate operating budget.

  ☑ **A.** ISACA audit standard 1002, "Organizational Independence," states the following: "The IS auditor's placement in the command-and-control structure of the organization should ensure that the IS auditor can act independently." This helps to avoid the possibility that the auditor is being coerced into providing a favorable audit opinion.

  ☒ **B** is incorrect because the audit standard does not require the auditor to work in a different organization. Indeed, internal audit departments in U.S. public companies are a part of the organization.

  ☒ **C** is incorrect because it is important to not only ensure the *appearance* of independence but the *fact* of independence.

  ☒ **D** is incorrect because a separate budget does not necessarily equate to independence.

28. An auditor is auditing an organization's risk management process. During the walkthrough, the auditor asked the auditee to list all of the sources of information that contribute to the process. The auditee cited penetration tests, vendor advisories, non-vendor advisories, and security incidents as all of the inputs. What conclusion should the auditor draw from this?

  A. The process is effective because risks are obtained from several disparate sources.

  B. The process is ineffective, as risk assessments apparently do not occur or contribute to the process.

  C. The process is effective because both internal and external sources are used.

  D. The process is ineffective because an anonymous tip line was not among the sources.

☑ **B.** The absence of risk assessments (or their omission as an input to the risk management process) constitutes an ineffective process. Risk assessments are among the most important input to the risk management process.

☒ **A** and **C** are incorrect because the process cannot be viewed as effective in the absence of risk assessments.

☒ **D** is incorrect because an anonymous tip line, while important, is not considered a key information source for a risk management process.

29. The capability wherein a server is constituted from backup media is known as which type of control?

   A. Primary control

   B. Manual control

   C. Compensating control

   D. Recovery control

   ☑ **D.** Restoration of a server from backup media is known as a recovery control.

   ☒ **A** is incorrect because "primary" is not considered a class of control.

   ☒ **B** is incorrect because while recovering a server may be manual, it could also be automated. Rebuilding a server from backup is generally considered a recovery control.

   ☒ **C** is incorrect because rebuilding a server is generally not considered a compensating control.

30. Prior to planning an audit, an auditor would need to conduct a risk assessment to identify high-risk areas in all of the following situations *except* for:

   A. When a client's most recent risk assessment is two years old

   B. When a client's risk assessment does not appear to be adequately rigorous

   C. A PCI "report on compliance" audit

   D. A SOC2 audit

   ☑ **C.** The PCI audit is not risk-based, and the presence or absence of a risk assessment will not alter the audit plan. This is despite the fact that PCI (as of version 3.2.1) requires an organization to conduct a risk assessment, although this has no bearing on the organization's obligation to implement all controls in the standard.

   ☒ **A, B,** and **D** are incorrect because these are valid reasons that would compel an auditor to conduct a risk assessment prior to developing the audit plan.

31. Which of the following audit types is appropriate for a financial services provider such as a payroll service?

   A. SSAE18

   B. SAS70

C. AUP

D. Sarbanes-Oxley

☑ **A.** An SSAE18 audit is specifically intended for financial service providers such as payroll, general accounting, expense management, and other financial services.

☒ **B** is incorrect because the SAS70 audit standard has been deprecated and replaced by the SSAE18 standard.

☒ **C** is incorrect because an AUP audit is general purpose in nature and not specifically designed for financial services.

☒ **D** is incorrect because a Sarbanes-Oxley audit is intended for the financial business processes of a U.S. public company.

32. Which of the following is the best method for ensuring that an audit project can be completed on time?

A. Distribute a "provided by client" evidence request list at the start of the audit.

B. Pre-populate the issues list with findings likely to occur.

C. Increase the number of auditors on the audit team.

D. Reduce the frequency of status meetings from weekly to monthly.

☑ **A.** Auditees sometimes take quite a long time to search for and provide requested evidence to auditors. By providing this request list at the beginning of the audit, auditors will obtain evidence earlier than if they wait until their walkthrough meetings.

☒ **B** is incorrect because this is not an accepted practice, and it would not save much time even in circumstances where auditors were sure that certain exceptions were going to occur.

☒ **C** is incorrect because it may not be feasible to increase the size of the audit team. Besides, the number of auditors is not always the factor that determines the duration of an audit.

☒ **D** is incorrect because reducing audit status meetings from weekly to monthly could have the opposite effect and increase the time for an audit project to complete, because of reduced communication.

33. An auditor is about to start an audit of a user account access request and fulfillment process. The audit covers a six-month period from January through June. The population contains 1,800 transactions. Which of the following sampling methodologies is best suited for this audit?

A. Examine the results of the client's control self-assessment (CSA).

B. Submit some user account access requests and observe how they are performed.

C. Request the first 30 transactions from the auditee.

D. Request the first five transactions from each month in the audit period.

☑ **D.** This methodology captures transactions through the entire audit period. In a period of this length, there could be personnel changes and other changes that could result in instances of acceptable or unacceptable performance throughout the period.

☒ **A** is incorrect because an auditee's CSA might not be of sufficient integrity to be relied upon. Further, specific audit rules or standards might preclude the use of a CSA.

☒ **B** is incorrect because reperformance assesses the current effectiveness of a control, not whether the control was effective throughout the audit period.

☒ **C** is incorrect because this will assess the process only at the beginning of the six-month audit period. If the process was effective in January but ineffective for the rest of the period, this technique would conceal this possibility.

34. An auditor is auditing an organization's personnel onboarding process and is examining the background check process. The auditor is mainly interested in whether background checks are performed for all personnel and whether background check results lead to no-hire decisions. Which of the following evidence collection techniques will support this audit objective?

   A. Request the full contents of background checks along with hire/no-hire decisions.

   B. Request the background check ledger that includes the candidates' names, results of background checks, and hire/no-hire decisions.

   C. Request the hire/no-hire decisions from the auditee.

   D. Examine the background check process and note which characteristics for each candidate are included.

   ☑ **B.** This evidence request will provide enough information for the auditor to understand whether background checks are performed for all positions requiring it, as well as whether any no-hire decisions are made.

   ☒ **A** is incorrect because the auditor should not need to see the details of individuals' background checks. This is highly sensitive information.

   ☒ **C** is incorrect because this does not reveal the correlation between pass/no-pass results and hire/no-hire decisions.

   ☒ **D** is incorrect because this audit requires examination of records, not just examination of the business process.

35. An auditor wants to audit the changes made to the DBMS configuration of a financial accounting system. What should the auditor use as the transaction population?

   A. All of the transactions in the database

   B. All of the requested changes in the change management process

   C. All of the changes made to the database

   D. All of the approved changes in the change management business process

☑ **C.** The total population is the total set of configuration changes present in the DBMS.

☒ **A** is incorrect because this would include all financial transactions, which is far larger than the desired population.

☒ **B** is incorrect because this would not include changes made to the system that were not requested.

☒ **D** is incorrect because this would not include changes made to the system that were not approved or requested.

36. A credit card payment processor undergoes an annual PCI report on compliance (ROC) audit. What evidence of a passing audit should the payment processor provide to merchant organizations and others?

   A. The signed report on compliance (ROC)

   B. The signed attestation of compliance (AOC)

   C. The signed report of validation (ROV)

   D. The signed self-assessment questionnaire (SAQ)

   ☑ **B.** It is entirely sufficient for the service provider to provide the signed attestation of compliance (AOC) to any merchant, customer, or other entity requesting evidence of PCI compliance.

   ☒ **A** is incorrect because the service provider should not need to provide the entire ROC, as this would provide excessive details of its internal operations. The AOC contains sufficient information regarding the pass or fail status of the audit and its PCI compliance.

   ☒ **C** is incorrect, as an ROV was not performed.

   ☒ **D** is incorrect because an SAQ was not completed.

37. Which of the following statements about the ISACA Audit Guidelines is correct?

   A. ISACA Audit Guidelines apply only to audit firms and not to internal audit departments.

   B. ISACA Audit Guidelines are required. Violations may result in fines for violators.

   C. ISACA Audit Guidelines are required. Violations may result in loss of certifications.

   D. ISACA Audit Guidelines are not required.

   ☑ **D.** ISACA Audit Guidelines are suggested implementation guidelines and not required of ISACA-certified personnel.

   ☒ **A** is incorrect because ISACA Audit Guidelines apply in all auditing situations.

   ☒ **B** and **C** are incorrect because ISACA Audit Guidelines are optional and not required.

38. An external auditor is auditing an organization's third-party risk management (TPRM) process. The auditor has observed that the organization has developed an ISO-based questionnaire that is sent to all third-party service providers annually. What value-added remarks can the auditor provide?

A. The process can be more efficient if the organization develops risk-based tiers to save time auditing low-risk vendors.

B. The organization should not be sending questionnaires to vendors every year.

C. The organization should structure its questionnaires based on CSA Star.

D. The organization should outsource its third-party management process.

☑ **A.** The TPRM process could indeed be more efficient if the organization stratifies its vendors based on risk. The highest-risk vendors would be assessed annually with the most rigorous questionnaire, while vendors at lower-risk tiers would be assessed with shorter questionnaires or not at all.

☒ **B** is incorrect because the organization should be sending questionnaires to its high-risk vendors annually.

☒ **C** is incorrect, as an ISO-based questionnaire may very possibly be sufficient.

☒ **D** is incorrect because there is no indication that suggests the TPRM process should be outsourced.

39. What is the difference between an SSAE18 Type I audit and an SSA18 Type II audit?

A. A Type I audit is an audit of process effectiveness, whereas a Type II audit is an audit of process effectiveness and process design.

B. A Type I audit is an audit of process design and process effectiveness, whereas a Type II audit is an audit of process design.

C. A Type I audit is an audit of process design, whereas a Type II audit is an audit of process design and process effectiveness.

D. A Type I audit is an audit of process design and effectiveness, whereas a Type II audit is an audit of process effectiveness.

☑ **C.** This is the correct definition of SSAE18 Type I and Type II audits.

☒ **A, B,** and **D** are incorrect because these are incorrect definitions of SSAE18 Type I and Type II audits.

40. An auditor is auditing the payment systems for a retail store chain that has 80 stores in the region. The auditor needs to observe and take samples from some of the stores' systems. The audit client has selected two stores that are located in the same city as the store chain headquarters and two stores in a nearby town. How should the audit of the store locations proceed?

A. The auditor should learn more about the stores' systems and practices before deciding what to do.

B. The auditor should audit the selected stores and proceed accordingly.

C. The auditor should accept the sampling but select additional stores.

D. The auditor should select which stores to examine and proceed accordingly.

☑ **A.** While the auditee's desire to select the stores to audit may seem proactive, the auditor needs to better understand the nature of each store's information systems before overruling the auditee. For instance, the systems in all stores may be identically configured, and the nearby store operators may be better equipped to explain audit processes. On the other hand, if store systems were not identically configured and operated, the client's desire to select samples may have to be overruled, so that the auditor retains independence in fact.

☒ **B** is incorrect. There may be reasons why the auditee selected the nearby stores; among them, their processes may be more disciplined than others that are farther away. Unless the auditor is confident that all stores' systems are identical, the auditor must select samples himself or herself.

☒ **C** is incorrect because there may be impropriety involved on the part of the auditee's desire to select samples.

☒ **D** is incorrect. However, if the auditor is unable to conclude that all stores' information systems are identically configured and run, he or she must select the samples.

41. As a part of an audit of a business process, the auditor has had a discussion with the control owner, as well as the control operators, and has collected procedure documents and records. The auditor is asking internal customers of the business process to describe in their own words how the business process is operated. What kind of evidence collection are these discussions with internal customers?

A. Reconciliation

B. Reperformance

C. Walkthrough

D. Corroborative inquiry

☑ **D.** An auditor having discussions about a business process with additional personnel outside the process is known as corroborative inquiry. This helps to give the auditor more confidence in the veracity of the evidence obtained from control owners and operators.

☒ **A** is incorrect because there is no audit collection technique known as reconciliation.

☒ **B** is incorrect because reperformance is defined as the auditor performing some of the control procedure himself or herself, such as recalculating a batch total.

☒ **C** is incorrect because a walkthrough is performed by the control owner or operator, who describes the business process to the auditor.

42. Three months after the completion of an audit, the auditor has contacted the auditee to inquire about the auditee's activities since the audit and whether the auditee has made any progress related to audit findings. What sort of a communication is this outreach from the auditor?

   A. The auditor is being a good audit partner and wants to ensure the auditee is successful.

   B. The auditor is acting improperly by contacting the auditee outside of an audit and should be censored for unethical behavior.

   C. The auditee should assume that the auditor's outreach is personal in nature since this kind of communication is forbidden.

   D. The auditor is clearly making sure that the auditee is happy with the auditor's work so that the auditor gets the next year's audit assignment.

   ☑ **A.** An auditor is free to contact an auditee after an audit to show concern for the auditee and be sure that the auditee is proceeding properly by working to resolve any findings identified by the auditor.

   ☒ **B** is incorrect, as the auditor is not acting improperly.

   ☒ **C** is incorrect, as the auditor is within his or her professional bounds to communicate with the auditee after the audit. In many cases, auditors are encouraged in this regard.

   ☒ **D** is incorrect because it is indeed hoped that the auditor is not "fishing for business" by feigning interest in the auditee's well-being.

43. According to ISACA Audit Standard 1202, which types of risks should be considered when planning an audit?

   A. Fraud risk

   B. Business risk

   C. Cybersecurity risk

   D. Financial risk

   ☑ **B.** All types of risks should be considered when planning an audit of a business process or system.

   ☒ **A** is incorrect because fraud risk is not the only risk that should be considered.

   ☒ **C** is incorrect, as cybersecurity risk is only one type of risk that should be considered.

   ☒ **D** is incorrect because financial risk is only one type of risk that should be considered.

44. An IT service desk department that provisions user accounts performs a monthly activity whereby all user account changes that occurred in the prior month are checked against the list of corresponding requests in the ticketing system. This activity is known as:

   A. An audit

   B. A monthly provisioning review

C. A control threat-assessment (CTA)

D. A risk assessment

☑ **B.** The service desk is performing a monthly review of user account provisioning to make sure that all such account provisioning activities were in fact requested.

☒ **A** is incorrect because this activity is not an audit, because the service desk is checking its own work.

☒ **C** is incorrect because threats are not being analyzed in this activity.

☒ **D** is incorrect because this activity is not a risk assessment, but an activity review.

45. An organization with video surveillance at a work center has placed visible notices on building entrances that inform people that video surveillance systems are in use. The notices are an example of:

A. Administrative controls

B. Preventive controls

C. Detective controls

D. Deterrent controls

☑ **D.** Visible notices announcing its presence is an example of a deterrent control.

☒ **A** is incorrect because visible notes are not examples of administrative controls. An example of an administrative control is a policy.

☒ **B** is incorrect because neither video surveillance nor visible notices are preventive controls. An example of a preventive control is a locked door.

☒ **C** is incorrect. While video surveillance itself is a detective control, a visible notice announcing video surveillance is a deterrent control.

46. An auditor is planning an audit of a financial planning application. Can the auditor rely on a recent penetration test of the application as a risk-based audit?

A. No, because a penetration test does not reveal risks.

B. No, because a penetration test is not a risk assessment.

C. Yes, the auditor can make use of the pen test, but a risk assessment is still needed.

D. Yes, the penetration test serves as a risk assessment in this case.

☑ **C.** A penetration test reveals a limited view of risks, although a full risk assessment is still needed if the audit is to be truly risk-driven.

☒ **A** is incorrect because penetration tests do reveal some risks.

☒ **B** is incorrect. While it is true that a penetration test is not a risk assessment, the auditor can still rely upon it in order to have a partial view of risk.

☒ **D** is incorrect because a penetration test is never considered a full risk assessment.

47. Which of the following is the best example of a control self-assessment of a user account provisioning process?

   A. An examination of Active Directory to ensure that only domain administrators can make user account permission changes

   B. Checks to see that only authorized personnel made user account changes

   C. Confirmation that all user account changes were approved by appropriate personnel

   D. Reconciliation of all user account changes against approved requests in the ticketing system

   ☑ **D.** A reconciliation of all user account changes with approved requests in the ticketing system ensures that all such changes were actually requested and approved.

   ☒ **A** is incorrect. Confirmation that only domain administrators can make user account changes does not reveal whether the user account provisioning process is effective.

   ☒ **B** is incorrect. Checks to see that only authorized personnel made user account changes does not reveal whether the user account provisioning process is effective.

   ☒ **C** is incorrect. Checking whether the approvers of user account changes were appropriate does not reveal whether the process is effective.

48. The proper sequence of an audit of an accounts payable process is:

   A. Identify control owners, make evidence requests, perform walkthroughs, do corroborative interviews.

   B. Make evidence requests, identify control owners, do corroborative interviews.

   C. Identify control owners, do corroborative interviews, make evidence requests, perform walkthroughs.

   D. Do corroborative interviews, identify control owners, make evidence requests, and perform walkthroughs.

   ☑ **A.** It is necessary to identify control owners so that evidence requests can be sent to the right personnel. Next, walkthroughs are performed, and finally corroborative interviews are held.

   ☒ **B** is incorrect. If control owners are not first identified, evidence requests will be sent to the wrong personnel.

   ☒ **C** is incorrect. Corroborative interviews are performed after walkthroughs.

   ☒ **D** is incorrect. Corroborative interviews are performed after evidence requests and walkthroughs.

49. An auditor is auditing an accounts payable process and has found no exceptions. The auditor has decided to select additional samples to see whether any exceptions may be found. Which type of sampling is the auditor performing?

   A. Stop-or-go sampling

   B. Discovery sampling

C. Judgmental sampling

D. Exception sampling

☑ **B.** Discovery sampling is used when an auditor is examining samples in the search for at least one exception.

☒ **A** is incorrect because stop-or-go sampling is used when the auditor feels there is a low risk of finding exceptions.

☒ **C** is incorrect because this is not judgmental sampling.

☒ **D** is incorrect because there is no such thing as exception sampling.

50. Which of the following methods is best suited for an auditee to deliver evidence to an auditor during the audit of a background check process?

A. FTP server

B. Secure file transfer portal

C. E-mail with SMTP over TLS

D. Courier

☑ **B.** A secure file transfer portal is the best choice, because sensitive information will be encrypted in transit, end to end, and can handle volumes of evidence that may be too large to e-mail.

☒ **A** is incorrect because an FTP server is not considered secure, since neither login credentials nor data in transit is encrypted.

☒ **C** is incorrect for two reasons. First, the evidence could well be too large to send over e-mail; second, SMTP over TLS only encrypts e-mail between mail servers, not end to end.

☒ **D** is incorrect because using a courier is inefficient, as evidence would first have to be printed and electronic analysis of the evidence would not be possible.

51. An auditor has completed an audit, and the deliverable is ready to give to the audit client. What is the best method for delivering the audit report to the client?

A. Courier

B. Secure file transfer portal

C. E-mail using SMTP over TLS

D. In person, in a close-out meeting

☑ **D.** The best way to deliver an audit report is face to face, so that the auditor can explain the audit project, provide the audit report, and answer any questions that the audit client might have. An in-person meeting provides the auditor with valuable body language cues from the audit client so that the auditor will better understand the audit client's response to the audit report and its description of findings.

☒ **A** is incorrect because courier delivery does not provide an opportunity for a face-to-face discussion of the audit project and its results.

☒ **B** is incorrect because e-mail delivery does not provide an opportunity for a face-to-face discussion of the audit project and its results.

☒ **C** is incorrect because a secure file transfer portal does not provide an opportunity for a face-to-face discussion of the audit project and its results.

52. What are the potential consequences if an IS auditor is a member of ISACA and is CISA certified and violates the ISACA Code of Professional Ethics?

   A. Fines

   B. Imprisonment

   C. Termination of employment

   D. Loss of ISACA certifications

   ☑ **D.** An ISACA member violating the ISACA Code of Professional Ethics "can result in an investigation into a member's or certification holder's conduct and, ultimately, in disciplinary measures," including loss of certifications.

   ☒ **A** is incorrect because fines are not a part of ISACA disciplinary action. However, if the matter also includes the violation of laws, there may be fines levied in that case.

   ☒ **B** is incorrect because imprisonment is not a part of ISACA disciplinary action. However, if the situation also includes the violation of laws, imprisonment is a possible outcome.

   ☒ **C** is incorrect, unless the matter is also seen as egregious by the IS auditor's employer, who may need to terminate the auditor's employment.

53. An auditor is auditing an accounts payable process and has discovered that a single individual has requested and also approved several payments to vendors. What kind of an issue has the auditor found?

   A. A separation of duties issue.

   B. A split custody issue.

   C. A dual custodian issue.

   D. No issue has been identified.

   ☑ **A.** The auditor has discovered a separation of duties (sometimes known as segregation of duties) issue. Payment request and approval should be handled by separate persons in accounts payable.

   ☒ **B** is incorrect because this is not a split custody issue, but a separation of duties issue.

   ☒ **C** is incorrect because this is not a dual custodian issue.

   ☒ **D** is incorrect because the auditor's discovery is indeed an audit exception.

54. An organization uses an automated workflow process for request, review, approval, and provisioning of user accounts. Anyone in the organization can request access. Specific persons are assigned to the review and approval steps. Provisioning is automated. What kind of control is the separation of duties between the review and approval steps?

    A. Compensating control

    B. Manual control

    C. Preventive control

    D. Administrative control

    ☑ **C.** This is a preventive control and also an automatic control. The workflow prevents a single individual from performing both the review and approval steps.

    ☒ **A** is incorrect because this is not a compensating control, but a preventive control.

    ☒ **B** is incorrect because this is not a manual control, but preventive and automatic.

    ☒ **D** is incorrect because this is not an administrative control. There may indeed be a policy that requires the separation of duties (and the policy would be an administrative control), but the implementation of the control in the workflow system is a preventive control.

55. An auditor is planning an audit of a monthly terminated users review procedure. The auditor is planning to ask the auditee for a list of current user accounts in Active Directory, as well as a list of current employees and a list of terminated employees from Human Resources, so that the auditor can compare the lists. What kind of an audit is the auditor planning to perform?

    A. Reperformance

    B. Observation

    C. Corroboration

    D. Walk-back

    ☑ **A.** Since the auditor is going to be essentially repeating the steps performed in the review, this is a reperformance audit.

    ☒ **B** is incorrect because the auditor is not observing the auditee perform the review.

    ☒ **C** is incorrect because the auditor is not interviewing additional parties to obtain corroborative evidence of the process.

    ☒ **D** is incorrect because "walk-back" is not a type of audit.

56. An IT service desk manager is the control owner for the IT department change control process. In an audit of the change control process, the auditor has asked the IT service desk manager to provide all change control tickets whose request numbers end with the digit "6." What sampling methodology has the auditor used?

    A. Judgmental sampling

    B. Statistical sampling

    C. Stratified sampling

    D. Stop-or-go sampling

☑ **B.** This is statistical sampling, where the auditor has requested 10 percent of the population, effectively random and spread throughout the audit period. This assumes, of course, that change control requests are serialized sequentially.

☒ **A** is incorrect because this is not judgmental sampling. Judgmental sampling occurs when an auditor is examining items in a population and using professional judgement to determine whether to include a specific item in the sample.

☒ **C** is incorrect because this is not stratified sampling. Stratified sampling occurs when an auditor selects items in various numeric ranges (such as purchase orders of high amounts and low amounts).

☒ **D** is incorrect because this is not stop-or-go sampling. Stop-or-go sampling is used when an auditor is confident there will be few or no exceptions and decides to stop sampling early.

57. An audit firm is planning an audit of an organization's asset management records. For what reason would the auditor request a copy of the entire asset database from the DBA versus a report of assets from the owner of the asset process?

   A. Honesty of the evidence provider

   B. Objectivity of the evidence provider

   C. Independence of the evidence provider

   D. Qualification of the evidence provider

   ☑ **C.** The DBA is an independent party from the asset process owner and has little or no interest in the outcome of the audit.

   ☒ **A** is incorrect because an auditor is not likely to suspect the honesty of a process owner.

   ☒ **B** is incorrect because this is not the best answer.

   ☒ **D** is incorrect because the DBA and asset process owner are both qualified to provide evidence.

58. An auditor has delivered a Sarbanes-Oxley audit report containing 12 exceptions to the audit client, who disagrees with the findings. The audit client is upset and is asking the auditor to remove any six findings from the report. A review of the audit findings resulted in the confirmation that all 12 findings are valid. How should the auditor proceed?

   A. Remove the three lowest-risk findings from the report.

   B. Remote the six lowest-risk findings from the report.

   C. Report the auditee to the Securities and Exchange Commission.

   D. Explain to the auditee that the audit report cannot be changed.

☑ **D.** The auditor has no choice but to stand by the audit report as is, particularly after a review upholds all findings.

☒ **A** and **B** are incorrect because the auditor cannot compromise himself or herself in this way.

☒ **C** is incorrect because this matter does not warrant reporting to the authorities. If the audit client was offering a bribe, then perhaps notifying the authorities would be more appropriate.

59. An auditor has delivered a Sarbanes-Oxley audit report containing 12 exceptions to the audit client, who disagrees with the findings. The audit client is upset and is asking the auditor to remove any six findings from the report in exchange for a payment of $25,000. A review of the audit findings resulted in the confirmation that all 12 findings are valid. How should the auditor proceed?

A. The auditor should report the matter to his or her manager.

B. The auditor should reject the payment and meet the auditee halfway by removing three of the findings.

C. The auditor should reject the payment and remove six of the findings.

D. The auditor should report the incident to the audit client's audit committee.

☑ **A.** The auditor should first report the matter to his or her manager, who will in turn decide how to handle it. More than likely, the audit manager will notify the audit client's audit committee, who can decide to refer the matter to regulatory authorities.

☒ **B** and **C** are incorrect because the auditor should stand by the report and not make any changes to it.

☒ **D** is incorrect because a better course of action is to first notify his or her manager, who will decide how to handle the matter further.

60. An auditor is auditing a change control process. During a walkthrough, the control owner described the process as follows: "Engineers plan their changes and send an e-mail about their changes to the IT manager before 5 P.M. on Wednesday. The engineers then proceed with their changes during the change window on Friday evening." What, if any, findings should the auditor identify?

A. The change control process is fine as is, but could be improved by creating a ledger of changes.

B. The change control process is fine as is.

C. The change control process lacks a review step.

D. The change control process lacks review and approval steps.

☑ **D.** The change control process lacks a step where requested changes are reviewed, discussed, and approved. As it stands, it appears that engineers unilaterally decide what changes to make.

☒ **A** is incorrect because the process lacks an approval step.

☒ **B** is incorrect because the process should include an approval step.

☒ **C** is incorrect because the more important finding is the lack of an approval step.

61. An organization utilizes a video surveillance system on all ingress and egress points in its work facility; surveillance cameras are concealed from view, and there are no visible notices. What type of control is this?

    A. Administrative control

    B. Secret control

    C. Detective control

    D. Deterrent control

☑ **C.** This is a detective control. The system is not a deterrent control, since the video surveillance system is not visible.

☒ **A** is incorrect because an example of an administrative control is a policy or standard.

☒ **B** is incorrect because controls are not typically classified as "secret."

☒ **D** is incorrect because this particular video surveillance control is not a deterrent control, since the cameras are not visible.

62. An auditor is selecting samples from records in the user access request process. While privileged access requests account for approximately 5 percent of all access requests, the auditor wants 20 percent of the samples to be requests for administrative access. What sampling technique has the auditor selected?

    A. Judgmental sampling

    B. Stratified sampling

    C. Statistical sampling

    D. Variable sampling

☑ **B.** This is stratified sampling, where an auditor is selecting samples from various classes or values—in this case, higher-risk privileged accounts.

☒ **A** is incorrect because the auditor is not examining samples to be selected.

☒ **C** is incorrect because statistical sampling would result in about 5 percent of the selected samples being related to privileged access requests.

☒ **D** is incorrect because variable sampling is used to estimate conclusions about the evidence population.

63. An auditor is auditing a change control process by examining change logs in a database management system and requesting change control records to show that those changes were approved. The auditor plans to proceed until the first exception is found. What sampling technique is being used here?

A. Discovery sampling

B. Stop-or-go sampling

C. Attribute sampling

D. Exception sampling

☑ **A.** This is an example of the discovery sampling technique, where an auditor examines samples until an exception is found.

☒ **B** is incorrect because stop-or-go sampling is a technique where an auditor will stop selecting samples when he or she determines that the risk is low enough.

☒ **C** is incorrect because attribute sampling is a technique where an auditor is trying to determine how many of different types of samples exist.

☒ **D** is incorrect because "exception sampling" is not a standard sampling technique.

IT Life Cycle Management

This chapter covers CISA Domain 3, "Information Systems Acquisition, Development, and Implementation," and includes questions from the following topics:

- Program and project management
- The systems development life cycle (SDLC)
- Infrastructure development and implementation
- Maintaining information systems
- Business processes and business process reengineering
- Managing third-party risk
- Application controls

The topics in this chapter represent 12 percent of the CISA examination.

To provide effective audits of an organization's information systems and related business processes, the IS auditor needs to understand how organizations develop and/or acquire information systems. The systems development life cycle (SDLC) has undergone significant changes in the past several years, as organizations are migrating away from developing line-of-business applications and instead are users of commercial off-the-shelf (COTS) software or Software-as-a-Service (SaaS) software. Regardless, the core components of an SDLC are largely unchanged in terms of feasibility study, requirements, testing, and implementation. As all of these forms of software development and acquisition are common today, IS auditors need to have a broad understanding of all of the forms of SDLC.

1. What is the best reason for considering a proof of concept?

   A. The system being considered is too expensive to implement all at once.

   B. The system being considered will be a fully customized solution.

   C. The system being considered is too complicated to evaluate fully.

   D. The system being considered is not yet available.

2. A formal process whereby the organization gathers all business and technical requirements and forwards them to several qualified vendors, who then respond to them, is called:

   A. Request for information (RFI)

   B. Request for proposals (RFP)

   C. Request for evaluation (RFE)

   D. Request for quote (RFQ)

3. An organization that wishes to acquire IT products or services that it fully understands should issue what kind of document?

   A. Request for proposals (RFP)

   B. Request for information (RFI)

   C. Statement of work (SOW)

   D. Bid schedule

4. Which SEI CMM maturity level states that there is some consistency in the ways that individuals perform tasks from one time to the next, as well as some management planning and direction to ensure that tasks and projects are performed consistently?

   A. Initial

   B. Defined

   C. Repeatable

   D. Managed

5. At what stage in the acquisition process should a project team develop requirements?

   A. After writing the test plan

   B. After operational process development

   C. Prior to writing the test plan

   D. Prior to operational process development

6. All of the following are activities a project manager must perform to ensure a project is progressing in accordance with its plan *except:*

   A. Designing and testing the system

   B. Tracking project expenditures

C. Recording task completion

D. Managing the project schedule

7. During which phase of the infrastructure development life cycle are all changes to the environment performed under formal processes, including incident management, problem management, defect management, change management, and configuration management?

   A. Testing

   B. Design

   C. Implementation

   D. Maintenance

8. Which management processes cover the post-implementation phase of the SDLC?

   A. Maintenance management and change management

   B. Change management and configuration management

   C. Service management and configuration management

   D. Incident management and problem management

9. Change management and configuration management are key to which phase of the SDLC?

   A. Requirement definition

   B. Design

   C. Maintenance

   D. Testing

10. Which of the following is a formal verification of system specifications and technologies?

    A. Design review

    B. User acceptance testing (UAT)

    C. Implementation review

    D. Quality assurance testing (QAT)

11. All of the following are considerations when selecting and evaluating a software vendor *except:*

    A. Source code languages

    B. Financial stability

    C. References

    D. Vendor supportability

12. Which type of quality assurance method involves the users rather than IT or IS personnel?

  A. System testing

  B. Functional testing

  C. Quality assurance testing (QAT)

  D. User acceptance testing (UAT)

13. All of the following are considered risks to a software development project *except:*

  A. Delivered software not adequately meeting business needs

  B. Delivered software not meeting efficiency needs

  C. Termination of the project manager

  D. Project falling behind schedule or exceeding budget

14. Analysis of regulations and market conditions normally takes place during which phase of the SDLC?

  A. Testing phase

  B. Feasibility study

  C. Design phase

  D. Requirements definition phase

15. Which term describes a Scrum project and is a focused effort to produce some portion of the total project deliverable?

  A. Milestone

  B. Objective

  C. Daily Scrum

  D. Sprint

16. For what reason would an Internet-based financial application record the IP address of users who log in?

  A. This permits application performance testing.

  B. This provides localization information to the application.

  C. This provides authentication information to the application.

  D. This provides forensic information that can be used later.

17. In the context of logical access controls, the terms "subject" and "object" refer to:

  A. "Subject" refers to the person who is accessing the data, and "object" refers to the data being accessed.

  B. "Subject" refers to the data being accessed, and "object" refers to the file that contains the data.

C. "Subject" refers to the security context, and "object" refers to the data.

D. "Subject" refers to the data, and "object" refers to the person or entity accessing the data.

18. In the context of logical access control, what does the term "fail closed" mean?

    A. In the event of a power outage, all access points are closed.

    B. If access is denied, a database table will be closed or locked to changes.

    C. If an access control mechanism fails, all access will be denied.

    D. If an access control mechanism fails, all access will be allowed.

19. When would you design an access control to "fail open"?

    A. In the case of fire suppression controls, which would need to activate immediately if a fire is detected.

    B. In the case of building access controls, which would need to permit evacuation of personnel in an emergency.

    C. In the event of an emergency, where data access controls would need to allow anyone access to data so it could be backed up successfully and removed from the site.

    D. In the case of an incident, where outside investigators would require immediate and complete access to restricted data.

20. What are the three levels of the Constructive Cost Model (COCOMO) method for estimating software development projects?

    A. Basic, Intermediate, and Detailed

    B. Levels I, II, and III

    C. Initial, Managed, and Optimized

    D. Organic, Semi-detached, and Embedded

21. The best source for requirements for an RFP project is:

    A. Published industry standards

    B. The incumbent system's specifications

    C. Vendors and suppliers

    D. The organization's own business, technical, and security requirements

22. An organization wants to build a new application, but it has not yet defined precisely how end-user interaction will work. Which application development technique should be chosen to determine end-user interaction?

    A. Prototyping

    B. RAD

    C. Waterfall

    D. Scrum

23. A project manager regularly sends project status reports to executive management. Executives are requesting that status reports include visual diagrams showing the project schedule and project-critical paths from week to week. Which type of a chart should the project manager use?

    A. WBS

    B. PRINCE2

    C. PERT

    D. Gantt

24. During which phase of the SDLC are functionality and design characteristics verified?

    A. Maintenance

    B. Implementation

    C. Testing

    D. Design

25. Which kind of testing ensures that data is being formatted properly and inserted into the new application from the old application?

    A. Unit testing

    B. Migration testing

    C. Regression testing

    D. Functional testing

26. Which entity commissions feasibility studies to support a business case?

    A. Project team

    B. Project manager

    C. CISO

    D. IT steering committee

27. What is the purpose of a configuration management database?

    A. Storage of every change made to system components

    B. Storage of available configurations for system components

    C. Storage of approvals for configuration changes to a system

    D. Storage of the most recent change made to system components

28. When is the best time for an organization to measure business benefits of a new system?

    A. During unit testing

    B. One year after implementation

C. During requirements definition

D. During user acceptance testing

29. Which of the following represents the components of the project in graphical or tabular form and is a visual or structural representation of the system, software, or application?

   A. Data flow diagram (DFD)

   B. Work breakdown structure (WBS)

   C. Zachman model

   D. Object breakdown structure (OBS)

30. Which type of tests will determine whether there are any failures or errors in input, processing, or output controls in an application?

   A. Referential integrity tests

   B. Data conversion tests

   C. Data integrity tests

   D. Static data storage tests

31. Which quantitative method of sizing software projects is repeatable for traditional programming languages, but is not as effective with newer, nontextual languages?

   A. Source lines of code (SLOC)

   B. Work breakdown structure (WBS)

   C. Object breakdown structure (OBS)

   D. Constructive Cost Model (COCOMO)

32. Which type of testing, usually performed by developers during the coding phase of the software development project, is used to verify that the code in various parts of the application works properly?

   A. Unit testing

   B. Regression testing

   C. Functional testing

   D. User acceptance testing

33. An organization is considering acquiring a key business application from a small software company. What business provision should the organization require of the software company?

   A. Bonding

   B. Liability insurance

   C. Developer background checks

   D. Place source code in escrow

34. Which phase of the SDLC is continually referenced during the development, acquisition, and testing phases to ensure that the system is meeting the required specifications?

   A. Testing

   B. Requirements definition

   C. Design

   D. Implementation

35. What is the purpose of the review process after each phase of the SDLC?

   A. To establish additional requirements

   B. To change existing requirements

   C. To ensure that project deliverables meet the agreed-upon requirements

   D. To provide end users with a progress check on system development

1. C	**13.** C	**25.** B
2. B	**14.** B	**26.** D
3. A	**15.** D	**27.** A
4. C	**16.** D	**28.** B
5. C	**17.** A	**29.** D
6. A	**18.** C	**30.** C
7. D	**19.** B	**31.** A
8. B	**20.** A	**32.** A
9. C	**21.** D	**33.** D
10. D	**22.** A	**34.** B
11. A	**23.** C	**35.** C
12. D	**24.** C	

1. What is the best reason for considering a proof of concept?

   A. The system being considered is too expensive to implement all at once.

   B. The system being considered will be a fully customized solution.

   C. The system being considered is too complicated to evaluate fully.

   D. The system being considered is not yet available.

   ☑ **C.** The system being evaluated is too complex to evaluate in a walkthrough or by analyzing its specifications.

   ☒ **A** is incorrect because the cost of a system is not a primary reason for considering a POC.

   ☒ **B** is incorrect because a fully customized solution would not yet exist for a POC to take place.

   ☒ **D** is incorrect because a solution that is not yet available cannot be evaluated in a POC.

2. A formal process whereby the organization gathers all business and technical requirements and forwards them to several qualified vendors, who then respond to them, is called:

   A. Request for information (RFI)

   B. Request for proposals (RFP)

   C. Request for evaluation (RFE)

   D. Request for quote (RFQ)

   ☑ **B.** An RFP is the formal process used to publish the organization's requirements to several vendors, who will then reply formally with proposals that will meet those requirements.

   ☒ **A** is incorrect because an RFI does not meet all of these requirements.

   ☒ **C** is incorrect because an RFE does not meet all of these requirements.

   ☒ **D** is incorrect because an RFQ does not meet all of these requirements.

3. An organization that wishes to acquire IT products or services that it fully understands should issue what kind of document?

   A. Request for proposals (RFP)

   B. Request for information (RFI)

   C. Statement of work (SOW)

   D. Bid schedule

   ☑ **A.** An organization that wishes to acquire a new IT system or service that it already fully understands should issue a request for proposals (RFP). If the organization does not yet understand the IT products or services it wants to acquire, it should first issue a request for information (RFI) in order to learn more about them.

☒ **B** is incorrect because an RFI does not meet all of these requirements.

☒ **C** is incorrect because an SOW is not issued by a customer organization, but by a product or service organization.

☒ **D** is incorrect because a bid schedule does not provide detailed information on IT products or services.

4. Which SEI CMM maturity level states that there is some consistency in the ways that individuals perform tasks from one time to the next, as well as some management planning and direction to ensure that tasks and projects are performed consistently?

   A. Initial

   B. Defined

   C. Repeatable

   D. Managed

   ☑ **C.** The repeatable level of the SEI CMM five-level model states that there is some consistency in the ways that individuals perform tasks from one time to the next, as well as some management planning and direction to ensure that tasks and projects are performed consistently.

   ☒ **A** is incorrect because the initial level of the SEI CMM model defines an ad hoc, unmanaged process.

   ☒ **B** is incorrect because the defined level of the SEI CMM model signifies a process that is documented but probably not measured.

   ☒ **D** is incorrect because the managed level of the SEI CMM model signifies a process that is more mature, with statistics and perhaps even metrics.

5. At what stage in the acquisition process should a project team develop requirements?

   A. After writing the test plan

   B. After operational process development

   C. Prior to writing the test plan

   D. Prior to operational process development

   ☑ **C.** Requirements should be developed early in the systems development/acquisitions life cycle. The best answer here is prior to writing the test plan, but, ideally, requirements will be developed far earlier than that—even before the solution is designed.

   ☒ **A** is incorrect because test plans are written directly from requirements, so that testing can confirm whether requirements have been met.

   ☒ **B** is incorrect because processes need to comply with requirements, which means requirements need to be developed before processes are designed.

   ☒ **D** is incorrect because this is still not early enough—requirements need to be developed prior to solution selection and design.

6. All of the following are activities a project manager must perform to ensure a project is progressing in accordance with its plan *except:*

    A. Designing and testing the system

    B. Tracking project expenditures

    C. Recording task completion

    D. Managing the project schedule

    ☑ **A.** It is not the project manager's job to design and test the system, but instead to coordinate those activities as performed by others.

    ☒ **B, C,** and **D** are incorrect. They all are activities the project manager must carry out to ensure a project is on track and meeting scheduling and budget requirements. System design and testing are not normally carried out by the project manager role.

7. During which phase of the infrastructure development life cycle are all changes to the environment performed under formal processes, including incident management, problem management, defect management, change management, and configuration management?

    A. Testing

    B. Design

    C. Implementation

    D. Maintenance

    ☑ **D.** After a system has been put into production, the maintenance phase involves activities relating to incident management, problems, defects, changes, and configuration.

    ☒ **A** is incorrect because testing is performed before the infrastructure is placed into production.

    ☒ **B** is incorrect because design precedes changes.

    ☒ **C** is incorrect because implementation is completed before subsequent changes are made.

8. Which management processes cover the post-implementation phase of the SDLC?

    A. Maintenance management and change management

    B. Change management and configuration management

    C. Service management and configuration management

    D. Incident management and problem management

    ☑ **B.** The post-implementation phase of the SDLC is carried out by the change management and configuration management processes.

    ☒ **A** is incorrect because maintenance management is not a formal operational term.

☒ **C** is incorrect because service management is not concerned with the management of an application after implementation.

☒ **D** is incorrect because incident and problem management are not concerned with the management of an application after implementation.

9. Change management and configuration management are key to which phase of the SDLC?

A. Requirement definition

B. Design

C. Maintenance

D. Testing

☑ **C.** Change management and configuration management are essential operational processes in the maintenance phase of the SDLC.

☒ **A** is incorrect because requirements definition is performed prior to initial implementation.

☒ **B** is incorrect because design is performed prior to initial implementation.

☒ **D** is incorrect because testing is performed during and immediately after initial development.

10. Which of the following is a formal verification of system specifications and technologies?

A. Design review

B. User acceptance testing (UAT)

C. Implementation review

D. Quality assurance testing (QAT)

☑ **D.** Quality assurance testing is a formal verification of system specifications and technologies. Users are usually not involved in QAT; instead, this testing is typically performed by IT or IS departments.

☒ **A** is incorrect because design review is not a verification of technologies, since development and implementation have not yet taken place.

☒ **B** is incorrect because UAT is a test of functionality, not of technologies.

☒ **C** is incorrect because implementation review does not verify specification, but the implementation process itself.

11. All of the following are considerations when selecting and evaluating a software vendor *except:*

A. Source code languages

B. Financial stability

C. References

D. Vendor supportability

☑ **A.** A software vendor's choice of source code languages is of lesser concern when selecting and evaluating software vendors.

☒ **B, C,** and **D** are incorrect. These all are considerations when evaluating and selecting a software or system vendor. Internal processes that the vendor may or may not have are not a factor in selection, but in the long run may affect the end product in terms of quality, support, and so on.

12. Which type of quality assurance method involves the users rather than IT or IS personnel?

   A. System testing

   B. Functional testing

   C. Quality assurance testing (QAT)

   D. User acceptance testing (UAT)

   ☑ **D.** User acceptance testing (UAT) should consist of a formal, written body of specific tests that permits application users to determine whether the application will operate properly.

   ☒ **A** is incorrect because users are not involved in system testing.

   ☒ **B** is incorrect because users are not involved in functional testing—this is performed by developers.

   ☒ **C** is incorrect because QAT is performed by alternative developers or software test personnel.

13. All of the following are considered risks to a software development project *except:*

   A. Delivered software not adequately meeting business needs

   B. Delivered software not meeting efficiency needs

   C. Termination of the project manager

   D. Project falling behind schedule or exceeding budget

   ☑ **C.** Termination of the project manager is not an anticipated risk in a software development project.

   ☒ **A, B,** and **D** are incorrect. Delivered software not meeting business needs or business efficiency needs are risks, as are cost and schedule overruns. Termination of a project manager is not considered a risk to a project, as they can be more easily replaced.

14. Analysis of regulations and market conditions normally takes place during which phase of the SDLC?

   A. Testing phase

   B. Feasibility study

   C. Design phase

   D. Requirements definition phase

☑ **B.** Changes in business conditions, including market changes and regulations, take place during the feasibility study, prior to requirements definition, design, and testing.

☒ **A** is incorrect because testing takes place after development has taken place.

☒ **C** is incorrect because the design phase is concerned with the logical design of the system.

☒ **D** is incorrect because requirements definition is concerned with ensuring that the system meets business needs.

15. Which term describes a Scrum project and is a focused effort to produce some portion of the total project deliverable?

   A. Milestone

   B. Objective

   C. Daily Scrum

   D. Sprint

☑ **D.** A typical Scrum project consists of several "sprints," which are focused efforts to produce some portion of the total project deliverable. A sprint usually lasts from two to four weeks.

☒ **A** is incorrect because a milestone is a point in a project when a key objective has been completed.

☒ **B** is incorrect because an objective is a goal of a project.

☒ **C** is incorrect because a Daily Scrum is a daily project status meeting in a Scrum project.

16. For what reason would an Internet-based financial application record the IP address of users who log in?

   A. This permits application performance testing.

   B. This provides localization information to the application.

   C. This provides authentication information to the application.

   D. This provides forensic information that can be used later.

☑ **D.** In an Internet-based financial application, it may be useful to record the IP address of each user who logs in. While it may be infeasible to restrict access by IP address (especially for traveling users), recording IP address at the time of login can be useful later on if there is a reason to believe that a user's account has been hijacked.

☒ **A** is incorrect because there is little or no correlation between a user's IP address and application performance.

☒ **B** is incorrect because IP addresses are not always a reliable indicator of location, particularly if the user is employing a VPN.

☒ **C** is incorrect because reliance on IP address as authentication is not the best available answer. Still, an IP address can provide information concerning the whereabouts of the subject. However, relying entirely on IP address for location information is not reliable since the subject could be using a VPN.

17. In the context of logical access controls, the terms "subject" and "object" refer to:

   A. "Subject" refers to the person who is accessing the data, and "object" refers to the data being accessed.

   B. "Subject" refers to the data being accessed, and "object" refers to the file that contains the data.

   C. "Subject" refers to the security context, and "object" refers to the data.

   D. "Subject" refers to the data, and "object" refers to the person or entity accessing the data.

   ☑ **A.** The terms "subject" and "object" are used in the context of access management. Subject refers to a person (or program or machine), and object refers to data (or other resource) being accessed.

   ☒ **B** is incorrect because this definition of "object" is too narrow.

   ☒ **C** is incorrect because "subject" and "object" are not used in this manner.

   ☒ **D** is incorrect because "subject" and "object" are not used in this manner.

18. In the context of logical access control, what does the term "fail closed" mean?

   A. In the event of a power outage, all access points are closed.

   B. If access is denied, a database table will be closed or locked to changes.

   C. If an access control mechanism fails, all access will be denied.

   D. If an access control mechanism fails, all access will be allowed.

   ☑ **C.** The correct definition of "fail closed" in an access control mechanism is one in which all requested accesses will be denied.

   ☒ **A, B,** and **D** are incorrect because these are incorrect definitions of "fail closed."

19. When would you design an access control to "fail open"?

   A. In the case of fire suppression controls, which would need to activate immediately if a fire is detected.

   B. In the case of building access controls, which would need to permit evacuation of personnel in an emergency.

   C. In the event of an emergency, where data access controls would need to allow anyone access to data so it could be backed up successfully and removed from the site.

   D. In the case of an incident, where outside investigators would require immediate and complete access to restricted data.

☑ **B.** A good example of an access control to "fail open" is the case of building access controls, which would need to permit evacuation of personnel in an emergency.

☒ **A, C,** and **D** are incorrect because these are not examples of "fail open."

20. What are the three levels of the Constructive Cost Model (COCOMO) method for estimating software development projects?

   A. Basic, Intermediate, and Detailed

   B. Levels I, II, and III

   C. Initial, Managed, and Optimized

   D. Organic, Semi-detached, and Embedded

   ☑ **A.** The three levels of the COCOMO method for estimating software development projects are Basic, Intermediate, and Detailed.

   ☒ **B** is incorrect because Levels I, II, and III are not the levels of COCOMO.

   ☒ **C** is incorrect because Initial, Managed, and Optimized are not the levels of COCOMO.

   ☒ **D** is incorrect because Organic, Semi-detached, and Embedded are not the levels of COCOMO.

21. The best source for requirements for an RFP project is:

   A. Published industry standards

   B. The incumbent system's specifications

   C. Vendors and suppliers

   D. The organization's own business, technical, and security requirements

   ☑ **D.** An organization that is developing requirements for an RFP (request for proposals) for products or services from vendors needs to develop these requirements internally.

   ☒ **A** is incorrect because there is no industry-standard list of requirements available, as every organization is different.

   ☒ **B** is incorrect because the incumbent system may no longer be meeting the organization's requirements, and hence should not be used for a replacement system.

   ☒ **C** is incorrect because requirements should definitely not come from vendors (who would develop requirements to ensure that only their products or services could be selected).

22. An organization wants to build a new application, but it has not yet defined precisely how end-user interaction will work. Which application development technique should be chosen to determine end-user interaction?

   A. Prototyping

   B. RAD

   C. Waterfall

   D. Scrum

☑ **A.** The best development methodology in a situation where the organization is unable to determine (in the design phase) how end-user interaction will work in a system is to build prototypes of various kinds until the most suitable one can be chosen.

☒ **B** is incorrect because RAD is more suited for situations where more is known about the desired function of the system.

☒ **C** is incorrect because waterfall is more suited for projects where requirements can all be developed in advance.

☒ **D** is incorrect because Scrum is not the *best* choice; however, Scrum is a good alternative.

23. A project manager regularly sends project status reports to executive management. Executives are requesting that status reports include visual diagrams showing the project schedule and project-critical paths from week to week. Which type of a chart should the project manager use?

   A. WBS

   B. PRINCE2

   C. PERT

   D. Gantt

   ☑ **C.** A PERT chart shows the project status and critical path for a given project.

   ☒ **A** is incorrect because WBS does not show project status or critical path, but instead the structure of the project.

   ☒ **B** is incorrect because PRINCE2 is a methodology, not a reporting tool.

   ☒ **D** is incorrect because Gantt does show project status but not critical path.

24. During which phase of the SDLC are functionality and design characteristics verified?

   A. Maintenance

   B. Implementation

   C. Testing

   D. Design

   ☑ **C.** Testing is the phase of a development process where functionality and design are verified in the test plan.

   ☒ **A** is incorrect because functionality and design are not verified during maintenance.

   ☒ **B** is incorrect because functionality and design are not verified during implementation.

   ☒ **D** is incorrect because functionality and design are not verified during the design phase of a project.

25. Which kind of testing ensures that data is being formatted properly and inserted into the new application from the old application?

   A. Unit testing

   B. Migration testing

   C. Regression testing

   D. Functional testing

   ☑ **B.** When one application is replacing another, data from the old application is often imported into the new application to eliminate the need for both old and new applications to function at the same time. Migration testing ensures that data is being properly formatted and inserted into the new application. This testing is often performed several times in advance of the real, live migration at cutover time.

   ☒ **A** is incorrect because unit testing is used to verify the functionality of small portions of code.

   ☒ **C** is incorrect because regression testing is used to verify that changes to a system do not alter functions that are intended to be unaffected by those changes.

   ☒ **D** is incorrect because functional testing is used to confirm proper operation of a system.

26. Which entity commissions feasibility studies to support a business case?

   A. Project team

   B. Project manager

   C. CISO

   D. IT steering committee

   ☑ **D.** An IT steering committee formally commissions the feasibility study, approves the project, assigns IT resources to the project, and approves the project schedule.

   ☒ **A** is incorrect because a project team's role is to complete assigned tasks, thereby ensuring the successful execution of a project.

   ☒ **B** is incorrect because a project manager's role is to coordinate project activities, thereby ensuring the successful execution of a project.

   ☒ **C** is incorrect because a CISO's role is to lead and manage an organization's cybersecurity program.

27. What is the purpose of a configuration management database?

   A. Storage of every change made to system components

   B. Storage of available configurations for system components

   C. Storage of approvals for configuration changes to a system

   D. Storage of the most recent change made to system components

☑ **A.** A configuration management database (CMDB) stores all changes made to a system. This makes it possible for system managers to know the precise configuration of every component at any point in time. This often proves useful during system troubleshooting.

☒ **B** is incorrect because a CMDB does not store available configurations, but actual configurations.

☒ **C** is incorrect because a CMDB's purpose is not to store approvals for changes to a system; this is done in the change control process.

☒ **D** is incorrect because a CMDB stores not only the most recent changes, but all historical changes.

28. When is the best time for an organization to measure business benefits of a new system?

   A. During unit testing

   B. One year after implementation

   C. During requirements definition

   D. During user acceptance testing

   ☑ **B.** The best time to measure business benefits of a new system is after implementation and when enough time has passed for business measurements to be collected and measured.

   ☒ **A** is incorrect because the system will not be running if unit testing is still in progress.

   ☒ **C** is incorrect because the system will not be running if requirements are still being defined.

   ☒ **D** is incorrect because the system will not be completed if UAT is still taking place.

29. Which of the following represents the components of the project in graphical or tabular form and is a visual or structural representation of the system, software, or application?

   A. Data flow diagram (DFD)

   B. Work breakdown structure (WBS)

   C. Zachman model

   D. Object breakdown structure (OBS)

   ☑ **D.** An OBS is a visual or structural representation of the system, software, or application, in a hierarchical form, from high level to fine detail.

   ☒ **A** is incorrect because a DFD depicts data flows in a system.

   ☒ **B** is incorrect because a WBS depicts all of the work required to complete a project.

   ☒ **C** is incorrect because a Zachman model shows the architecture of a system.

30. Which type of tests will determine whether there are any failures or errors in input, processing, or output controls in an application?

    A. Referential integrity tests

    B. Data conversion tests

    C. Data integrity tests

    D. Static data storage tests

    ☑ **C.** Data integrity testing is used to confirm whether an application properly accepts, processes, and stores information. Data integrity tests will determine whether there are any failures or errors in input, processing, or output controls in an application.

    ☒ **A** is incorrect because referential integrity tests confirm the correct function of primary and foreign keys in a relational database management system.

    ☒ **B** is incorrect because data conversion tests confirm whether data is properly converted from one system to another.

    ☒ **D** is incorrect because static data storage tests confirm the correctness of data storage.

31. Which quantitative method of sizing software projects is repeatable for traditional programming languages, but is not as effective with newer, nontextual languages?

    A. Source lines of code (SLOC)

    B. Work breakdown structure (WBS)

    C. Object breakdown structure (OBS)

    D. Constructive Cost Model (COCOMO)

    ☑ **A.** Sizing for software projects has traditionally relied upon source lines of code (SLOC) estimates. A similar measuring unit is kilo lines of code (KLOC). The advantage of SLOC and KLOC is that they are quantitative and somewhat repeatable for a given computer language, such as COBOL, FORTRAN, or BASIC. However, these methods are falling out of favor because many of the languages in use today are not textual in nature.

    ☒ **B** is incorrect because WBS is a depiction of the work required to successfully complete a project.

    ☒ **C** is incorrect because OBS is a depiction of the components of a system.

    ☒ **D** is incorrect because COCOMO is used to calculate the cost, not the size, of a development project.

32. Which type of testing, usually performed by developers during the coding phase of the software development project, is used to verify that the code in various parts of the application works properly?

  A. Unit testing

  B. Regression testing

  C. Functional testing

  D. User acceptance testing

  ☑ A. Unit testing is usually performed by developers during the coding phase of the software development project. When each developer is assigned the task of building a section of an application, the specifications that are given to the developer should include test plans or test cases that the developer will use to verify that the code works properly.

  ☒ B is incorrect because regression testing is used to verify the system continues to work properly.

  ☒ C is incorrect because functional testing is used to verify the correct operation of a system.

  ☒ D is incorrect because user acceptance testing is used to confirm that user-facing features of a system work properly.

33. An organization is considering acquiring a key business application from a small software company. What business provision should the organization require of the software company?

  A. Bonding

  B. Liability insurance

  C. Developer background checks

  D. Place source code in escrow

  ☑ D. Software escrow ensures that the customer organization will be able to continue using and maintaining an application even if the vendor goes out of business.

  ☒ A is incorrect because bonding is related to operational liability, not survival of the vendor.

  ☒ B is incorrect because liability insurance has little or no bearing on the survival of the vendor.

  ☒ C is incorrect because developer background checks do not measurably help ensure the survival of the vendor.

34. Which phase of the SDLC is continually referenced during the development, acquisition, and testing phases to ensure that the system is meeting the required specifications?

   A. Testing

   B. Requirements definition

   C. Design

   D. Implementation

   ☑ **B.** The requirements definition phase, and the system requirements developed during this phase, is continually referenced throughout the SDLC to ensure that the system meets the requirements that were agreed upon.

   ☒ **A** is incorrect because testing is not referenced during all of these phases.

   ☒ **C** is incorrect because design is not referenced during all phases of the SDLC.

   ☒ **D** is incorrect because implementation is not referenced throughout the SDLC.

35. What is the purpose of the review process after each phase of the SDLC?

   A. To establish additional requirements

   B. To change existing requirements

   C. To ensure that project deliverables meet the agreed-upon requirements

   D. To provide end users with a progress check on system development

   ☑ **C.** Post-phase reviews are used to ensure that any project deliverables due at the end of each phase meet requirements. These reviews are sometimes called "gate reviews" because they represent a gating process where a project is not permitted to progress to a later phase until an earlier phase is reviewed and approved by management.

   ☒ **A** is incorrect because additional requirements are not introduced in post-phase reviews.

   ☒ **B** is incorrect because requirements are not altered in post-phase reviews.

   ☒ **D** is incorrect because the main purpose of post-phase reviews is to review project status and performance, not inform end users of the same.

CHAPTER 5

IT Service Management and Continuity

This chapter covers CISA Domain 4, "Information Systems Operations and Business Resilience" and includes questions from the following topics:

- Information systems operations
- Information systems hardware
- Information systems architecture and software
- Network infrastructure, technologies, models, and protocols
- Business continuity and disaster recovery planning
- Auditing infrastructure, operations, and business continuity and disaster recovery planning

The topics in this chapter represent 23 percent of the CISA examination.

IT organizations are effective if their operations are effective. Management needs to be in control of information systems operations, which means that all aspects of operations need to be measured, those measurements and reports reviewed, and management-directed changes carried out to ensure continuous improvement.

IT organizations are service organizations—they exist to serve the organization and support its business processes. IT's service management operations need to be well designed, adequately measured, and reviewed by management.

In the age of digital transformation (DX), organizations are more dependent than ever before on information technology for execution of core business processes. This, in turn, changes the business resilience conversation and increases the emphasis on business continuity and disaster recovery planning, which has moved to this domain in the 2019 CISA job practice.

In addition to being familiar with IT business processes, IS auditors need to have a keen understanding of the workings of computer hardware, operating systems, and network communications technology. This knowledge will help the auditor better understand many aspects of service management and operations.

1. A device that forwards packets to their destination based on their destination IP address is known as a:

   A. Bridge

   B. Gateway

   C. Router

   D. Switch

2. A security manager is planning to implement a first-time use of a vulnerability scanning tool in an organization. What method should the security manager use to confirm that all assets are scanned?

   A. Compare the scan results with the accounting department asset inventory.

   B. Compare the scan results with the contents of the CMDB.

   C. Compare the scan results with a discovery scan performed by the vulnerability scanning tool.

   D. Compare the scan results with the latest network diagram.

3. Which of the following methods should be used to create a point-in-time copy of a large production database?

   A. Storage system snapshot

   B. Storage system replication

   C. E-vaulting

   D. Export to a flat file that is backed up to tape

4. All of the following protocols are used for federated authentication *except:*

   A. OAuth

   B. SAML

   C. WSDL

   D. HMAC

5. What is typically the most significant risk associated with end users being local administrators on their workstations?

   A. End users will have access to all confidential information.

   B. End users can install unauthorized software.

   C. Malware can run at the highest privilege level.

   D. End users can use tools to crack all domain passwords.

6. Which of the following persons is best suited to approve users' access to sensitive data in a customer database?

   A. Customer service manager

   B. IT service desk personnel

   C. Information security manager

   D. IT manager

7. An organization is planning a new SaaS service offering and is uncertain about the resources required to support the service. How should the organization proceed?

   A. Calculate projected performance using CMMI tools.

   B. Calculate projected performance using Zachman tools.

   C. Measure actual performance metrics in production.

   D. Build a working prototype and perform load tests.

8. What is the best definition of a problem in ITIL-based service management?

   A. Chronic exceptions in audits of IT systems

   B. The same incident that occurs repeatedly

   C. Repeated unscheduled downtime

   D. Unscheduled downtime that exceeds SLAs

9. Which of the following is the best relationship between system security and the use of vulnerability scanning tools?

   A. Vulnerability scanning is performed proactively, and it drives the security patching and hardening functions.

   B. Vulnerability scanning is performed proactively, and it drives the security patching function.

   C. Patching and hardening are performed proactively, and vulnerability scanning is used to verify their effectiveness.

   D. Patching is performed proactively, and vulnerability scanning is used to verify its effectiveness.

10. A SaaS provider and a customer are having a dispute about the availability of service, quality of service, and issue resolution provided by the SaaS provider. What type of a legal agreement should the parties add to their contract to better define these problems and their resolution?

    A. Pricing table

    B. Exit clause

    C. Performance addendum

    D. Service level agreement

11. What is the purpose of a business impact analysis?

   A. It defines the most critical business processes.

   B. It defines the most critical IT applications.

   C. It defines the most critical service providers.

   D. It defines the disaster recovery plan.

12. An IT architect needs to increase the resilience of a single application server. Which of the following choices will *least* benefit the server's resilience?

   A. Active-active cluster

   B. Active-passive cluster

   C. Geo-cluster

   D. Redundant power supply

13. Which of the following backup schemes best protects an organization from ransomware?

   A. Storage system replication

   B. Storage system mirroring

   C. Storage system snapshots

   D. RAID-5

14. A mail order organization wants to develop procedures to be followed in the event that the main office building cannot be occupied, so that customer orders can still be fulfilled. What kind of a plan does the organization need to develop?

   A. Business impact analysis

   B. Business continuity plan

   C. Disaster recovery plan

   D. Emergency evacuation plan

15. An IT department is planning on implementing disaster recovery capabilities in some of its business systems. What means should be used to determine which applications require DR capabilities and to what level of recoverability?

   A. Business continuity plan

   B. Disaster recovery plan

   C. Risk assessment

   D. Business impact analysis

16. Which of the following is the most compelling reason for an organization to *not* automate its data purging jobs in support of data retention policies?

   A. DR planning

   B. Referential integrity

C. Privacy breaches

D. Legal holds

17. Which of the following schemes is most likely to be successful for workstations used by a mobile workforce?

A. Automated patching followed by a system restart that the end user can control

B. Automated patching and restarts

C. End-user-initiated patching and restarts

D. Applying only those patches not requiring a system restart

18. An IT department completed a data discovery assessment and found that numerous users were saving files containing sensitive information on organization-wide readable file shares. Which of the following is the best remediation for this matter?

A. Remove the offending files from the org-wide share.

B. Announce to users that the org-wide readable share is not for sensitive data.

C. Change the org-wide readable share to read-only for most users.

D. Change the org-wide readable share to write-only for most users.

19. For which users or groups should the SQL listener on a database management system be accessible?

A. For the application accounts only

B. For the application and DBA accounts only

C. For DBA accounts only

D. For DBA accounts plus all users of the application

20. An organization's financial accounting system crashes every Friday night after backups have completed. In ITIL terms, what process should be invoked?

A. Problem management

B. Incident management

C. Capacity management

D. Business continuity management

21. An IT organization is investigating a problem in its change management process whereby many changes have to be backed out because they could not be completed or because verifications failed. Which is the best remedy for this situation?

A. Increase the size of change windows.

B. Require a separate person to verify changes.

C. Require change requests to have better backout procedures.

D. Require more rigorous testing in a test environment prior to scheduling changes in production.

22. Which language is used to change the schema in a database management system?

   A. DDL

   B. SQL

   C. Stored procedures

   D. JCL

23. A DBA has been asked to limit the tables, rows, or columns that are visible to some users with direct database access. Which solution would best fulfill this request?

   A. Create alternative user accounts.

   B. Move those users into different AD groups.

   C. Create one or more views.

   D. Change the schema for those users.

24. An organization's IT department developed DR capabilities for some business applications prior to a BIA ever being performed. Now that a BIA has been performed, it has been determined that some IT applications' DR capabilities exceed what is called for in the BIA and that other applications fall short. What should be done to remedy this?

   A. Redo the BIA, using existing DR capabilities as inputs.

   B. Make no changes, as this is the expected result.

   C. Change IT application DR capabilities to align with the BIA.

   D. Change the BIA to align with IT application DR capabilities.

25. What is the purpose of hot-pluggable drives in a storage system?

   A. Ability to replace drives that have crashed or overheated

   B. Ability to replace drives while the storage system is still running

   C. Ability to replace drives without the risk of harm to personnel

   D. Ability to install additional drives without powering down the system

26. What is the primary purpose for data restoration testing?

   A. To meet regulatory requirements

   B. To prove that bare-metal restores can be performed

   C. To see how long it takes to restore data from backup

   D. To ensure that backups are actually being performed

27. Which of the following should approve RTO and RPO targets?

   A. Senior business executives

   B. Board of directors

   C. CISO

   D. CIO

28. An organization has developed its first-ever disaster recovery plan. What is the best choice for the first round of testing of the plan?

    A. Cutover test

    B. Walkthrough

    C. Simulation

    D. Parallel test

29. Which of the following best describes the purpose of a hypervisor?

    A. It creates and manages virtual desktops.

    B. It creates and manages containers.

    C. It installs software on virtual machines.

    D. It creates and manages virtual machines.

30. Which of the following best fits the definition of a set of structured tables with indexes, primary keys, and foreign keys?

    A. Hierarchical database

    B. Object database

    C. Relational database

    D. Network database

31. An organization uses its vulnerability scanning tool as its de facto asset management system. What is the biggest risk associated with this approach?

    A. Network engineers could build new IP networks not included in the scanning tool's configuration.

    B. System engineers could implement new servers that the scanning tool won't see.

    C. System engineers could implement new virtual machines that the scanning tool won't see.

    D. IP source routing could prevent the scanning tool from seeing all networks.

32. Which of the following systems should be used for populating the IT asset database in an elastic cloud environment?

    A. Hypervisor

    B. Vulnerability scanning tool

    C. Patch management tool

    D. CMDB

33. What is a typical frequency for running a job that checks Active Directory for unused user accounts?

    A. Every hour

    B. Every 24 hours

    C. Every 7 days

    D. Every 90 days

34. The system interface standard that includes process control, IPC, and shared memory is known as:

A. Unix

B. POSIX

C. ActiveX

D. Ultrix

35. An environment consisting of centralized servers running end-user operating systems that display on users' computers is known as:

A. Hosted hypervisor

B. Bare-metal hypervisor

C. Virtual desktop infrastructure

D. Reverse Telnet

36. A data privacy officer recently commissioned a data discovery exercise to understand the extent to which sensitive data is present on the company's world-readable file share. The exercise revealed that dozens of files containing large volumes of highly sensitive data were present on the file share. What is the best first step the data privacy officer should take?

A. Remove all instances of files containing large volumes of highly sensitive data.

B. Investigate each instance to see whether any files are a part of business processes.

C. Sanction the users who placed the files there for violations of internal privacy policy.

D. Do nothing, as this is an acceptable practice for files of this type.

37. A new IT manager is making improvements in the organization's management of unplanned outages. The IT manager has built a new process where repeated cases of similar outages are analyzed in order to identify their cause. What process has the IT manager created?

A. Problem management

B. Incident management

C. Root cause analysis

D. Security event management

38. A new IT manager is making improvements in the organization's management of the detailed settings on servers and network devices. The process that the IT manager has made is a part of:

A. Vulnerability management

B. System hardening

C. Configuration management

D. Performance management

39. A new IT manager is making improvements in the organization's management of the detailed settings on servers and network devices. The process includes the creation of a repository for storing details about this information. This repository is known as:

    A. An asset management database

    B. A vulnerability management database

    C. A configuration management database

    D. A system hardening standard

40. A new IT manager is making improvements to the organization's need to make its systems and devices more resilient to attacks. The IT manager should update:

    A. The vulnerability management process

    B. The system and device hardening standard

    C. The configuration management database

    D. The security incident response plan

41. A customer of a SaaS provider is complaining about the SaaS provider's lack of responsiveness in resolving security issues. What portion of the contract should the customer refer to when lodging a formal complaint?

    A. Service description

    B. System availability

    C. Service level agreement

    D. Security controls

42. Computer code that is found within the contents of a database is known as a:

    A. Blob

    B. Function

    C. Stored procedure

    D. Subroutine

43. An organization is starting its first-ever effort to develop a business continuity and disaster recovery plan. What is the best first step to perform in this effort?

    A. Criticality analysis

    B. Business impact analysis

    C. Setting recovery targets

    D. Selecting a DR site

44. What is the purpose for connecting two redundant power supplies to separate electrical circuits?

    A. System resilience in case one electrical circuit fails

    B. To balance electrical load between the circuits

    C. To balance the phasing between the circuits

    D. To avoid overloading a single electrical circuit

45. An IT organization is modernizing its tape backup system by replacing its tape library system with a storage array, while keeping its tape backup software system. What has the organization implemented?

 A. E-vaulting

 B. S-vaulting

 C. Virtual tape library

 D. Mirroring

46. An IT organization is modernizing its tape backup system by sending data to a cloud storage provider. What has the organization implemented?

 A. Replication

 B. Mirroring

 C. Virtual tape library

 D. E-vaulting

47. A city government department that accepts payments for water use has developed a procedure to be followed when the IT application for processing payments is unavailable. What type of procedure has been developed?

 A. Business continuity plan

 B. Disaster recovery plan

 C. Business impact analysis

 D. Backout plan

48. A city government IT department has developed a procedure to be followed when the primary application for accepting water usage payments has been incapacitated. The procedure calls for the initiation of a secondary application in a different data center. What type of procedure has been developed?

 A. Business continuity plan

 B. Backout plan

 C. Security incident response plan

 D. Disaster recovery plan

49. What is the most important factor to consider in the development of a disaster recovery plan?

 A. The safety of personnel

 B. The availability of critical data

 C. Notification of civil authorities

 D. The continuity of critical operations

50. An SSD is most commonly used as:

   A. Backup storage

   B. Removable storage

   C. Main storage

   D. Secondary storage

51. The phrase "you can't protect what you don't know about" refers to which key IT process?

   A. Vulnerability management

   B. License management

   C. Patching

   D. Asset management

52. The SOAP protocol is related to:

   A. The patch management process

   B. The exchange of data through an API

   C. The vulnerability management process

   D. Memory garbage collection

53. Restricting USB attached storage on end-user workstations addresses all of the following *except:*

   A. Leakage of intellectual property

   B. Malware infection

   C. System capacity management

   D. Personal use of a workstation

54. The primary purpose of a dynamic DLP system is:

   A. To detect unauthorized personal use of a workstation

   B. To detect unauthorized use of personal web mail

   C. To control unauthorized access to sensitive information

   D. To control unauthorized movement of sensitive information

55. What is the suitability for the use of a SIEM to alert personnel of system capacity and performance issues?

   A. If syslog events are generated, use cases related to performance and capacity can be developed.

   B. A SIEM can only be used to alert personnel of security events.

   C. Use cases for non-security-related events do not function on a SIEM.

   D. Alerts for non-security-related events do not function on a SIEM.

56. After analyzing events and incidents from the past year, an analyst has declared the existence of a problem. To what is the analyst referring?

    A. One or more controls are in a state of failure.

    B. The analyst is unable to access all incident data for the entire year.

    C. One or more high-criticality incidents have occurred.

    D. A specific type of incident is recurring.

57. A DBA has determined that it is not feasible to directly back up a large database. What is the best remedy for this?

    A. Defragment the database to permit a linear backup.

    B. Change the database to read-only during a backup to preserve integrity.

    C. Compress the database to recover free space.

    D. Export the database to a flat file and back up the flat file.

58. What is the feasibility for using the results of a BIA in the creation of a system classification plan?

    A. A BIA will indicate sensitivity of specific data that is associated with critical business processes.

    B. A BIA will indicate operational criticality of specific data that is associated with critical business processes.

    C. A BIA does not correlate to specific information systems.

    D. A BIA does not correlate to specific data sets.

59. A system engineer is reviewing critical systems in a data center and mapping them to individual electrical circuits. The engineer identified a system with two power supplies that are connected to the same plug strip. What should the engineer conclude from this?

    A. It is an acceptable practice to connect both power supplies to the same circuit.

    B. It is an acceptable practice to connect both power supplies to the same plug strip.

    C. The two power supplies should not be connected to the same circuit.

    D. The two power supplies should not be connected to the same plug strip.

60. An IT architect is proposing a plan for improving the resilience of critical data in the organization. The architect proposes that applications be altered so that they confirm that transactions have been successfully written to two different storage systems. What scheme has been proposed?

    A. Journaling

    B. Mirroring

    C. Data replication

    D. Two-phase commit

61. A department has completed a review of its business continuity plan through a moderated discussion that followed a specific, scripted disaster scenario. What kind of a review was performed?

A. Walkthrough

B. Simulation

C. Parallel test

D. Peer review

62. What is the purpose of salvage operations in a disaster recovery plan?

A. To identify the damage to, and recoverability of, critical equipment and assets

B. To determine the scrap value of critical equipment and assets

C. To ensure that all personnel are accounted for

D. To identify business processes that can be resumed

63. RAM is most commonly used as:

A. Secondary storage

B. Main storage

C. Virtual disk

D. CPU instruction cache

64. All of the following are valid reasons for removing end users' local administrators privileges on their workstations *except:*

A. To reduce malware attack impact

B. To prevent the use of personal web mail

C. To prevent installation of unauthorized software

D. To reduce the number of service desk support calls

65. The primary mission of data governance is:

A. To ensure the availability of sensitive and critical information

B. To ensure the integrity of sensitive and critical information

C. To control and monitor all uses of sensitive or critical information

D. To ensure compliance with applicable privacy laws

66. Many of the backout plans in the records of a change control process simply read, "Reverse previous steps." What conclusion can be drawn from this?

A. Backout plans are only relevant for emergency changes.

B. Backout plans are not a part of a change management process.

C. Backout plans are adequate.

D. Backout plans are not as rigorous as they should be.

67. The purpose of a business impact analysis (BIA) is primarily:

    A. To calculate risk in a risk assessment

    B. To determine the impact of a breach

    C. To determine process criticalities

    D. To determine process dependencies

68. The purpose for pre-writing public statements describing the impact, response, and recovery from a disaster include all of the following *except:*

    A. During a disaster is not a good time to write such statements from scratch.

    B. Key personnel who would write such statements may not be available.

    C. Such public statements can be issued more quickly.

    D. Pre-written public statements are required by regulation.

1. C	24. C	47. A
2. B	25. B	48. D
3. A	26. D	49. A
4. C	27. A	50. D
5. C	28. B	51. D
6. A	29. D	52. B
7. D	30. C	53. C
8. B	31. A	54. D
9. C	32. A	55. A
10. D	33. D	56. D
11. A	34. B	57. D
12. D	35. C	58. B
13. C	36. B	59. C
14. B	37. A	60. D
15. D	38. C	61. B
16. D	39. C	62. A
17. A	40. B	63. B
18. C	41. C	64. B
19. B	42. C	65. C
20. A	43. B	66. D
21. D	44. A	67. D
22. A	45. C	68. D
23. C	46. D	

1. A device that forwards packets to their destination based on their destination IP address is known as a:

    A. Bridge

    B. Gateway

    C. Router

    D. Switch

    ☑ **C.** A router is a network device that forwards packets towards their destination.

    ☒ **A** is incorrect because a bridge forwards all packets regardless of their destination.

    ☒ **B** is incorrect because a gateway is an application-layer device that transforms packets from one protocol to another.

    ☒ **D** is incorrect because a switch forwards packets based on their MAC or IP address.

2. A security manager is planning to implement a first-time use of a vulnerability scanning tool in an organization. What method should the security manager use to confirm that all assets are scanned?

    A. Compare the scan results with the accounting department asset inventory.

    B. Compare the scan results with the contents of the CMDB.

    C. Compare the scan results with a discovery scan performed by the vulnerability scanning tool.

    D. Compare the scan results with the latest network diagram.

    ☑ **B.** The best option to confirm that a vulnerability scan is catching all known assets is to compare it with a well-managed configuration management database (CMDB). In organizations lacking a CMDB, reconciliation of the scan results can be performed against other tools such as configuration management tools, anti-malware tools, or network management tools.

    ☒ **A** is incorrect because business asset inventories are not regarded as accurately reflecting all working systems in an environment. Further, a business asset inventory will not account for virtual machines.

    ☒ **C** is incorrect because a discovery scan will only find what is present on the network at the time the scan is performed. Assets that are not running at the time of the scan, and assets not reachable because of network ACLs, will not be identified in the discovery scan. Further, unauthorized devices will show up in a discovery scan.

    ☒ **D** is incorrect because network diagrams often do not include every individual device in an environment.

3. Which of the following methods should be used to create a point-in-time copy of a large production database?

    A. Storage system snapshot

    B. Storage system replication

C. E-vaulting

D. Export to a flat file that is backed up to tape

☑ **A.** A storage system snapshot is nearly instantaneous and is the best method for producing a "point-in-time" backup of a large database.

☒ **B** is incorrect because replication is not used to create a backup copy, but rather a live second copy of a data set.

☒ **C** is incorrect because e-vaulting does not necessarily create a point-in-time backup.

☒ **D** is incorrect because an export to a flat file and backup to tape would not be a point-in-time backup unless the database management system was quiesced.

4. All of the following protocols are used for federated authentication *except:*

A. OAuth

B. SAML

C. WSDL

D. HMAC

☑ **C.** WSDL is a protocol used to describe the functionality of a web service.

☒ **A** is incorrect because OAuth is a protocol found in federated authentication.

☒ **B** is incorrect because SAML is a protocol found in federated authentication.

☒ **D** is incorrect because HMAC is a protocol found in federated authentication, although it has fallen out of common use.

5. What is typically the most significant risk associated with end users being local administrators on their workstations?

A. End users will have access to all confidential information.

B. End users can install unauthorized software.

C. Malware can run at the highest privilege level.

D. End users can use tools to crack all domain passwords.

☑ **C.** If malware is introduced by the end user in a phishing or watering hole attack, the malware will run as an administrator, which is the highest privilege level on the system. Malware would have access to all files, data, and devices on the machine.

☒ **A** is incorrect because local administrative privileges should not ever result in end users having access to data on other systems.

☒ **B** is incorrect. While it is correct that end users who are local administrators can install software, this is generally not as severe a risk as a malware infection.

☒ **D** is incorrect because end users should not be able to access the encrypted password file for all users in the organization.

6. Which of the following persons is best suited to approve users' access to sensitive data in a customer database?

   A. Customer service manager

   B. IT service desk personnel

   C. Information security manager

   D. IT manager

   ☑ **A.** The customer service manager is the best available choice because a business leader is almost always more familiar with business processes than are IT and information security personnel. Further, because the customer service manager is responsible for customer service, this is the person who should be specifying which persons in the organization are permitted to access customer service data.

   ☒ **B, C,** and **D** are incorrect. These all are IT and IT security–related personnel who are not going to be as familiar with business unit or business department operations as the leaders of business units or business departments.

7. An organization is planning a new SaaS service offering and is uncertain about the resources required to support the service. How should the organization proceed?

   A. Calculate projected performance using CMMI tools.

   B. Calculate projected performance using Zachman tools.

   C. Measure actual performance metrics in production.

   D. Build a working prototype and perform load tests.

   ☑ **D.** The best choice here is to build a prototype system that closely resembles the network, computing, and database activities and perform load testing. This will give the organization an idea of the capacity of the planned system. But because this technique is imperfect, load tests should be performed throughout the development process.

   ☒ **A** is incorrect because CMMI tools are used to measure process maturity, not system performance.

   ☒ **B** is incorrect because Zachman tools are used to develop an enterprise architecture, not system performance.

   ☒ **C** is incorrect because, while this technique will provide the most accurate data, it is better to get estimates earlier in the development process so that changes in architecture, coding, or business models can be made prior to completion of the project.

8. What is the best definition of a problem in ITIL-based service management?

   A. Chronic exceptions in audits of IT systems

   B. The same incident that occurs repeatedly

C. Repeated unscheduled downtime

D. Unscheduled downtime that exceeds SLAs

☑ **B.** The definition of a problem in ITIL is a recurrence of the same type of incident. This indicates that there is something wrong with a business process or information system that needs to be corrected.

☒ **A** is incorrect because this is too narrow a definition. A problem can indeed be caused by repeated audit exceptions, but also with many other types of incidents.

☒ **C** is incorrect because this is too narrow a definition. A problem can definitely be behind repeated downtime incidents, but also other types of incidents.

☒ **D** is incorrect because this is too narrow a definition. Downtime that exceeds SLAs is indeed a problem, but many other types of chronic incidents also fit the definition of a problem in ITIL.

9. Which of the following is the best relationship between system security and the use of vulnerability scanning tools?

A. Vulnerability scanning is performed proactively, and it drives the security patching and hardening functions.

B. Vulnerability scanning is performed proactively, and it drives the security patching function.

C. Patching and hardening are performed proactively, and vulnerability scanning is used to verify their effectiveness.

D. Patching is performed proactively, and vulnerability scanning is used to verify its effectiveness.

☑ **C.** The best use of vulnerability scanning is its functioning as a quality assurance activity, to ensure that security patching and system hardening are being performed effectively.

☒ **A** is incorrect because system security should not be driven by the vulnerability scanning function. Instead, system security should be proactively performed, with vulnerability scanning serving as a means for verifying that they are effective.

☒ **B** is incorrect because system security should not be driven by vulnerability scanning. Instead, patching and hardening should be proactive, with scanning used to verify their effectiveness.

☒ **D** is incorrect because system hardening should also be proactive.

10. A SaaS provider and a customer are having a dispute about the availability of service, quality of service, and issue resolution provided by the SaaS provider. What type of a legal agreement should the parties add to their contract to better define these problems and their resolution?

A. Pricing table

B. Exit clause

C. Performance addendum

D. Service level agreement

☑ **D.** A service level agreement (SLA) is used to define the quantity and quality of service to be provided by a service provider to its customers. An SLA can cover issues such as transaction volume, service quality, issue resolution, and service availability.

☒ **A** is incorrect because pricing is not the core problem in this example.

☒ **B** is incorrect because an exit clause only addresses terms in which the parties can terminate the agreement; it does not address service quality.

☒ **C** is incorrect because a performance addendum is not the appropriate term for an agreement that addresses these problems.

11. What is the purpose of a business impact analysis?

A. It defines the most critical business processes.

B. It defines the most critical IT applications.

C. It defines the most critical service providers.

D. It defines the disaster recovery plan.

☑ **A.** A business impact analysis (BIA) defines the most critical business processes in the organization. The BIA reveals which business processes warrant the development of emergency contingency planning and disaster recovery planning.

☒ **B** is incorrect because a BIA does not directly define the most critical IT applications.

☒ **C** is incorrect because a BIA does not directly define the most critical service providers; however, a BIA will reveal service providers required by the most critical business processes.

☒ **D** is incorrect because the BIA does not define the disaster recovery plan (DRP), but the BIA will help to drive development of the DRP.

12. An IT architect needs to increase the resilience of a single application server. Which of the following choices will *least* benefit the server's resilience?

A. Active-active cluster

B. Active-passive cluster

C. Geo-cluster

D. Redundant power supply

☑ **D.** A redundant power supply only addresses the problem of a power supply failure but does not address other failures such as storage or CPU.

☒ **A, B,** and **C** are incorrect because an active-active cluster, active-passive cluster, and geo-cluster all adequately address the complete failure of a single-server system, through the resumption of services by the other server(s) in the cluster.

13. Which of the following backup schemes best protects an organization from ransomware?

A. Storage system replication

B. Storage system mirroring

C. Storage system snapshots

D. RAID-5

☑ **C.** Storage system snapshots effectively store the state of a storage system from time to time; if ransomware destroys files in the storage system, the system can be rolled back to a recent snapshot, effectively restoring damaged files.

☒ **A** is incorrect because replication will effectively replicate the damaging effects of ransomware from the primary storage system to other storage systems through their replication.

☒ **B** is incorrect because mirroring will effectively replicate the damaging effects of ransomware from primary storage to mirrored storage.

☒ **D** is incorrect because RAID-5 is used to improve storage system performance and would effectively allow ransomware to damage files more quickly.

14. A mail order organization wants to develop procedures to be followed in the event that the main office building cannot be occupied, so that customer orders can still be fulfilled. What kind of a plan does the organization need to develop?

A. Business impact analysis

B. Business continuity plan

C. Disaster recovery plan

D. Emergency evacuation plan

☑ **B.** A business continuity plan is the document that describes procedures to be followed when events such as local and regional disasters prevent normal business operations.

☒ **A** is incorrect because a business impact analysis is used to determine which business processes are most critical and warrant the development of business continuity plans.

☒ **C** is incorrect because a disaster recovery plan is used to survey damage and salvage business equipment, as well as direct the initiation of procedures to activate alternative resources, such as IT systems in alternative locations if IT equipment in primary locations is inoperable.

☒ **D** is incorrect because an emergency evacuation plan, while important during disasters, does not contribute to the ability for an organization to continue the fulfillment of customer orders.

15. An IT department is planning on implementing disaster recovery capabilities in some of its business systems. What means should be used to determine which applications require DR capabilities and to what level of recoverability?

A. Business continuity plan

B. Disaster recovery plan

C. Risk assessment

D. Business impact analysis

☑ **D.** A business impact analysis (BIA) is used to determine which business processes are most critical, and this leads to the development of recovery objectives, which in turn leads to the development of DR capabilities that meet those objectives.

☒ **A** is incorrect because, while a business continuity plan and a disaster recovery plan are closely related, the BIA is the tool that defines which business processes warrant the development of supporting DR capabilities.

☒ **B** is incorrect because a DR plan does not define which systems are to be covered or what recovery targets are to be met.

☒ **C** is incorrect because a risk assessment, while valuable, does not define which business processes warrant the development of DR plans.

16. Which of the following is the most compelling reason for an organization to *not* automate its data purging jobs in support of data retention policies?

A. DR planning

B. Referential integrity

C. Privacy breaches

D. Legal holds

☑ **D.** Legal holds in most organizations are manual processes and involve the cessation of data purging for arbitrary sets of information. A better approach would be a manually initiated data purging process that is started only after it is determined that no legal holds exist for the data to be purged.

☒ **A** is incorrect because DR planning has little or no bearing on automatic purging of stale data.

☒ **B** is incorrect because referential integrity is a matter that can often be solved through structured data removal, but it's not relevant to the automated starting of purge jobs.

☒ **C** is incorrect because privacy breaches on their own should have no bearing on the automatic purging of data.

17. Which of the following schemes is most likely to be successful for workstations used by a mobile workforce?

A. Automated patching followed by a system restart that the end user can control

B. Automated patching and restarts

C. End-user-initiated patching and restarts

D. Applying only those patches not requiring a system restart

☑ **A.** Automated patching, together with giving end users some control over restarts, is most likely to be successful, as this gives users an option to defer restarts (for a while) so that important work is not interrupted.

☒ **B** is incorrect because automated restarts are likely to disrupt critical business activities (such as an executive presentation) from time to time.

☒ **C** is incorrect because end users are not inclined or likely to be diligent about initiating patching jobs.

☒ **D** is incorrect because this plan will result in the absence of many critical patches, which could lead to an increased frequency and impact of malware attacks.

18. An IT department completed a data discovery assessment and found that numerous users were saving files containing sensitive information on organization-wide readable file shares. Which of the following is the best remediation for this matter?

A. Remove the offending files from the org-wide share.

B. Announce to users that the org-wide readable share is not for sensitive data.

C. Change the org-wide readable share to read-only for most users.

D. Change the org-wide readable share to write-only for most users.

☑ **C.** In most organizations, few people truly need to write to the organization-wide readable share (for example, HR, legal, and IT). This will drive users to using department shares for saving sensitive data, which will result in lower risk to the business since sensitive data would then be readable only by personnel in their respective departments instead of the entire organization. Further improvement opportunities may be found after that.

☒ **A** is incorrect because simply removing the files containing sensitive information is not likely to solve the problem, as similar files may soon reappear.

☒ **B** is incorrect because many users typically ignore such reminders, and many do not read them at all.

☒ **D** is incorrect because making the share write-only would result in the org-wide share being unreadable.

19. For which users or groups should the SQL listener on a database management system be accessible?

A. For the application accounts only

B. For the application and DBA accounts only

C. For DBA accounts only

D. For DBA accounts plus all users of the application

☑ **B.** Applications that need to access the database need to be able to access the SQL listener on a database server, as do DBAs who need to perform maintenance on the system.

☒ **A** is incorrect because this would deprive the DBA from being able to access the SQL listener.

☒ **C** is incorrect because this would deprive applications that need to access the database management system.

☒ **D** is incorrect because application end users should not be given direct access to the SQL listener. Instead, capabilities in the application should be provided that give users the access they need.

20. An organization's financial accounting system crashes every Friday night after backups have completed. In ITIL terms, what process should be invoked?

   A. Problem management

   B. Incident management

   C. Capacity management

   D. Business continuity management

   ☑ **A.** Problem management is the correct ITIL process to be invoked when similar incidents are recurring.

   ☒ **B** is incorrect because incident management is used to manage individual incidents, but not the recurrence of similar incidents.

   ☒ **C** is incorrect because capacity management is not the correct response, unless problem management reveals that the crashes are occurring as a result of a capacity issue.

   ☒ **D** is incorrect because business continuity management is concerned with the continuation of business processes during disasters.

21. An IT organization is investigating a problem in its change management process whereby many changes have to be backed out because they could not be completed or because verifications failed. Which is the best remedy for this situation?

   A. Increase the size of change windows.

   B. Require a separate person to verify changes.

   C. Require change requests to have better backout procedures.

   D. Require more rigorous testing in a test environment prior to scheduling changes in production.

   ☑ **D.** Repeated implementation failures should first call for more rigorous testing in a test or staging environment in order to iron out any issues that may occur when changes are applied in production environments.

☒ **A** is incorrect because the problem does not appear to be one where there is insufficient time to implement changes.

☒ **B** is incorrect because using a different person to verify changes does not appear to be at the heart of the issue.

☒ **C** is incorrect because improved backout procedures are not likely the remedy for failed implementations.

22. Which language is used to change the schema in a database management system?

    A. DDL

    B. SQL

    C. Stored procedures

    D. JCL

    ☑ **A.** DDL, or Data Definition Language, is most commonly used to change the schema (or architecture of a database) in a database management system.

    ☒ **B** is incorrect because SQL is not often used to change the schema of a DBMS.

    ☒ **C** is incorrect because stored procedures play a different role in a database management system.

    ☒ **D** is incorrect because JCL is a batch control language on mainframe computers.

23. A DBA has been asked to limit the tables, rows, or columns that are visible to some users with direct database access. Which solution would best fulfill this request?

    A. Create alternative user accounts.

    B. Move those users into different AD groups.

    C. Create one or more views.

    D. Change the schema for those users.

    ☑ **C.** A view provides the appearance of virtual tables that are parts of real tables.

    ☒ **A** is incorrect because creating alternative user accounts is not the best solution for this request.

    ☒ **B** is incorrect because access permissions may not fully fulfill this request.

    ☒ **D** is incorrect because it's not possible to change the schema for users, other than creating one or more views.

24. An organization's IT department developed DR capabilities for some business applications prior to a BIA ever being performed. Now that a BIA has been performed, it has been determined that some IT applications' DR capabilities exceed what is called for in the BIA and that other applications fall short. What should be done to remedy this?

    A. Redo the BIA, using existing DR capabilities as inputs.

    B. Make no changes, as this is the expected result.

C. Change IT application DR capabilities to align with the BIA.

D. Change the BIA to align with IT application DR capabilities.

☑ **C.** DR capabilities need to align with the results of the BIA, including established recovery objectives.

☒ **A** is incorrect because the BIA does not need to be redone. It is the IT DR capabilities that require adjustment.

☒ **B** is incorrect because this misalignment between the BIA and DR capabilities is not an expected result.

☒ **D** is incorrect because the BIA should not be changed to align with DR capabilities. It is the reverse that should be performed.

25. What is the purpose of hot-pluggable drives in a storage system?

A. Ability to replace drives that have crashed or overheated

B. Ability to replace drives while the storage system is still running

C. Ability to replace drives without the risk of harm to personnel

D. Ability to install additional drives without powering down the system

☑ **B.** The term "hot-pluggable drives" refers to the ability to remove and replace drives in a storage system while the system is still running. Together with RAID capabilities, there would be no interruption in the storage system's ability to read and write data to the drives.

☒ **A** is incorrect because this reason is too limited: while hot-pluggable drives would indeed permit personnel to replace drives that have crashed or overheated, they also permit personnel to remove and replace them for any reason.

☒ **C** is incorrect because this is not the definition of hot-pluggable drives.

☒ **D** is incorrect because this definition is too limiting: while it is true that hot-pluggable drives permit additional drives to be added to the system, they also permit faulty drives to be removed and replaced.

26. What is the primary purpose for data restoration testing?

A. To meet regulatory requirements

B. To prove that bare-metal restores can be performed

C. To see how long it takes to restore data from backup

D. To ensure that backups are actually being performed

☑ **D.** Restoration testing proves that data is actually being written to backup media. It also demonstrates that personnel know how to restore data.

☒ **A** is incorrect because regulatory requirements are a minor consideration here.

☒ **B** is incorrect because restoration testing does not necessarily test bare-metal restores.

☒ **C** is incorrect because the time required to restore data is not a major consideration.

27. Which of the following should approve RTO and RPO targets?

    A. Senior business executives

    B. Board of directors

    C. CISO

    D. CIO

    ☑ **A.** Senior business executives should approve RTO and RPO targets. As business leaders, senior executives are in the best position to decide how much downtime the organization will tolerate in the event of a minor or major disaster. Further, senior executives are going to be in the best position to fund and provide resources for IT to implement DR capabilities to meet these objectives.

    ☒ **B** is incorrect because the board of directors does not usually become involved in operational matters.

    ☒ **C** is incorrect because the CISO is responsible for cybersecurity, not business resilience related to disasters.

    ☒ **D** is incorrect because the CIO is responsible for implementing DR capabilities to support RPO and RTO targets, but does not select the targets.

28. An organization has developed its first-ever disaster recovery plan. What is the best choice for the first round of testing of the plan?

    A. Cutover test

    B. Walkthrough

    C. Simulation

    D. Parallel test

    ☑ **B.** The best choice here is for participants to walk through the plan and discuss all of the steps in detail.

    ☒ **A** is incorrect because a cutover test is the highest-risk test available and should be performed only after successful walkthroughs, simulations, and parallel tests.

    ☒ **C** is incorrect because a simulation should be performed after walkthroughs have identified improvement areas.

    ☒ **D** is incorrect because a parallel test should not be performed until at least a walkthrough and simulation have first been performed.

29. Which of the following best describes the purpose of a hypervisor?

    A. It creates and manages virtual desktops.

    B. It creates and manages containers.

    C. It installs software on virtual machines.

    D. It creates and manages virtual machines.

☑ **D.** A hypervisor, whether hosted or bare-metal, is used to create, manage, and run virtual machines.

☒ **A** is incorrect because a hypervisor is not typically used to create virtual desktops.

☒ **B** is incorrect because a hypervisor is not used to create containers.

☒ **C** is incorrect because hypervisors are not used to install software on virtual machines.

30. Which of the following best fits the definition of a set of structured tables with indexes, primary keys, and foreign keys?

   A. Hierarchical database

   B. Object database

   C. Relational database

   D. Network database

   ☑ **C.** A relational database is one with structured tables containing rows and columns, with indexes, primary keys, and foreign keys.

   ☒ **A** is incorrect because a hierarchical database has a different structure than the one described.

   ☒ **B** is incorrect because an object database has a different structure than the one described.

   ☒ **D** is incorrect because a network database has a different structure than the one described.

31. An organization uses its vulnerability scanning tool as its de facto asset management system. What is the biggest risk associated with this approach?

   A. Network engineers could build new IP networks not included in the scanning tool's configuration.

   B. System engineers could implement new servers that the scanning tool won't see.

   C. System engineers could implement new virtual machines that the scanning tool won't see.

   D. IP source routing could prevent the scanning tool from seeing all networks.

   ☑ **A.** The biggest risk of using a vulnerability scanning tool as a tool for tracking assets is that these tools are generally configured to scan a list of IP networks. If a network engineer creates a new IP network and does not inform the personnel who manage the scanning tool, the tool won't detect the new IP network or any systems and devices that reside in it.

   ☒ **B** is incorrect because vulnerability scanning tools generally scan IP networks and would generally detect new systems and devices automatically.

   ☒ **C** is incorrect because new virtual machines should be detected, provided they reside on an existing IP network and are active.

   ☒ **D** is incorrect because IP source routing would not necessarily interfere with a vulnerability scanning tool's operation.

32. Which of the following systems should be used for populating the IT asset database in an elastic cloud environment?

   A. Hypervisor

   B. Vulnerability scanning tool

   C. Patch management tool

   D. CMDB

   ☑ **A.** The hypervisor is the system that manages the creation and use of virtual machines in an environment where virtual machines are created dynamically to support workload.

   ☒ **B** is incorrect because a vulnerability scanning tool is only going to detect virtual machines that are active during the scan.

   ☒ **C** is incorrect because the patch management tool may not be automatically aware of new virtual machines.

   ☒ **D** is incorrect because the CMDB is an IT asset database.

33. What is a typical frequency for running a job that checks Active Directory for unused user accounts?

   A. Every hour

   B. Every 24 hours

   C. Every 7 days

   D. Every 90 days

   ☑ **D.** Ninety days is the most typical interval for checking for dormant user accounts.

   ☒ **A** is incorrect because checking for dormant user accounts every hour is excessive.

   ☒ **B** is incorrect because checking for dormant user accounts every day is excessive.

   ☒ **C** is incorrect because checking for dormant user accounts every week is excessive.

34. The system interface standard that includes process control, IPC, and shared memory is known as:

   A. Unix

   B. POSIX

   C. ActiveX

   D. Ultrix

   ☑ **B.** POSIX is the system interface standard that includes several components, such as process control, interprocess communication (IPC), named pipes, and files and file systems.

   ☒ **A** is incorrect because Unix is not an interface standard, but an operating system.

   ☒ **C** is incorrect because ActiveX does not include all of these components.

   ☒ **D** is incorrect because Ultrix is not an interface standard, but an operating system.

35. An environment consisting of centralized servers running end-user operating systems that display on users' computers is known as:

A. Hosted hypervisor

B. Bare-metal hypervisor

C. Virtual desktop infrastructure

D. Reverse Telnet

☑ **C.** A virtual desktop infrastructure (VDI) consists of one or more centralized servers that run end-user desktop operating systems that display on users' computers.

☒ **A** is incorrect because a hosted hypervisor does not match the environment description.

☒ **B** is incorrect because a bare-metal hypervisor does not match the environment description.

☒ **D** is incorrect because reverse Telnet does not describe the environment description.

36. A data privacy officer recently commissioned a data discovery exercise to understand the extent to which sensitive data is present on the company's world-readable file share. The exercise revealed that dozens of files containing large volumes of highly sensitive data were present on the file share. What is the best first step the data privacy officer should take?

A. Remove all instances of files containing large volumes of highly sensitive data.

B. Investigate each instance to see whether any files are a part of business processes.

C. Sanction the users who placed the files there for violations of internal privacy policy.

D. Do nothing, as this is an acceptable practice for files of this type.

☑ **B.** The most prudent move is for the DPO to investigate the files that were found to better understand why they are there. Possibly, some are part of vital business processes (which, in many cases, would need to be adjusted to avoid exposing the information).

☒ **A** is incorrect because removing all files may inadvertently disrupt an existing important business process (which may need to be adjusted to avoid exposing this data).

☒ **C** is incorrect because there may be some legitimate files among those that were found.

☒ **D** is incorrect because inaction would unnecessarily expose the organization to potential privacy violations. Files containing large volumes of sensitive information probably should not be present on file shares readable by the entire organization.

37. A new IT manager is making improvements in the organization's management of unplanned outages. The IT manager has built a new process where repeated cases of similar outages are analyzed in order to identify their cause. What process has the IT manager created?

A. Problem management

B. Incident management

C. Root cause analysis

D. Security event management

☑ **A.** Analysis of repeated incidents is known as problem management.

☒ **B** is incorrect because incident management is the management of individual incidents.

☒ **C** is incorrect. While root cause analysis may be a part of the process described, the overall process is better known as problem management.

☒ **D** is incorrect because security event management is concerned with the response to security events and incidents.

38. A new IT manager is making improvements in the organization's management of the detailed settings on servers and network devices. The process that the IT manager has made is a part of:

A. Vulnerability management

B. System hardening

C. Configuration management

D. Performance management

☑ **C.** The IT manager is making improvements to the configuration management process.

☒ **A** is incorrect because vulnerability management is the process of identifying and mitigating vulnerabilities on systems and devices.

☒ **B** is incorrect because system hardening is the process of making systems more resistant to attack.

☒ **D** is incorrect because performance management is concerned with improving the efficiency of systems.

39. A new IT manager is making improvements in the organization's management of the detailed settings on servers and network devices. The process includes the creation of a repository for storing details about this information. This repository is known as:

A. An asset management database

B. A vulnerability management database

C. A configuration management database

D. A system hardening standard

☑ **C.** A repository containing the configuration of systems is known as a configuration management database (CMDB).

☒ **A** is incorrect because an asset management database is going to contain basic information about an organization's assets.

☒ **B** is incorrect because a vulnerability management database (which is not a common term) might contain information about vulnerabilities in systems and devices.

☒ **D** is incorrect because a system hardening standard specifies the configuration for making systems more resistant to attack.

40. A new IT manager is making improvements to the organization's need to make its systems and devices more resilient to attacks. The IT manager should update:

   A. The vulnerability management process

   B. The system and device hardening standard

   C. The configuration management database

   D. The security incident response plan

   ☑ **B.** A system and device hardening standard specifies the configurations to be used to make systems and devices more resistant to attack.

   ☒ **A** is incorrect because a vulnerability management process is concerned with techniques used to identify and remediate vulnerabilities on systems and devices.

   ☒ **C** is incorrect because a configuration management database contains information about the configuration of systems and devices.

   ☒ **D** is incorrect because a security incident response plan contains procedures to follow when a security incident occurs.

41. A customer of a SaaS provider is complaining about the SaaS provider's lack of responsiveness in resolving security issues. What portion of the contract should the customer refer to when lodging a formal complaint?

   A. Service description

   B. System availability

   C. Service level agreement

   D. Security controls

   ☑ **C.** A service level agreement (SLA) defines terms of responsiveness to various types of services and service issues.

   ☒ **A** is incorrect because a service description is more likely to describe services rendered, but not about resolving security issues.

   ☒ **B** is incorrect because this is not an issue about system availability.

   ☒ **D** is incorrect because this is not a matter of security controls, but of service levels.

42. Computer code that is found within the contents of a database is known as a:

   A. Blob

   B. Function

   C. Stored procedure

   D. Subroutine

☑ **C.** A stored procedure is computer code that is stored in a database and executed when called.

☒ **A** is incorrect because a blob, or binary large object, does not typically store code, but instead is usually a video, image, or audio recording.

☒ **B** is incorrect because a function is a segment of a computer program.

☒ **D** is incorrect because a subroutine is a segment of a computer program.

43. An organization is starting its first-ever effort to develop a business continuity and disaster recovery plan. What is the best first step to perform in this effort?

A. Criticality analysis

B. Business impact analysis

C. Setting recovery targets

D. Selecting a DR site

☑ **B.** A business impact analysis (BIA) is used to enumerate business processes and their dependencies upon other processes, assets, personnel, and service providers.

☒ **A** is incorrect. A criticality analysis is performed after the business impact analysis to determine the criticality of business processes identified in the BIA.

☒ **C** is incorrect because recovery targets are established after the maximum tolerable downtime (MTD) and BIA are completed.

☒ **D** is incorrect because a DR site is not selected until the BIA, CA, and recovery targets are established.

44. What is the purpose for connecting two redundant power supplies to separate electrical circuits?

A. System resilience in case one electrical circuit fails

B. To balance electrical load between the circuits

C. To balance the phasing between the circuits

D. To avoid overloading a single electrical circuit

☑ **A.** A system with redundant power supplies will be more resilient if the power supplies are connected to separate electrical circuits (and even more resilient if the circuits lead to separate PDUs, UPSs, electrical feeds, and generators). In the event of a failure in any of these components, the others will still supply power to the system.

☒ **B** is incorrect because this is not a primary purpose for connecting power supplies to separate circuits.

☒ **C** is incorrect because this is not a primary purpose for connecting power supplies to separate circuits.

☒ **D** is incorrect because circuit loading is not usually performed using this technique.

45. An IT organization is modernizing its tape backup system by replacing its tape library system with a storage array, while keeping its tape backup software system. What has the organization implemented?

A. E-vaulting

B. S-vaulting

C. Virtual tape library

D. Mirroring

☑ **C.** A virtual tape library (VTL) is a storage system that emulates a tape library system. A VTL is used when an organization wishes to retain its tape backup software platform while modernizing the actual backup storage.

☒ **A** is incorrect because e-vaulting is the practice of sending backup data to a cloud storage provider.

☒ **B** is incorrect because s-vaulting is not a valid term.

☒ **D** is incorrect because mirroring involves real-time duplication of data stored on a primary storage system to a secondary or tertiary storage system.

46. An IT organization is modernizing its tape backup system by sending data to a cloud storage provider. What has the organization implemented?

A. Replication

B. Mirroring

C. Virtual tape library

D. E-vaulting

☑ **D.** E-vaulting is the process of backing up data to a cloud storage provider using backup software created for that purpose.

☒ **A** is incorrect because replication is the near-real-time copying of disk storage transactions from a primary storage system to a secondary storage system.

☒ **B** is incorrect because mirroring is a block-by-block duplication of data stored on a primary storage system onto a secondary storage system.

☒ **C** is incorrect because a virtual tape library (VTL) is a disk-based storage system that emulates a tape library system.

47. A city government department that accepts payments for water use has developed a procedure to be followed when the IT application for processing payments is unavailable. What type of procedure has been developed?

A. Business continuity plan

B. Disaster recovery plan

C. Business impact analysis

D. Backout plan

☑ **A.** The procedure developed is a business continuity plan, which is an emergency operations procedure to be followed when one or more critical assets required for the business-as-usual procedure are unavailable.

☒ **B** is incorrect because a disaster recovery plan is a set of procedures to be followed to assess damage and restore operation of critical assets such as IT systems and other business equipment.

☒ **C** is incorrect because a business impact analysis is a study to enumerate critical business processes and their dependencies.

☒ **D** is incorrect because a backout plan is a procedure in the change management process used to restore a system to its pre-changed state in the event that the change was unsuccessful.

48. A city government IT department has developed a procedure to be followed when the primary application for accepting water usage payments has been incapacitated. The procedure calls for the initiation of a secondary application in a different data center. What type of procedure has been developed?

   A. Business continuity plan

   B. Backout plan

   C. Security incident response plan

   D. Disaster recovery plan

☑ **D.** The procedure created is a disaster recovery plan.

☒ **A** is incorrect because a business continuity plan is a business-level procedure to be followed in the event that critical assets or personnel are unavailable to continue operations of important business processes.

☒ **B** is incorrect because a backout plan is a procedure in the change management process used to restore a system to its pre-changed state in the event that the change was unsuccessful.

☒ **C** is incorrect because a security incident response plan is a procedure to be followed in the event of a security incident or breach.

49. What is the most important factor to consider in the development of a disaster recovery plan?

   A. The safety of personnel

   B. The availability of critical data

   C. Notification of civil authorities

   D. The continuity of critical operations

☑ **A.** The safety of personnel should always be the highest priority in any disaster recovery plan.

☒ **B** is incorrect because the availability of critical data, while important, is less critical than the safety of personnel.

☒ **C** is incorrect because the notification of civil authorities is important, but less important than the safety of personnel.

☒ **D** is incorrect because the continuity of critical operations is key to the resilience of the organization, but less important than the safety of personnel.

50. An SSD is most commonly used as:

   A. Backup storage

   B. Removable storage

   C. Main storage

   D. Secondary storage

   ☑ **D.** Solid-state drives (SSDs) are most commonly used as secondary storage. Prior to SSDs, hard-disk drives (HDDs) were used as secondary storage.

   ☒ **A** is incorrect because SSDs are not most commonly used as backup storage.

   ☒ **B** is incorrect because SSDs are not most commonly used as removable storage.

   ☒ **C** is incorrect because RAM (random access memory) is used as a system's main storage.

51. The phrase "you can't protect what you don't know about" refers to which key IT process?

   A. Vulnerability management

   B. License management

   C. Patching

   D. Asset management

   ☑ **D.** Asset management is a critical process that other processes, such as vulnerability management, patch management, and license management, depend upon. It is the author's opinion that asset management is the #1 control objective in the CIS Critical Controls for this reason.

   ☒ **A** is incorrect because vulnerability management is dependent upon sound asset management to ensure that all assets are identified and their vulnerabilities remediated timely.

   ☒ **B** is incorrect because license management is not related to the protection of assets.

   ☒ **C** is incorrect because patching is dependent upon vulnerability management and asset management.

52. The SOAP protocol is related to:

   A. The patch management process

   B. The exchange of data through an API

   C. The vulnerability management process

   D. Memory garbage collection

☑ **B.** SOAP, or Simple Object Access Protocol, is a network API for exchanging data between systems over a network.

☒ **A** is incorrect because SOAP is not related to the patch management process.

☒ **C** is incorrect because SOAP is not related to the vulnerability management process.

☒ **D** is incorrect because SOAP is not related to memory garbage collection.

53. Restricting USB attached storage on end-user workstations addresses all of the following *except:*

    A. Leakage of intellectual property

    B. Malware infection

    C. System capacity management

    D. Personal use of a workstation

☑ **C.** Restrictions of USB storage often address leakage of intellectual property or personally sensitive information, malware infection, and personal uses of a workstation. Restricting USB has little or nothing to do with system capacity management.

☒ **A** is incorrect because leakage of intellectual property is often a primary reason for restricting USB attached storage on workstations.

☒ **B** is incorrect because malware control is often a primary reason for restricting USB attached storage.

☒ **D** is incorrect because personal use of a workstation is sometimes a reason for restricting the use of USB attached storage—for example, to prevent a user from downloading personal documents onto a work-related computer.

54. The primary purpose of a dynamic DLP system is:

    A. To detect unauthorized personal use of a workstation

    B. To detect unauthorized use of personal web mail

    C. To control unauthorized access to sensitive information

    D. To control unauthorized movement of sensitive information

☑ **D.** The main purpose of dynamic DLP (data loss prevention) is the unauthorized movement of sensitive information. For example, a dynamic DLP solution can prevent sensitive information from being stored on an external USB attached storage device or transmitted through e-mail.

☒ **A** is incorrect because a dynamic DLP solution is not used to detect personal use of a workstation.

☒ **B** is incorrect because a primary purpose of dynamic DLP is not to detect or block personal web mail. However, a dynamic DLP system can prevent the transmission of sensitive data via personal web mail.

☒ **C** is incorrect because system access controls are more commonly used to prevent unauthorized access to sensitive information.

55. What is the suitability for the use of a SIEM to alert personnel of system capacity and performance issues?

    A. If syslog events are generated, use cases related to performance and capacity can be developed.

    B. A SIEM can only be used to alert personnel of security events.

    C. Use cases for non-security-related events do not function on a SIEM.

    D. Alerts for non-security-related events do not function on a SIEM.

    ☑ **A.** A SIEM is a general-purpose system used to ingest log data from systems and devices and to create alerts when specific types of log entries are received. There is no limit to the types of log data and alerts that can be employed in a SIEM.

    ☒ **B** is incorrect because a SIEM can be used for security and non-security events.

    ☒ **C** is incorrect because a SIEM can be used for security and non-security events.

    ☒ **D** is incorrect because a SIEM can generate alerts for any type of event. However, for non-security-related events, an administrator may need to develop a custom use case to detect a non-security-related event and generate an alert for it.

56. After analyzing events and incidents from the past year, an analyst has declared the existence of a problem. To what is the analyst referring?

    A. One or more controls are in a state of failure.

    B. The analyst is unable to access all incident data for the entire year.

    C. One or more high-criticality incidents have occurred.

    D. A specific type of incident is recurring.

    ☑ **D.** In ITIL terminology, a problem is an incident that keeps occurring. This means that there is some root cause for these incidents that needs to be investigated, and a plan needs to be developed to eliminate the root cause so that the incidents no longer occur.

    ☒ **A** is incorrect because a problem, in ITIL terminology, does not specifically indicate a control failure.

    ☒ **B** is incorrect because a problem, in ITIL terminology, does not indicate an inability to access historical event data.

    ☒ **C** is incorrect because a problem in ITIL terminology does not indicate the severity of incidents that are occurring, but only that similar incidents that are all potentially related to a single root cause are occurring.

57. A DBA has determined that it is not feasible to directly back up a large database. What is the best remedy for this?

    A. Defragment the database to permit a linear backup.

    B. Change the database to read-only during a backup to preserve integrity.

C. Compress the database to recover free space.

D. Export the database to a flat file and back up the flat file.

☑ **D.** The best remedy when a database cannot be directly backed up is the creation of an export, which itself can be backed up.

☒ **A** is incorrect because defragmentation of a database is not a common operation.

☒ **B** is incorrect because changing a database to read-only would certainly disrupt business operations.

☒ **C** is incorrect because compression of a database is not a common practice.

58. What is the feasibility for using the results of a BIA in the creation of a system classification plan?

A. A BIA will indicate sensitivity of specific data that is associated with critical business processes.

B. A BIA will indicate operational criticality of specific data that is associated with critical business processes.

C. A BIA does not correlate to specific information systems.

D. A BIA does not correlate to specific data sets.

☑ **B.** A BIA identifies critical business processes in an organization, including the organization's dependencies upon IT systems and their data sets. Critical processes can be mapped to the systems they depend upon, which can contribute to system classification.

☒ **A** is incorrect because a BIA does not typically identify data by sensitivity, but instead identifies data by operational criticality.

☒ **C** is incorrect because a BIA does in fact correlate business processes to information systems.

☒ **D** is incorrect because a BIA does in fact correlate business processes to specific data sets.

59. A system engineer is reviewing critical systems in a data center and mapping them to individual electrical circuits. The engineer identified a system with two power supplies that are connected to the same plug strip. What should the engineer conclude from this?

A. It is an acceptable practice to connect both power supplies to the same circuit.

B. It is an acceptable practice to connect both power supplies to the same plug strip.

C. The two power supplies should not be connected to the same circuit.

D. The two power supplies should not be connected to the same plug strip.

☑ **C.** The main issue at stake here is that the power supplies are both connected to the same electrical circuit. If the electrical circuit fails, the system will be powered down. A better practice is to connect the two power supplies to separate circuits.

☒ **A** and **B** are incorrect because it is not a recommended practice to connect both power supplies to the same plug strip or the same circuit. The plug strip and electrical circuit represent a single failure path, somewhat negating the purpose of multiple power supplies.

☒ **D** is incorrect because the bigger issue is not whether the power supplies are connected to the same plug strip, but that they are connected to the same circuit.

60. An IT architect is proposing a plan for improving the resilience of critical data in the organization. The architect proposes that applications be altered so that they confirm that transactions have been successfully written to two different storage systems. What scheme has been proposed?

   A. Journaling

   B. Mirroring

   C. Data replication

   D. Two-phase commit

   ☑ **D.** Two-phase commit is the act of writing a transaction to separate storage systems and not completing the transaction until confirmation of successful write operations has been received.

   ☒ **A** is incorrect because journaling is the process of recording storage transactions in another part of a file system for redundancy and integrity purposes.

   ☒ **B** is incorrect because mirroring is a storage system function that applications are unaware of.

   ☒ **C** is incorrect because data replication is a storage system function that applications are unaware of.

61. A department has completed a review of its business continuity plan through a moderated discussion that followed a specific, scripted disaster scenario. What kind of a review was performed?

   A. Walkthrough

   B. Simulation

   C. Parallel test

   D. Peer review

   ☑ **B.** A simulation is a type of review where a moderator reveals a realistic scenario, and test participants talk through the steps they would be taking should an actual disaster of this type be occurring. A simulation is more realistic than a walkthrough, as it helps to bring a disaster to life.

   ☒ **A** is incorrect because a walkthrough does not attempt to simulate a disaster scenario.

   ☒ **C** is incorrect because a parallel test involves the actual deployment of business continuity procedures to see whether they can be operated properly.

⊠ **D** is incorrect because a peer review involves other personnel, possibly those in another organization.

62. What is the purpose of salvage operations in a disaster recovery plan?

    A. To identify the damage to, and recoverability of, critical equipment and assets

    B. To determine the scrap value of critical equipment and assets

    C. To ensure that all personnel are accounted for

    D. To identify business processes that can be resumed

    ☑ **A.** The primary purpose of salvage is to determine the extent of damage of critical business equipment and to determine what is still functional, which assets can be repaired, and which are damaged beyond repair.

    ⊠ **B** is incorrect because the primary purpose of salvage is to determine the extent of damage of critical business equipment and to determine what is still functional, which assets can be repaired, and which are damaged beyond repair. A secondary purpose is to determine whether the equipment that is damaged beyond repair can be scrapped.

    ⊠ **C** is incorrect because the purpose of salvage is related to business equipment, not personnel.

    ⊠ **D** is incorrect because the purpose of salvage is related to business equipment, not business processes.

63. RAM is most commonly used as:

    A. Secondary storage

    B. Main storage

    C. Virtual disk

    D. CPU instruction cache

    ☑ **B.** RAM, or random access memory, is the primary technology used for a computer's main storage.

    ⊠ **A** is incorrect because SSDs and HDDs are most commonly used for secondary storage.

    ⊠ **C** is incorrect because a virtual disk is a secondary use of RAM, not a primary use.

    ⊠ **D** is incorrect because a CPU has its own instruction cache built in.

64. All of the following are valid reasons for removing end users' local administrators privileges on their workstations *except:*

    A. To reduce malware attack impact

    B. To prevent the use of personal web mail

    C. To prevent installation of unauthorized software

    D. To reduce the number of service desk support calls

☑ **B.** Removing local administrator access from an end user would not impact a user's ability to access personal web mail in most cases.

☒ **A, C,** and **D** are incorrect because these are primary reasons for removing local administrator privileges from end users.

65. The primary mission of data governance is:

A. To ensure the availability of sensitive and critical information

B. To ensure the integrity of sensitive and critical information

C. To control and monitor all uses of sensitive or critical information

D. To ensure compliance with applicable privacy laws

☑ **C.** The primary mission of data governance is the control and monitoring of all uses of sensitive and/or critical information in an organization, both in structured and unstructured storage.

☒ **A** is incorrect because data governance is not primarily concerned with the availability of information.

☒ **B** is incorrect because data governance is not primarily concerned with the integrity of information.

☒ **D** is incorrect because compliance with applicable laws should be an outcome of data governance, but not its main purpose.

66. Many of the backout plans in the records of a change control process simply read, "Reverse previous steps." What conclusion can be drawn from this?

A. Backout plans are only relevant for emergency changes.

B. Backout plans are not a part of a change management process.

C. Backout plans are adequate.

D. Backout plans are not as rigorous as they should be.

☑ **D.** "Reverse previous steps" is wholly inadequate for most changes, as this represents unpreparedness for situations where changes are unsuccessful.

☒ **A** is incorrect because backout plans are needed for all changes.

☒ **B** is incorrect because backout plans are a key part of a change management process.

☒ **C** is incorrect because a backout plan that states simply "reverse previous steps" is not adequate. Complex changes may not be so easily reversed.

67. The purpose of a business impact analysis (BIA) is primarily:

A. To calculate risk in a risk assessment

B. To determine the impact of a breach

C. To determine process criticalities

D. To determine process dependencies

☑ **D.** The purpose of business impact analysis (BIA) is to determine the dependencies of business processes—what assets, staff, and outside parties are required to sustain a process. Subsequent to a BIA is the criticality assessment (CA), which determines the criticality of business processes analyzed in the BIA.

☒ **A** is incorrect because a BIA is not used in a general risk assessment.

☒ **B** is incorrect because a BIA is not used in a breach assessment.

☒ **C** is incorrect because it is the criticality assessment (CA) that is used to determine process criticality, once the BIA itself has been completed.

68. The purpose for pre-writing public statements describing the impact, response, and recovery from a disaster include all of the following *except:*

A. During a disaster is not a good time to write such statements from scratch.

B. Key personnel who would write such statements may not be available.

C. Such public statements can be issued more quickly.

D. Pre-written public statements are required by regulation.

☑ **D.** Few, if any, regulations require organizations to pre-write their public statements describing a disaster and the details about impact, response, and recovery.

☒ **A, B,** and **C** are incorrect because these are some of the advantages of writing out the templates for such statements in advance.

Information Asset Protection

This chapter covers CISA Domain 5, "Protection of Information Assets," and includes questions from the following topics:

- Information security management
- Logical access controls
- Network security
- Environmental security
- Physical security
- Privacy

The topics in this chapter represent 27 percent of the CISA examination.

Information assets consist of information and information systems. Information includes software, tools, and data. Information system is an inclusive term that encompasses servers, workstations, mobile devices, network devices, gateways, appliances, IoT devices, and applications. An information system can be a single device or a collection of systems that work together for some business purpose.

1. A new information security manager has examined the systems in the production environment and has found that their security-related configurations are inadequate and inconsistent. To improve this situation, the security manager should create a:

   A. Jump server

   B. Firewall rule

   C. Hardening standard

   D. CMDB

2. Which U.S. government agency enforces retail organizations' information privacy policy?

   A. National Institute of Standards and Technology

   B. Federal Trade Commission

   C. Office of Civil Rights

   D. United States Secret Service

3. While useful for detecting fires, what is one known problem associated with the use of smoke detectors under a raised computer room floor?

   A. False alarms due to the accumulation of dust

   B. Higher cost of maintenance

   C. Lack of visual reference

   D. Lower sensitivity due to stagnant air

4. An organization is seeking to establish a protocol standard for federated authentication. Which of the following protocols is *least* likely to be selected?

   A. OAuth

   B. SAML

   C. SOAP

   D. HMAC

5. What is one distinct disadvantage of the use of on-premises web content filtering?

   A. End users can no longer inspect URLs in e-mail messages.

   B. End users can easily circumvent it with a local IPS.

   C. Mobile devices are unprotected when off-network.

   D. It is labor intensive to manage exceptions.

6. What is the purpose of data classification?

   A. To establish rules for data protection and use

   B. To discover sensitive data on unstructured shares

   C. To enforce file access rules

   D. To gather statistics on data usage

7. Blockchain is best described as:

   A. A cryptographic algorithm

   B. A data confidentiality technique using cryptography

   C. A popular cryptocurrency

   D. A list of records that are linked using cryptography

8. The private keys for a well-known web site have been compromised. What is the best approach for resolving this matter?

   A. Change the IP address of the web server.

   B. Add an entry to a CRL for the web site's SSL keys.

   C. Recompile the web site's application.

   D. Reboot the web server.

9. A web application stores unique codes on each user's system in order to track the activities of each visitor. What is a common term for these codes?

   A. Http-only cookie

   B. Super cookie

   C. Session cookie

   D. Persistent cookie

10. The term "virtual memory" refers to what mechanism?

    A. The main storage allocated to a guest of a hypervisor

    B. Memory management that isolates running processes

    C. Memory that is shared between guests of a hypervisor

    D. Main storage space that exceeds physical memory and is extended to secondary storage

11. What is the effect of suppressing the broadcast of SSID?

    A. Network is not listed, but no difference in security.

    B. Only registered users are able to connect.

    C. Stronger (AES vs. TKIP) cryptography.

    D. Administrators can track users more easily.

12. What is the purpose of recordkeeping in a security awareness training program?

    A. It prevents users from repeating the training.

    B. Compliance with training provider licensing requirements.

    C. Recordkeeping is required by ISO 27001.

    D. Users cannot later claim no knowledge of content if they violate policy.

13. An attack technique in which an attacker attempts to place arbitrary code into the instruction space of a running process is known as:

    A. Cross-site scripting

    B. A time-of-check to time-of-use attack

    C. A buffer overflow attack

    D. A race condition

14. A security analyst who is troubleshooting a security issue has asked another engineer to obtain a PCAP file associated with a given user's workstation. What is the security analyst asking for?

    A. A copy of the workstation's registry file

    B. A copy of the network traffic to and from the workstation

    C. An image of the workstation's main memory (RAM)

    D. An image of the workstation's secondary memory (hard drive)

15. A development lab employs a syslog server for security and troubleshooting issues. The information security office has recently implemented a SIEM and has directed that all log data be sent to the SIEM. How can the development lab continue to employ its local syslog server while complying with this request?

    A. Build a proxy server that will clone the log data.

    B. The development lab will have to shut down its syslog server.

    C. Export syslog data every hour and send it to the SIEM.

    D. Direct servers to send their syslog data to the local server and to the SIEM.

16. The best time to assign roles and responsibilities for computer security incident response is:

    A. During training

    B. During tabletop testing

    C. While responding to an incident

    D. While writing the incident response plan

17. Chain of custody is employed in which business process?

    A. Internal investigation

    B. Asset management

    C. Access management

    D. Penetration testing

18. Canada's ITSG-33 is a similar to which standard?

    A. SSAE18

    B. HIPAA

C. NIST SP800-53

D. ISO/IEC 27001

19. The process of ensuring proper protection and use of PII is known as:

A. Security

B. Privacy

C. Data loss prevention

D. Data discovery

20. A CIO is investigating the prospect of a hosting center for its IT infrastructure. A specific hosting center claims to have "N+1 HVAC Systems." What is meant by this term?

A. The hosting center has one more HVAC system than is necessary for adequate cooling.

B. The hosting center has the "N+1" brand of HVAC systems designed for hosting centers.

C. The hosting center has recently installed a new HVAC system.

D. The hosting center HVAC systems meet the N+1 reliability standard.

21. An organization has updated its identity and access management infrastructure so that users use their AD credentials to log in to the network as well as internal business applications. What has the organization implemented?

A. Credential vaulting

B. Single sign-on

C. Federated identity

D. Reduced sign-on

22. The primary advantage of a firewall on a laptop computer is:

A. Laptop computers are protected when outside the enterprise network.

B. End users have more control over their network security.

C. Improved performance of enterprise network firewalls.

D. Redundancy in the event the enterprise firewall is overloaded.

23. An organization's data classification policy includes guidelines for placing footers with specific language in documents and presentations. What activity does this refer to?

A. Digital signatures

B. Digital envelopes

C. Document marking

D. Document tagging

24. What technique does PGP use to permit multiple users to read an encrypted document?

    A. Key fingerprints

    B. Symmetric cryptography

    C. Digital envelope

    D. Digital signature

25. What feature permits enterprise users of Microsoft Outlook to digitally sign e-mail messages?

    A. PGP

    B. AD PKI

    C. Local administrative privileges

    D. Password vaulting

26. A URL starting with shttp:// signifies what technology?

    A. Self-signed content

    B. Encryption with 3DES

    C. Encryption with SSL or TLS

    D. SET, or Secure Electronic Transaction

27. A recent audit of an IT operation included a finding stating that the organization experiences virtualization sprawl. What is the meaning of this term?

    A. The process related to the creation of new virtual machines is not effective.

    B. Virtual machines are contending for scarce resources.

    C. The organization has too many virtual machines.

    D. Resource requirements for virtual machines are growing.

28. Reasons for placing all IoT-type devices on isolated VLANs include all of the following *except:*

    A. Use of a different network access method

    B. Compatibility with IPv4

    C. Risks associated with unpatched and unpatchable devices

    D. Protection from malware present in end-user environments

29. What is the best reason for including competency quizzes in security awareness training courses?

    A. Quizzes are needed in order to improve users' knowledge.

    B. Quizzes are required by regulations such as PCI and HIPAA.

    C. It gives users an opportunity to test their skills.

    D. It provides evidence of retention of course content.

30. In the context of information technology and information security, what is the purpose of fuzzing?

    A. To assess a physical server's resilience through a range of humidity settings

    B. To assess a physical server's ability to repel static electricity

    C. To assess a program's resistance to attack via the UI

    D. To assess a program's performance

31. An attacker who is attempting to infiltrate an organization has decided to employ a DNS poison cache attack. What method will the attacker use to attempt this attack?

    A. Send forged query replies to a DNS server.

    B. Send forged query replies to end-user workstations.

    C. Send forged PTR replies to end-user workstations.

    D. Send forced PTR replies to DNS servers.

32. What is the Unix command to dynamically view the end of a text logfile?

    A. tail -f

    B. tail -e

    C. less -f

    D. more -f

33. In the United States, what are organizations required to do when discovering child pornography on a user's workstation?

    A. Contact law enforcement after the user has admitted to viewing child porn.

    B. Contact law enforcement when the user's workstation has been retired.

    C. Contact law enforcement after terminating the user.

    D. Immediately contact law enforcement.

34. An organization suspects one of its employees of a security violation regarding the use of their workstation. The workstation, a laptop computer that is powered down, has been delivered to a forensic expert. What is the first thing the expert should do?

    A. Remove the hard drive.

    B. Photograph the laptop.

    C. Power up the laptop.

    D. Remove the RAM from the laptop.

35. Which of the following statements is true regarding the Payment Card Industry Data Security Standard (PCI-DSS)?

   A. All organizations processing more than US$6,000,000 in credit card transactions annually must undergo an annual audit.

   B. Organizations using chip-and-PIN terminals are exempt from PCI requirements.

   C. Organizations processing fewer than six million merchant transactions annually are usually permitted to provide annual self-assessments.

   D. Organizations are permitted to opt out of low-risk controls via Compensating Control Worksheets.

36. According to the European General Data Protection Regulation (GDPR), what is the requirement for organizations' use of a Data Protection Officer (DPO)?

   A. All organizations storing EU citizen data are required to have an employee designated as the DPO.

   B. All organizations storing large volumes of EU citizen data are required to use a DPO.

   C. All organizations storing EU citizen data are required to retain the services of a DPO consultant.

   D. Only organizations based in Europe are required to have a DPO.

37. What is the biggest risk associated with access badges that show the name of the organization?

   A. Someone who finds the badge may know where it can be used.

   B. An attacker can look up the organization's public key and create forged badges.

   C. An attacker would know what brand of access badge technology is being used.

   D. Someone who finds a lost badge would be able to return it to the company.

38. A user at work logs on to a web site that includes links to various business applications. Once the user logs on to the web site, the user does not need to log on to individual business applications. What mechanism provides this capability?

   A. Public key infrastructure

   B. Reduced sign-on

   C. Single sign-on

   D. Key vaulting

39. What is the primary advantage of cloud-based web content filtering versus on-premises web content filtering:

   A. Cloud-based web content filtering systems are less expensive.

   B. Exceptions can be processed more quickly.

   C. Off-network users are protected just as in-office users are.

   D. Users are unable to circumvent this protection.

40. An organization is investigating the use of an automated DLP solution that controls whether data files can be sent via e-mail or stored on USB drives based on their tags. What is the advantage of the use of tags for such a solution?

   A. Users are easily able to tag files so that they can be properly handled in e-mail.

   B. Data files are automatically processed based on tags instead of their data content.

   C. Tags are a better solution than the use of digital envelopes.

   D. Tags are human readable and can be altered as needed.

41. All of the following are appropriate uses of digital signatures *except:*

   A. Verification of message authenticity

   B. Verification of message integrity

   C. Verification of message confidentiality

   D. Verification of message origin

42. The entity that accepts requests for new public keys in a PKI is known as the:

   A. Reservation authority (RA)

   B. Validation authority (VA)

   C. Registration authority (RA)

   D. Certificate authority (CA)

43. What method is used by a transparent proxy filter to prevent a user from visiting a site that has been blacklisted?

   A. Proxy sends an HTTP 400 Bad Request to the user's browser.

   B. User is directed to a "web site blocked" splash page.

   C. Proxy filter simply drops the packets and the user's browser times out.

   D. User's workstation is quarantined to prevent malware from spreading.

44. In a virtualized environment, which method is the fastest way to ensure rapid recovery of servers at an alternative processing center?

   A. Copy snapshots of virtual machine images to alternative processing center storage system.

   B. Provide build instructions for all servers and make master server images available.

   C. Perform full and incremental backups of all servers on a daily basis.

   D. Perform grandfather-father-son backups of all servers on a daily basis.

45. In an environment where users are not local administrators of their workstations, which of the following methods ensures that end users are not able to use their mobile devices as mobile Wi-Fi hotspots for circumventing network security controls such as web content filters and IPS?

   A. Require employees to turn off their mobile devices at work.

   B. Jam the signals of unauthorized Wi-Fi networks.

   C. Create a whitelist of permitted Wi-Fi networks.

   D. Create a blacklist of forbidden Wi-Fi networks.

46. What is the most effective method for training users to more accurately detect and delete phishing messages?

    A. Block access to personal webmail and permit corporate e-mail only.

    B. Include phishing information in regular security awareness training.

    C. Conduct phishing tests and publicly inform offenders of their mistakes.

    D. Conduct phishing tests and privately inform offenders of their mistakes.

47. An attacker has targeted an organization in order to steal specific information. The attacker has found that the organization's defenses are strong and that very few phishing messages arrive at end-user inboxes. The attacker has decided to try a watering hole attack. What first steps should the hacker use to ensure a successful watering hole attack?

    A. Determine which web sites are frequently visited by the organization's end users.

    B. Determine which restaurants the organization's end users visit after working hours.

    C. Determine which protocols are blocked by the organization's Internet firewalls.

    D. Determine the IP addresses of public-facing web servers that can be attacked.

48. Which of the following techniques most accurately describes a penetration test?

    A. Manual exploitation tools and techniques

    B. Security scan, with results tabulated into a formal report that includes an executive summary

    C. Security scan, with results validated to remove any false positives

    D. Security scan, followed by manual exploitation tools and techniques

49. A security analyst spends most of her time on a system that collects log data and correlates events from various systems to deduce potential attacks in progress. What kind of a system is the security analyst using?

    A. SIEM

    B. IPS

    C. IDS

    D. AV console

50. The general counsel is becoming annoyed with notifications of minor security events occurring in the organization. This is most likely due to:

    A. Careless users clicking on too many phishing e-mails

    B. Ineffective defenses allowing frequent attacks

    C. Improper classification of security incidents

    D. Lack of a security incident severity scheme

51. A forensic investigator is seen to be creating a detailed record of artifacts that are collected, analyzed, controlled, transferred to others, and stored for safekeeping. What kind of a written record is this?

    A. Storage inventory

    B. Investigation report

    C. Evidence collection log

    D. Chain of custody record

52. Which controls framework is suggested by the ISO/IEC 27001 standard?

    A. ISO/IEC 27001

    B. ISO/IEC 27002

    C. NIST SP800-53

    D. Any framework that is applicable to the organization

53. The default principle in the European General Data Protection Regulation for marketing communications from organizations to citizens is:

    A. Citizens are included and cannot opt out.

    B. Citizens are included until they explicitly opt out.

    C. Citizens are excluded until they explicitly opt in.

    D. Citizens are excluded and cannot opt in.

54. The primary purpose of a mantrap is:

    A. To catch an individual attempting to enter a room without authorization

    B. To hold an offender in custody until charged or released

    C. To permit entry of one authorized person at a time

    D. To permit entry or exit of one authorized person at a time

55. What is the purpose of locking a user account that has not been used for long periods of time?

    A. Reduction of the risk of compromised credentials

    B. Free up space for others to use the system

    C. Avoidance of audit exceptions

    D. Recycle license keys and cost reduction

56. What is the best approach for implementing a new blocking rule in an IPS?

    A. First implement a firewall rule and then activate the IPS rule.

    B. Use the change control process so that stakeholders are aware of the new rule.

    C. Implement a new rule during a change window.

    D. Put the rule in learn mode and analyze the results.

57. A security leader needs to develop a data classification program. After developing the data classification and handling policy, what is the best next step to perform?

    A. Configure DLP systems to monitor and enforce compliance.

    B. Configure DLP systems to monitor compliance.

    C. Announce the new policy to the organization.

    D. Work with business departments to socialize the policy.

58. An organization wants to implement an IPS that utilizes SSL inspection. What must first be implemented so that the IPS will function?

    A. A span port on the Internet switch must be configured.

    B. A new root certificate must be pushed to all user workstations.

    C. Users must sign a consent for their personal traffic to be monitored.

    D. All end-user private keys must be refreshed.

59. In what manner does a PKI support whole disk encryption on end-user workstations?

    A. PKI stores the bootup passwords used on each end-user workstation.

    B. PKI detects unauthorized use of data on end-user workstations.

    C. PKI stores decryption keys in the event an end-user forgets their bootup password.

    D. PKI records encryption and decryption operations.

60. A browser contacts a web server and requests a web page. The web server responds with a status code 200. What is the meaning of this status code?

    A. The user has been redirected to another URL on the same domain.

    B. The user has been redirected to another URL on a different domain.

    C. The requested page requires prior authentication.

    D. The request is valid and has been accepted.

61. For what reason would an engineer choose to use a hosted hypervisor versus a bare-metal hypervisor?

    A. There are insufficient resources available for a bare-metal hypervisor.

    B. Features available only in a host operating system are required.

    C. Guest OS monitoring is required.

    D. The hypervisor is supporting a VDI environment.

62. The laboratory environment of a pharmaceutical research organization contains many scientific instruments that contain older versions of Windows and Linux operating systems that cannot be patched. What is the best remedy for this?

    A. Isolate the scientific instruments on a separate, protected network.

    B. Upgrade the OSs on the scientific instruments to current OS versions.

    C. Disconnect the OSs from the network.

    D. Audit user accounts on the OSs periodically.

63. Which of the following is the best policy for a security awareness training course?

    A. Users are not required to take competency quizzes.

    B. Users are required to repeat modules when they fail competency quizzes.

    C. Users are required to take competency quizzes only one time, regardless of score.

    D. Users can skip training if they pass competency quizzes.

64. Guessing that an intended victim has a particular online banking session open, an attacker attempts to trick the victim into clicking on a link that will attempt to execute a transaction on the online banking site. This type of an attack is known as:

    A. Cross-site scripting

    B. Cross-site request forgery

    C. Man in the middle

    D. Man in the browser

65. Which of the following tools is considered a search engine that can be used to list vulnerabilities in devices?

    A. OpenVAS

    B. Burp Suite

    C. Shodan

    D. John the Ripper

66. All of the following tools are used to detect changes in static files *except:*

    A. Blacklight

    B. OSSEC

    C. Tripwire

    D. Firesheep

67. Which of the following correctly describes the correct sequence for computer security incident response?

    A. Protect, detect, respond, recover

    B. Identify, protect, detect, respond, recover

    C. Evaluate, detect, eradicate, contain, recover, closure

    D. Detect, initiate, evaluate, contain, eradicate, recover, remediate

68. Which of the following devices is needed for the creation of a forensically identical hard disk drive?

    A. Diode

    B. Bit locker

    C. Read blocker

    D. Write blocker

69. Which of the following statements about NIST CSF is true?

    A. NIST CSF is a security controls framework.

    B. NIST CSF is a policy framework for cybersecurity.

    C. NIST CSF is a computer security incident response framework.

    D. NIST CSF is a software development framework.

70. The "right to be forgotten" was first implemented by:

    A. GDPR

    B. Google

    C. NYDFS

    D. Facebook

71. The term "tailgating" most often refers to:

    A. Personnel who prop or shim doors so that others can enter a protected facility without authentication

    B. Personnel who permit others to follow them into a protected facility without authentication

    C. Personnel who follow others into a protected facility without authentication

    D. Personnel who loan their keycards to others to enter a protected facility

72. A security manager in a large organization has found that the IT department has no central management of privileged user accounts. What kind of a tool should the security manager introduce to remedy this practice?

    A. FAM tools

    B. FIM tools

    C. PAM tools

    D. SIEM tools

73. A security analyst has determined that some of the OS configuration file alterations have taken place without proper authorization. Which tool did the security analyst use to determine this?

    A. FAM

    B. FIM

    C. PAM

    D. SIEM

74. An employee notes that a company document is marked "Confidential." Is it acceptable for the employee to e-mail the document to a party outside the company?

   A. Yes, but the document must be encrypted first.

   B. Yes, the document can be e-mailed to an outside party in plaintext.

   C. This cannot be determined without first consulting the data classification and handling policy.

   D. No, the document cannot be e-mailed to any inside or outside party.

75. An auditor has completed an audit of an organization's use of a tool that generates SSL certificates for its external web sites. The auditor has determined that key management procedures are insufficient and that split custody of the key generation procedure is required. How might this be implemented?

   A. Of two engineers, one creates the certificate and the other verifies its creation.

   B. Of two engineers, each performs half of the procedure used to create a new certificate.

   C. Of two engineers, each has one half of the password required to create a new certificate.

   D. Of two engineers, one approves the creation of the certificate and the other creates the certificate.

76. An organization that issues digital certificates recently discovered that a digital certificate was issued to an unauthorized party. What is the appropriate response?

   A. Create a CRLF entry.

   B. Create a CRL entry.

   C. Notify all certificate holders.

   D. Call a press conference.

77. Why is it important for a web session cookie to be encrypted?

   A. Parties that can observe the communication will not be able to hijack the session.

   B. Parties that observe the communication will not be able to view the user's password.

   C. Third parties will not be able to push unsolicited advertising to the user.

   D. The web site operator will not be able to record the user's session.

78. Why would a hypervisor conceal its existence from a guest OS?

   A. To prevent the guest OS from breaking out of the container.

   B. To improve the performance of the guest OS.

   C. To avoid letting an intruder know that the OS is part of a virtualized environment.

   D. To let an intruder know that the OS is part of a virtualized environment.

79. How can an organization prevent employees from connecting to the corporate Exchange e-mail environment with personally owned mobile devices?

   A. Implement multifactor authentication.

   B. Permit only Outlook clients to connect to the Exchange server.

   C. Encrypt OWA traffic.

   D. Put the OWA server behind the firewall and VPN switch.

80. What is the purpose of the Firesheep tool?

   A. It demonstrates the dangers of non-encrypted web sessions.

   B. It is used as an alternative browser to Firefox to illustrate security concepts.

   C. It is used to analyze firewall rules.

   D. It is used to back up firewall rules.

81. An organization is implementing a new SIEM. How must engineers get log data from systems and devices to the SIEM?

   A. Install agents on all systems and devices.

   B. Send them via Windows events.

   C. Send them via syslog.

   D. Send them via syslog and Windows events.

82. What is the appropriate consequence of SOC operators declaring incidents that turn out to be false positives?

   A. Additional training to improve their incident-handling skills.

   B. Termination of employment.

   C. Removal of incident declaration privileges.

   D. No consequence, as false positives are a part of business as usual.

1. C	29. D	57. D
2. B	30. C	58. B
3. A	31. A	59. C
4. C	32. A	60. D
5. C	33. D	61. B
6. A	34. B	62. A
7. D	35. C	63. B
8. B	36. B	64. B
9. C	37. A	65. C
10. D	38. C	66. D
11. A	39. C	67. D
12. D	40. B	68. D
13. C	41. C	69. B
14. B	42. C	70. A
15. D	43. B	71. C
16. D	44. A	72. C
17. A	45. C	73. B
18. C	46. D	74. C
19. B	47. A	75. C
20. A	48. D	76. B
21. D	49. A	77. A
22. A	50. D	78. C
23. C	51. D	79. D
24. C	52. B	80. A
25. B	53. C	81. D
26. D	54. D	82. A
27. A	55. A	
28. B	56. D	

1. A new information security manager has examined the systems in the production environment and has found that their security-related configurations are inadequate and inconsistent. To improve this situation, the security manager should create a:

   A. Jump server

   B. Firewall rule

   C. Hardening standard

   D. CMDB

   ☑ **C.** A hardening standard will define the security-related configurations applicable to information systems and devices. Note that automation may also need to be implemented if there are large numbers of servers.

   ☒ **A** is incorrect because a jump server will not address this situation.

   ☒ **B** is incorrect because firewall rules will not adequately address this situation.

   ☒ **D** is incorrect because a CMDB may already exist in this situation; regardless, it is the strong and consistent configuration of servers that is necessary. A CMDB will assist in the management of server configuration.

2. Which U.S. government agency enforces retail organizations' information privacy policy?

   A. National Institute of Standards and Technology

   B. Federal Trade Commission

   C. Office of Civil Rights

   D. United States Secret Service

   ☑ **B.** The Federal Trade Commission (FTC) has historically been enforcing retail organizations' information privacy policy and has brought legal suit against organizations knowingly violating these policies.

   ☒ **A** is incorrect because the National Institute of Standards and Technology (NIST) develops standards and guidelines but does not perform enforcement.

   ☒ **C** is incorrect because the Office of Civil Rights (OCR) enforces HIPAA and related laws in the health-care industry.

   ☒ **D** is incorrect because the U.S. Secret Service (USSS) protects U.S. currency as well as the president.

3. While useful for detecting fires, what is one known problem associated with the use of smoke detectors under a raised computer room floor?

   A. False alarms due to the accumulation of dust

   B. Higher cost of maintenance

   C. Lack of visual reference

   D. Lower sensitivity due to stagnant air

☑ **A.** Dust can accumulate under the raised floor in a computer room environment. Changes in airflow can cause the dust to circulate in the air, causing false-positive smoke detection.

☒ **B** is incorrect because there is no difference in maintenance costs for smoke detectors above or below a raised floor.

☒ **C** is incorrect because it is not necessary for personnel to be able to see smoke detectors below a raised floor.

☒ **D** is incorrect because the air under a raised floor is not stagnant, but instead serves as a plenum for cooling and air circulation.

4. An organization is seeking to establish a protocol standard for federated authentication. Which of the following protocols is *least* likely to be selected?

   A. OAuth

   B. SAML

   C. SOAP

   D. HMAC

   ☑ **C.** SOAP is a protocol used for distributed object instantiation and communication.

   ☒ **A** is incorrect because OAuth is a protocol found in federated authentication.

   ☒ **B** is incorrect because SAML is a protocol found in federated authentication.

   ☒ **D** is incorrect because HMAC is a protocol found in federated authentication. HMAC has fallen out of common use.

5. What is one distinct disadvantage of the use of on-premises web content filtering?

   A. End users can no longer inspect URLs in e-mail messages.

   B. End users can easily circumvent it with a local IPS.

   C. Mobile devices are unprotected when off-network.

   D. It is labor intensive to manage exceptions.

   ☑ **C.** On-premises web content filtering protects devices on the internal network, as well as remote devices when they have established VPNs without split tunneling. Mobile devices connected to the Internet without VPN receive no protection from on-premises web content filtering systems.

   ☒ **A** is incorrect because web content filtering systems do not interact with the content of e-mail messages.

   ☒ **B** is incorrect because users would not be able to circumvent web content filtering with a local IPS; on the contrary, a local IPS would further improve endpoint security, particularly when off-network.

   ☒ **D** is incorrect because the management of rule exceptions is not necessarily a problem.

6. What is the purpose of data classification?

   A. To establish rules for data protection and use

   B. To discover sensitive data on unstructured shares

   C. To enforce file access rules

   D. To gather statistics on data usage

   ☑ A. The purpose of a data classification program is to define the classes, or categories, of data and define usage guidelines for data at each classification level. This helps personnel to understand and follow handling guidelines, which results in improved data protection.

   ☒ B is incorrect because data classification is not used in data discovery.

   ☒ C is incorrect because data classification does not directly contribute to the enforcement of file access rules. Data classification, however, may state what file access rules should be.

   ☒ D is incorrect because data classification does not contribute to data usage statistics.

7. Blockchain is best described as:

   A. A cryptographic algorithm

   B. A data confidentiality technique using cryptography

   C. A popular cryptocurrency

   D. A list of records that are linked using cryptography

   ☑ D. A blockchain is a series of records that are linked using cryptography. Specifically, each successive record in a blockchain contains a hash of the previous record; this makes data in a blockchain resistant to alteration.

   ☒ A is incorrect because blockchain is not a cryptographic algorithm; blockchain uses crypto algorithms, however.

   ☒ B is incorrect because blockchain does not protect the confidentiality of data.

   ☒ C is incorrect because blockchain is not a cryptocurrency.

8. The private keys for a well-known web site have been compromised. What is the best approach for resolving this matter?

   A. Change the IP address of the web server.

   B. Add an entry to a CRL for the web site's SSL keys.

   C. Recompile the web site's application.

   D. Reboot the web server.

   ☑ B. Adding an entry to the certificate revocation list (CRL) is the most effective solution. The certificate authority (CA) that issued the original SSL keys would perform this action. Subsequent attempts to connect with the compromised keys would be unsuccessful—at least for all software that checks the CRL first.

☒ **A** is incorrect because changing the web server's IP address does not address the problem of the compromised private key.

☒ **C** is incorrect because recompiling the web site's application does not address the problem of the compromised private key.

☒ **D** is incorrect because rebooting the web server does not change anything about the encryption keys in use.

9. A web application stores unique codes on each user's system in order to track the activities of each visitor. What is a common term for these codes?

A. Http-only cookie

B. Super cookie

C. Session cookie

D. Persistent cookie

☑ **C.** A session cookie is used to uniquely identify each visitor to a web site and is used to manage user sessions.

☒ **A** is incorrect because an http-only cookie is one that cannot be read by client-side software such as JavaScript.

☒ **B** is incorrect because a super cookie is one issued by a top-level domain such as .com.

☒ **D** is incorrect because a persistent cookie is used to store user preferences such as language and time zone.

10. The term "virtual memory" refers to what mechanism?

A. The main storage allocated to a guest of a hypervisor

B. Memory management that isolates running processes

C. Memory that is shared between guests of a hypervisor

D. Main storage space that exceeds physical memory and is extended to secondary storage

☑ **D.** Virtual memory is the technique of creating memory space that exceeds the physical main memory of a system; memory is extended onto secondary storage.

☒ **A, B,** and **C** are incorrect because virtual memory is not correctly described in these terms.

11. What is the effect of suppressing the broadcast of SSID?

A. Network is not listed, but no difference in security.

B. Only registered users are able to connect.

C. Stronger (AES vs. TKIP) cryptography.

D. Administrators can track users more easily.

☑ **A.** Suppressing the broadcast of SSID in a Wi-Fi network makes no difference in terms of the security of the network. Some believe that suppressing SSID is better for security, but there are numerous tools available that show all available networks, whether they are broadcasting SSID or not.

☒ **B** is incorrect because suppressing SSID broadcast has no effect on the users who are able to connect.

☒ **C** is incorrect because suppressing SSID broadcast is not related to the selection of cryptography.

☒ **D** is incorrect because suppressing SSID broadcast does not affect administration or monitoring of the Wi-Fi network.

12. What is the purpose of recordkeeping in a security awareness training program?

    A. It prevents users from repeating the training.

    B. Compliance with training provider licensing requirements.

    C. Recordkeeping is required by ISO 27001.

    D. Users cannot later claim no knowledge of content if they violate policy.

    ☑ **D.** When a user completes security awareness training and there is evidence of this completion in business records, the user cannot easily refute knowledge of the training content if they later are found to violate policy. Competency quizzes as a part of security awareness training helps even more in this regard.

    ☒ **A** is incorrect because an organization would not normally deny a user from repeating security awareness training.

    ☒ **B** is incorrect because license requirements are enforced through access controls.

    ☒ **C** is incorrect because recordkeeping is not necessarily required by ISO 27001.

13. An attack technique in which an attacker attempts to place arbitrary code into the instruction space of a running process is known as:

    A. Cross-site scripting

    B. A time-of-check to time-of-use attack

    C. A buffer overflow attack

    D. A race condition

    ☑ **C.** A buffer overflow attack is a technique where the attacker attempts to overflow a running program's input buffer, resulting in arbitrary code overwriting other instructions in the program. Successful exploitation of a buffer overflow vulnerability gives the attacker complete control over the target program.

    ☒ **A** is incorrect because a cross-site scripting attack does not overwrite code in the instruction space of a running program, but instead is a technique where the attacker attempts to place client-side scripts into web pages so that a user's browser will execute the attacker's code.

☒ **B** and **D** are incorrect because a time-of-check to time-of-use attack (also known as a race condition) is an attack that exploits a software bug that allows two programs to control a resource that only one resource should be able to control.

14. A security analyst who is troubleshooting a security issue has asked another engineer to obtain a PCAP file associated with a given user's workstation. What is the security analyst asking for?

   A. A copy of the workstation's registry file

   B. A copy of the network traffic to and from the workstation

   C. An image of the workstation's main memory (RAM)

   D. An image of the workstation's secondary memory (hard drive)

   ☑ **B.** A PCAP (packet capture) file is a file containing a copy of network traffic associated with one or more devices on a network.

   ☒ **A** is incorrect because a PCAP is not a copy of the workstation's registry file.

   ☒ **C** and **D** are incorrect because a PCAP is not an image of a workstation's main or secondary memory.

15. A development lab employs a syslog server for security and troubleshooting issues. The information security office has recently implemented a SIEM and has directed that all log data be sent to the SIEM. How can the development lab continue to employ its local syslog server while complying with this request?

   A. Build a proxy server that will clone the log data.

   B. The development lab will have to shut down its syslog server.

   C. Export syslog data every hour and send it to the SIEM.

   D. Direct servers to send their syslog data to the local server and to the SIEM.

   ☑ **D.** Servers and devices can send syslog data to multiple destinations.

   ☒ **A** is incorrect because a proxy server is unnecessary, as systems and devices can send syslog data to multiple destinations.

   ☒ **B** is incorrect because the development lab can continue using its syslog server and comply with the request by configuring its systems and devices to send syslog data to both the local syslog server and the SIEM.

   ☒ **C** is incorrect because exporting syslog data and forwarding it to the SIEM is unnecessary, since systems and devices can send syslog data to multiple destinations.

16. The best time to assign roles and responsibilities for computer security incident response is:

   A. During training

   B. During tabletop testing

   C. While responding to an incident

   D. While writing the incident response plan

☑ **D.** The best time to establish and assign roles and responsibilities for computer security incident response is at the time of incident response plan development.

☒ **A** is incorrect because responsible parties for computer security incident response should be established well before training, in the plan development stage.

☒ **B** is incorrect because responsible parties for computer security incident response should be established well before tabletop testing, in the plan development stage.

☒ **C** is incorrect because roles and responsibilities should be established well before an incident actually occurs, ideally in the plan development stage.

17. Chain of custody is employed in which business process?

    A. Internal investigation

    B. Asset management

    C. Access management

    D. Penetration testing

    ☑ **A.** Chain of custody is employed whenever there is an investigation, including forensics and security incidents, where evidence needs to be collected and retained for later legal proceedings.

    ☒ **B** and **C** are incorrect because chain of custody is not used in asset or access management processes.

    ☒ **D** is incorrect because chain of custody is not used in penetration tests.

18. Canada's ITSG-33 is a similar to which standard?

    A. SSAE18

    B. HIPAA

    C. NIST SP800-53

    D. ISO/IEC 27001

    ☑ **C.** Canada's ITSG-33 is nearly a clone of the U.S. standard NIST SP800-53.

    ☒ **A, B,** and **D** are incorrect because ITSG-33 is not similar to SSAE18, HIPAA, or ISO/IEC 27001.

19. The process of ensuring proper protection and use of PII is known as:

    A. Security

    B. Privacy

    C. Data loss prevention

    D. Data discovery

    ☑ **B.** Privacy is primarily concerned with the protection of PII (personally identifiable information), as well as its uses in and by an organization.

☒ **A** is incorrect because security is primarily concerned only with the protection of PII, but not with its use.

☒ **C** is incorrect because data loss prevention is mainly concerned with the use of PII and other sensitive information such as intellectual property.

☒ **D** is incorrect because data discovery is the process of examining storage systems to determine the nature of the data that resides there.

20. A CIO is investigating the prospect of a hosting center for its IT infrastructure. A specific hosting center claims to have "N+1 HVAC Systems." What is meant by this term?

    A. The hosting center has one more HVAC system than is necessary for adequate cooling.

    B. The hosting center has the "N+1" brand of HVAC systems designed for hosting centers.

    C. The hosting center has recently installed a new HVAC system.

    D. The hosting center HVAC systems meet the N+1 reliability standard.

    ☑ **A.** N+1 refers to any of several critical systems, including incoming power, HVAC, and Internet connectivity, where at least one additional component is available so that the failure of one component will not interrupt hosting center services.

    ☒ **B** is incorrect because N+1 is not an HVAC brand, but an expression of resilience.

    ☒ **C** is incorrect because N+1 is an expression of resilience through redundancy.

    ☒ **D** is incorrect because N+1 is an expression of resilience through the number of components in use, generally one more than is necessary to sustain operations.

21. An organization has updated its identity and access management infrastructure so that users use their AD credentials to log in to the network as well as internal business applications. What has the organization implemented?

    A. Credential vaulting

    B. Single sign-on

    C. Federated identity

    D. Reduced sign-on

    ☑ **D.** Reduced sign-on is the result of integrating a central identity store such as Active Directory (AD) with applications and networks. The term "reduced sign-on" refers to the reduction in the numbers of login credentials users need to access networks and systems.

    ☒ **A** is incorrect because credential vaulting is a technique of storing login credentials in an encrypted repository.

    ☒ **B** is incorrect because single sign-on (SSO) is a mechanism that permits a user to log in once to an environment containing multiple applications and systems. The logged-in state of each user is known to systems and applications that are a part of the SSO environment.

    ☒ **C** is incorrect because federated identity is the process of permitting users to authenticate to systems in participating organizations.

22. The primary advantage of a firewall on a laptop computer is:

A. Laptop computers are protected when outside the enterprise network.

B. End users have more control over their network security.

C. Improved performance of enterprise network firewalls.

D. Redundancy in the event the enterprise firewall is overloaded.

☑ **A.** The firewall on a laptop computer will provide some network protection in cases where the laptop is connected to the Internet at a location outside of the enterprise and its firewalls.

☒ **B** is incorrect because end users should not be able to configure the firewalls on their workstations.

☒ **C** and **D** are incorrect because the use of laptop firewalls will not affect the performance of enterprise firewalls.

23. An organization's data classification policy includes guidelines for placing footers with specific language in documents and presentations. What activity does this refer to?

A. Digital signatures

B. Digital envelopes

C. Document marking

D. Document tagging

☑ **C.** Document marking is the process of placing human-readable text in a document that advises a reader of its sensitivity.

☒ **A** is incorrect because the use of digital signatures is a process of cryptographically signing a document to ensure its authenticity and integrity.

☒ **B** is incorrect because the use of digital envelopes is a technique of encapsulating encryption keys.

☒ **D** is incorrect because document tagging, while similar to document marking, is used to place machine-readable tags on documents for use by automated systems.

24. What technique does PGP use to permit multiple users to read an encrypted document?

A. Key fingerprints

B. Symmetric cryptography

C. Digital envelope

D. Digital signature

☑ **C.** PGP uses a digital envelope to encapsulate multiple public keys that permits multiple users to read an encrypted document.

☒ **A** is incorrect because key fingerprints are used to verify a user's public key.

☒ **B** is incorrect because symmetric cryptography, while used at the core of PGP to encrypt and decrypt files, does not itself facilitate access by multiple users.

☒ **D** is incorrect because a digital signature is used to verify the authenticity and integrity of a document.

25. What feature permits enterprise users of Microsoft Outlook to digitally sign e-mail messages?

   A. PGP

   B. AD PKI

   C. Local administrative privileges

   D. Password vaulting

   ☑ **B.** The PKI capabilities in Active Directory facilitate the use of digital signatures, and encryption, of e-mail messages in Outlook.

   ☒ **A** is incorrect because PGP is not commonly used any more for this purpose.

   ☒ **C** is incorrect because local administrative privileges do not directly facilitate the use of digital signatures in e-mail. While a local administrator may be able to generate a keypair locally, a recipient of a digitally signed or encrypted message would probably not be able to verify or decrypt it.

   ☒ **D** is incorrect because password vaulting is used to protect passwords.

26. A URL starting with shttp:// signifies what technology?

   A. Self-signed content

   B. Encryption with 3DES

   C. Encryption with SSL or TLS

   D. SET, or Secure Electronic Transaction

   ☑ **D.** SHTTP:// signifies the use of the now-deprecated SET (Secure Electronic Transaction) protocol, which is no longer in wide use.

   ☒ **A** is incorrect because shttp:// does not signify the use of self-signed content.

   ☒ **B** and **C** are incorrect because shttp:// does not determine the encryption protocol to be used.

27. A recent audit of an IT operation included a finding stating that the organization experiences virtualization sprawl. What is the meaning of this term?

   A. The process related to the creation of new virtual machines is not effective.

   B. Virtual machines are contending for scarce resources.

   C. The organization has too many virtual machines.

   D. Resource requirements for virtual machines are growing.

☑ **A.** Virtualization sprawl is the phenomenon whereby new virtual machines are created without adequate management control. Because new servers can be created in a virtual environment without requiring the purchase of server hardware, organizations without effective controls will find that they have far more virtual machines than management intends.

☒ **B** is incorrect because virtualization sprawl does not refer to VMs contending for scarce resources. However, VMs contending for resources is a likely result of virtualization sprawl.

☒ **C** is incorrect because an organization with too many virtual machines is a *result* of ineffective virtual machine management controls.

☒ **D** is incorrect because virtualization sprawl does not refer to the growing need for resources, but to the loss of control over the creation of virtual machines.

28. Reasons for placing all IoT-type devices on isolated VLANs include all of the following *except:*

    A. Use of a different network access method

    B. Compatibility with IPv4

    C. Risks associated with unpatched and unpatchable devices

    D. Protection from malware present in end-user environments

    ☑ **B.** Compatibility with IPv4 is rarely, if ever, a reason for isolating IoT devices onto a separate VLAN.

    ☒ **A, C,** and **D** are incorrect because these are all potential considerations for placing IoT devices in isolated VLANs.

29. What is the best reason for including competency quizzes in security awareness training courses?

    A. Quizzes are needed in order to improve users' knowledge.

    B. Quizzes are required by regulations such as PCI and HIPAA.

    C. It gives users an opportunity to test their skills.

    D. It provides evidence of retention of course content.

    ☑ **D.** Quizzes help to reinforce learning and provide evidence that users learned the content. Some online courses are able to require users to pass quizzes with an arbitrary minimum score in order to complete the course. Finally, a user accused of policy violation cannot rightfully claim their lack of understanding of policies if quiz scores demonstrate they did understand them at the time of their training.

    ☒ **A** is incorrect because quizzes don't necessarily improve users' knowledge, but are used to test their knowledge.

    ☒ **B** is incorrect because PCI and HIPAA do not necessarily require quizzes in security awareness training courses.

☒ **C** is incorrect because the primary purposes of quizzes is to measure competency, not provide opportunities to practice.

30. In the context of information technology and information security, what is the purpose of fuzzing?

    A. To assess a physical server's resilience through a range of humidity settings

    B. To assess a physical server's ability to repel static electricity

    C. To assess a program's resistance to attack via the UI

    D. To assess a program's performance

    ☑ **C.** Fuzzing refers to techniques where numerous iterations of data input combinations are offered to input fields to assess the presence and exploitability of security vulnerabilities.

    ☒ **A** and **B** are incorrect because fuzzing is not related to humidity or static electricity in a server environment.

    ☒ **D** is incorrect because fuzzing is not used to assess a program's performance.

31. An attacker who is attempting to infiltrate an organization has decided to employ a DNS poison cache attack. What method will the attacker use to attempt this attack?

    A. Send forged query replies to a DNS server.

    B. Send forged query replies to end-user workstations.

    C. Send forged PTR replies to end-user workstations.

    D. Send forced PTR replies to DNS servers.

    ☑ **A.** A DNS poison cache attack works by sending forged DNS query replies to a DNS server in an attempt to plant false information in the server's cache. The purpose of this attack is to direct users to the wrong server when their workstations query the DNS server in attempts to obtain IP addresses for target servers. When the attacker has successfully poisoned the DNS server's cache, the DNS server provides falsified replies and users are sent to imposter servers.

    ☒ **B** is incorrect because DNS poison cache attacks involve sending forged replies to DNS servers, not to workstations.

    ☒ **C** and **D** are incorrect because DNS poison cache attacks do not utilize the sending of PTR replies.

32. What is the Unix command to dynamically view the end of a text logfile?

    A. tail -f

    B. tail -e

    C. less -f

    D. more -f

☑ **A.** The "tail -f" command will dynamically display the end of a text logfile. When new entries appear in the logfile, tail will automatically show the new entries with no user intervention required.

☒ **B** is incorrect because "tail -e" is not the proper command to display the end of a logfile dynamically.

☒ **C** is incorrect because "less -f" is not the proper command to display the end of a logfile.

☒ **D** is incorrect because "more -f" is not the proper command to display the end of a logfile.

33. In the United States, what are organizations required to do when discovering child pornography on a user's workstation?

    A. Contact law enforcement after the user has admitted to viewing child porn.

    B. Contact law enforcement when the user's workstation has been retired.

    C. Contact law enforcement after terminating the user.

    D. Immediately contact law enforcement.

    ☑ **D.** Organizations in the United States are required to contact law enforcement immediately upon discovery of child porn on any computer or workstation.

    ☒ **A** is incorrect because there is no requirement for users to admit anything.

    ☒ **B** is incorrect because law enforcement must be notified immediately.

    ☒ **C** is incorrect because law enforcement must be notified immediately.

34. An organization suspects one of its employees of a security violation regarding the use of their workstation. The workstation, a laptop computer that is powered down, has been delivered to a forensic expert. What is the first thing the expert should do?

    A. Remove the hard drive.

    B. Photograph the laptop.

    C. Power up the laptop.

    D. Remove the RAM from the laptop.

    ☑ **B.** Prior to removing the hard drive to make a forensically identical copy for analysis, the forensic expert should first photograph the laptop to show its state prior to any disassembly.

    ☒ **A** is incorrect because the laptop should be photographed prior to removing the hard drive in order to document its pre-investigation state.

    ☒ **C** is incorrect because the laptop should not be powered up until after it has been photographed and its hard drive forensically copied.

    ☒ **D** is incorrect because the laptop should be photographed prior to any disassembly to document its pre-investigation state.

35. Which of the following statements is true regarding the Payment Card Industry Data Security Standard (PCI-DSS)?

   A. All organizations processing more than US$6,000,000 in credit card transactions annually must undergo an annual audit.

   B. Organizations using chip-and-PIN terminals are exempt from PCI requirements.

   C. Organizations processing fewer than six million merchant transactions annually are usually permitted to provide annual self-assessments.

   D. Organizations are permitted to opt out of low-risk controls via Compensating Control Worksheets.

   ☑ C. Merchant organizations with fewer than six million credit card transactions annually are usually permitted to complete annual self-assessment questionnaires.

   ☒ A is incorrect because compliance levels are determined by the number of transactions, not the value of transactions.

   ☒ B is incorrect because organizations using chip-and-PIN terminals are still subject to PCI-DSS standards; however, such organizations have fewer requirements to comply with.

   ☒ D is incorrect because organizations are not permitted to opt out of controls.

36. According to the European General Data Protection Regulation (GDPR), what is the requirement for organizations' use of a Data Protection Officer (DPO)?

   A. All organizations storing EU citizen data are required to have an employee designated as the DPO.

   B. All organizations storing large volumes of EU citizen data are required to use a DPO.

   C. All organizations storing EU citizen data are required to retain the services of a DPO consultant.

   D. Only organizations based in Europe are required to have a DPO.

   ☑ B. According to Article 37 of the GDPR, those organizations with large volumes of EU citizen data are required to have a DPO, which may be an employee or a consultant.

   ☒ A is incorrect because only organizations with a large volume of data, or operations requiring monitoring, are required to have a DPO.

   ☒ C is incorrect because organizations are not required to have a DPO consultant; they are also permitted to appoint an employee as the DPO, or not have a DPO at all if requirements in Article 37, Section 1 are met.

   ☒ D is incorrect because organizations based outside of Europe but with operations in Europe are required to have a DPO if requirements in Article 37, Section 1 deem it necessary.

37. What is the biggest risk associated with access badges that show the name of the organization?

   A. Someone who finds the badge may know where it can be used.

   B. An attacker can look up the organization's public key and create forged badges.

   C. An attacker would know what brand of access badge technology is being used.

   D. Someone who finds a lost badge would be able to return it to the company.

   ☑ **A.** An access badge bearing the name of the organization would give someone finding the badge valuable information about where the badge may be used. If the organization does not use multifactor access controls, anyone finding a badge may be able to enter buildings, parking garages, and even data centers.

   ☒ **B** is incorrect because encryption keys for access badge systems are not publicly available.

   ☒ **C** is incorrect because the organization's name does not reveal the brand of access card in use. However, often the brand of access card is visible on the front or rear of a card.

   ☒ **D** is incorrect because this is not a risk associated with an organization's name on the badge, but a benefit.

38. A user at work logs on to a web site that includes links to various business applications. Once the user logs on to the web site, the user does not need to log on to individual business applications. What mechanism provides this capability?

   A. Public key infrastructure

   B. Reduced sign-on

   C. Single sign-on

   D. Key vaulting

   ☑ **C.** The user has logged on to a single sign-on (SSO) portal, which provides easy access to many business applications without the user having to log on to each one.

   ☒ **A** is incorrect because a PKI is not the primary agent providing this capability. PKI is not required for an SSO portal.

   ☒ **B** is incorrect because reduced sign-on lets users remember fewer login credentials, but those credentials must be used when logging on to each application.

   ☒ **D** is incorrect because key vaulting is a mechanism for storing encryption keys, not for facilitating single sign-on.

39. What is the primary advantage of cloud-based web content filtering versus on-premises web content filtering:

   A. Cloud-based web content filtering systems are less expensive.

   B. Exceptions can be processed more quickly.

   C. Off-network users are protected just as in-office users are.

   D. Users are unable to circumvent this protection.

☑ **C.** The primary advantage of cloud-based web content filtering is that all users are protected, whether they are on the organization's internal network or off-network, either at home or traveling.

☒ **A** is incorrect because cloud-based solutions are not necessarily less expensive.

☒ **B** is incorrect because the process of handling exceptions does not vary based on whether the solution is on-premises or cloud-based.

☒ **D** is incorrect because users are unable to circumvent protection, whether the solution is on-premises or cloud-based.

40. An organization is investigating the use of an automated DLP solution that controls whether data files can be sent via e-mail or stored on USB drives based on their tags. What is the advantage of the use of tags for such a solution?

    A. Users are easily able to tag files so that they can be properly handled in e-mail.

    B. Data files are automatically processed based on tags instead of their data content.

    C. Tags are a better solution than the use of digital envelopes.

    D. Tags are human readable and can be altered as needed.

    ☑ **B.** Automated systems can take action based on the tags in a file. However, this is only as good as the mechanism used to apply tags in the first place, which could be highly accurate or inaccurate.

    ☒ **A** is incorrect because users do not necessarily have the ability to tag files (and if they did, one should expect that many errors will be made that will result in mishandling of data).

    ☒ **C** is incorrect because digital envelopes have not been used in DLP solutions.

    ☒ **D** is incorrect because tags are not easily human readable, and they are not intended to be easily changed, except by approved means.

41. All of the following are appropriate uses of digital signatures *except:*

    A. Verification of message authenticity

    B. Verification of message integrity

    C. Verification of message confidentiality

    D. Verification of message origin

    ☑ **C.** Verification of message confidentiality is *not* a use of digital signatures.

    ☒ **A, B,** and **D** are incorrect because these *are* legitimate and intended uses of digital signatures.

42. The entity that accepts requests for new public keys in a PKI is known as the:

    A. Reservation authority (RA)

    B. Validation authority (VA)

C. Registration authority (RA)

D. Certificate authority (CA)

☑ **C.** A registration authority (RA) is the entity that receives and accepts requests for new public keys or digital certificates in a PKI such as an SSL certificate issuer for securing web site communication.

☒ **A** is incorrect because reservation authority is not the term used; further, the PKI model does not have an entity called a reservation authority.

☒ **B** is incorrect because a validation authority (VA), usually a third party such as a government, serves to ensure that the request is genuine.

☒ **D** is incorrect because a certificate authority (CA) is the entity that creates and issues a public key or digital certificate.

43. What method is used by a transparent proxy filter to prevent a user from visiting a site that has been blacklisted?

A. Proxy sends an HTTP 400 Bad Request to the user's browser.

B. User is directed to a "web site blocked" splash page.

C. Proxy filter simply drops the packets and the user's browser times out.

D. User's workstation is quarantined to prevent malware from spreading.

☑ **B.** A transparent proxy server will usually direct a user to a "splash page," informing the user that their request to access a forbidden web site has been blocked. Some organizations include information on the splash page that can direct the user to make a request to unblock access to the desired site.

☒ **A** is incorrect. A transparent proxy generally does not return error codes to the user's browser, but instead displays a splash page that informs the user that access has been blocked.

☒ **C** is incorrect because this inelegant method will cause the user to believe that there is a technical problem that potentially requires tech support.

☒ **D** is incorrect because this situation does not cite a suspected or confirmed malware infection that warrants quarantining the workstation.

44. In a virtualized environment, which method is the fastest way to ensure rapid recovery of servers at an alternative processing center?

A. Copy snapshots of virtual machine images to alternative processing center storage system.

B. Provide build instructions for all servers and make master server images available.

C. Perform full and incremental backups of all servers on a daily basis.

D. Perform grandfather-father-son backups of all servers on a daily basis.

☑ **A.** Copying snapshots of actual server images ensures that recent server images are available at the alternative processing center for rapid restoration.

☒ **B** is incorrect, as using procedures to recover servers may be accurate but will take more time than restoring snapshots of virtual server images.

☒ **C** and **D** are incorrect because restoring server images from multiple generations of backup media may be accurate, but will be far more time consuming than employing snapshots of server images.

45. In an environment where users are not local administrators of their workstations, which of the following methods ensures that end users are not able to use their mobile devices as mobile Wi-Fi hotspots for circumventing network security controls such as web content filters and IPS?

   A. Require employees to turn off their mobile devices at work.

   B. Jam the signals of unauthorized Wi-Fi networks.

   C. Create a whitelist of permitted Wi-Fi networks.

   D. Create a blacklist of forbidden Wi-Fi networks.

☑ **C.** The best workable solution is to create a whitelist of Wi-Fi networks that workstations are permitted to connect to. These networks would include all corporate Wi-Fi networks, as well as any trusted non-corporate networks.

☒ **A** is incorrect because a policy requiring employees to turn off their mobile devices is not likely to be successful.

☒ **B** is incorrect because jamming signals of unauthorized Wi-Fi networks is not likely to be successful, and may possibly even be illegal in some jurisdictions. Also, many mobile devices also permit Bluetooth and USB connections for tethering Internet connectivity for workstations.

☒ **D** is incorrect because managing blacklists is a never-ending game of whack-a-mole.

46. What is the most effective method for training users to more accurately detect and delete phishing messages?

   A. Block access to personal webmail and permit corporate e-mail only.

   B. Include phishing information in regular security awareness training.

   C. Conduct phishing tests and publicly inform offenders of their mistakes.

   D. Conduct phishing tests and privately inform offenders of their mistakes.

☑ **D.** Well-managed phishing testing campaigns can help employees learn how to spot phishing messages. Providing a "I think this is a phish" reporting capability gives end users the ability to affirm that test messages are phishing tests, and it's also a good method for reporting actual phishing messages.

☒ **A** is incorrect because blocking personal web mail does not address the matter of phishing messages that are sent to users' corporate e-mail addresses.

☒ **B** is incorrect. While including phishing information in security awareness training is a good practice, this is not as effective as conducting phishing tests.

☒ **C** is incorrect because publicly shaming users who make mistakes is not good for morale.

47. An attacker has targeted an organization in order to steal specific information. The attacker has found that the organization's defenses are strong and that very few phishing messages arrive at end-user inboxes. The attacker has decided to try a watering hole attack. What first steps should the hacker use to ensure a successful watering hole attack?

   A. Determine which web sites are frequently visited by the organization's end users.

   B. Determine which restaurants the organization's end users visit after working hours.

   C. Determine which protocols are blocked by the organization's Internet firewalls.

   D. Determine the IP addresses of public-facing web servers that can be attacked.

   ☑ **A.** In order to conduct a successful watering hole attack, the attacker must first determine which web sites are frequently visited by employees in the organization. This will include cloud-based applications used for primary business processes such as accounting, sales, human resources, and file storage.

   ☒ **B** is incorrect because a watering hole attack involves attacks on web sites frequently visited by the target organization's personnel.

   ☒ **C** and **D** are incorrect because the attacker has already dismissed frontal attack techniques such as compromising exploitable server vulnerabilities.

48. Which of the following techniques most accurately describes a penetration test?

   A. Manual exploitation tools and techniques

   B. Security scan, with results tabulated into a formal report that includes an executive summary

   C. Security scan, with results validated to remove any false positives

   D. Security scan, followed by manual exploitation tools and techniques

   ☑ **D.** A penetration test most commonly begins with a security scan that enumerates assets and provides a big-picture attack profile. This is followed by an array of manual attack techniques that attempt to exploit vulnerabilities in the systems and services identified by the security scan.

   ☒ **A** is incorrect because a penetration test usually begins with a security scan to enumerate the environment, which identifies targets to attack.

   ☒ **B** is incorrect because this method lacks the manual tools and techniques that are central to a penetration test. What is described here is simply a security scan and nothing more.

   ☒ **C** is incorrect because a penetration test also includes numerous manual exploitation techniques. What is described here is simply a validated security scan and nothing more.

49. A security analyst spends most of her time on a system that collects log data and correlates events from various systems to deduce potential attacks in progress. What kind of a system is the security analyst using?

A. SIEM

B. IPS

C. IDS

D. AV console

☑ **A.** The security analyst is using a SIEM, or security information and event management system. A SIEM collects log data from devices throughout the environment and then correlates seemingly disparate events to deduce potential attacks. When such attacks are discerned, the SIEM will produce an alert that directs the security analyst to further investigate the matter and take possible action.

☒ **B** is incorrect because an IPS is an inline device that is used to detect and block unwanted network traffic. An IPS does not collect log data from devices in the network.

☒ **C** is incorrect because an IDS is a device that is used to monitor network traffic and detect unwanted traffic. An IDS does not collect log data from devices in the network.

☒ **D** is incorrect because an AV console is used to monitor antivirus software that is running on servers and endpoints.

50. The general counsel is becoming annoyed with notifications of minor security events occurring in the organization. This is most likely due to:

A. Careless users clicking on too many phishing e-mails

B. Ineffective defenses allowing frequent attacks

C. Improper classification of security incidents

D. Lack of a security incident severity scheme

☑ **D.** The most likely reason the general counsel is being notified of minor incidents is the lack of an incident classification scheme in the organization's security incident response plan. Without a severity classification scheme, all incidents are treated as equal, regardless of their actual severity. In this case, the result is executives being notified of minor incidents that should be of little or no concern to them.

☒ **A** is incorrect because this is too narrow a scenario.

☒ **B** is incorrect because the scenario here involves minor incidents, not successful attacks on outer defenses.

☒ **C** is incorrect because improper classification of incidents would likely be resolved quickly.

51. A forensic investigator is seen to be creating a detailed record of artifacts that are collected, analyzed, controlled, transferred to others, and stored for safekeeping. What kind of a written record is this?

A. Storage inventory

B. Investigation report

C. Evidence collection log

D. Chain of custody record

☑ **D.** The recordkeeping described is a chain of custody record, which provides a detailed account for each artifact collected and analyzed.

☒ **A** is incorrect because a storage inventory record would not include information about transfer of custody or analysis of items.

☒ **B** is incorrect because an investigative report would describe conclusions of an investigation.

☒ **C** is incorrect because an evidence collection log would not include analysis, control, and transfers.

52. Which controls framework is suggested by the ISO/IEC 27001 standard?

A. ISO/IEC 27001

B. ISO/IEC 27002

C. NIST SP800-53

D. Any framework that is applicable to the organization

☑ **B.** ISO/IEC 27001 suggests the use of the ISO/IEC 27002 standard for controls. Annex A of ISO/IEC 27001 contains a summary list of the controls found in the ISO/IEC 27002 standard.

☒ **A** is incorrect because the controls listed in Annex A of ISO/IEC 27001 are from the ISO/IEC 27002 standard.

☒ **C** is incorrect because ISO/IEC 27001 does not suggest the use of NIST SP800-53.

☒ **D** is incorrect because ISO/IEC 27001 contains a summary of the controls in ISO/IEC 27002.

53. The default principle in the European General Data Protection Regulation for marketing communications from organizations to citizens is:

A. Citizens are included and cannot opt out.

B. Citizens are included until they explicitly opt out.

C. Citizens are excluded until they explicitly opt in.

D. Citizens are excluded and cannot opt in.

☑ **C.** Under the GDPR, organizations are not permitted to market to individual citizens unless the citizens first opt in.

☒ **A** is incorrect because citizens are not included, but excluded, and they are permitted to opt out.

☒ **B** is incorrect because citizens are not included, but excluded, and they can opt out.

☒ **D** is incorrect because although citizens are excluded, they can opt in.

54. The primary purpose of a mantrap is:

A. To catch an individual attempting to enter a room without authorization

B. To hold an offender in custody until charged or released

C. To permit entry of one authorized person at a time

D. To permit entry or exit of one authorized person at a time

☑ **D.** A mantrap is a special controlled entrance or exit that permits only one person at a time to enter or exit an area.

☒ **A** is incorrect because a mantrap does not intend to entrap persons attempting to enter or exit an area.

☒ **B** is incorrect because a mantrap is not a holding cell, but an access control.

☒ **C** is incorrect because a mantrap can be used for both entrance and exit.

55. What is the purpose of locking a user account that has not been used for long periods of time?

A. Reduction of the risk of compromised credentials

B. Free up space for others to use the system

C. Avoidance of audit exceptions

D. Recycle license keys and cost reduction

☑ **A.** If a user has not logged in to an application for long periods of time, then perhaps the user account for that application can be locked. This would reduce the impact of compromised credentials by preventing an unauthorized party from logging in to a system.

☒ **B** is incorrect because freeing up space is generally not the primary reason for removing user accounts.

☒ **C** is incorrect because avoidance of audit exceptions would be a secondary result. Many organizations have a control that requires dormant (unused) user accounts to be locked or removed, and that control is sometimes audited.

☒ **D** is incorrect because the harvesting of unused licenses is not generally a primary reason for locking a user account. If an organization needed to harvest licenses, the user account would probably need to be removed and not just locked.

56. What is the best approach for implementing a new blocking rule in an IPS?

    A. First implement a firewall rule and then activate the IPS rule.

    B. Use the change control process so that stakeholders are aware of the new rule.

    C. Implement a new rule during a change window.

    D. Put the rule in learn mode and analyze the results.

    ☑ **D.** The best approach is to first create the rule in learn mode, where the rule will detect and log rule activations, but not actually block traffic. Analysis of the log will help analysts understand whether the new rule would inadvertently block legitimate traffic and disrupt system operation. If no such interference is observed, the rule can be safely put into block mode.

    ☒ **A** is incorrect because firewalls generally lack the sophistication of an IPS and instead can only block packets based on source and destination IP addresses and port numbers.

    ☒ **B** is incorrect because even the change control process is not always going to detect potential negative consequences of a new IPS blocking rule.

    ☒ **C** is incorrect because this approach provides no opportunity to first learn whether the new blocking rule will disrupt legitimate activities.

57. A security leader needs to develop a data classification program. After developing the data classification and handling policy, what is the best next step to perform?

    A. Configure DLP systems to monitor and enforce compliance.

    B. Configure DLP systems to monitor compliance.

    C. Announce the new policy to the organization.

    D. Work with business departments to socialize the policy.

    ☑ **D.** The best next step is to work with various business departments to discuss the new policy and handling guidelines to understand the potential impact of the policy. A badly implemented data classification program can cause business disruption and erode goodwill.

    ☒ **A** is incorrect because enforcing data classification policy as a first step is highly likely to disrupt business processes.

    ☒ **B** is incorrect because monitoring data classification policy is highly likely to produce numerous false-positive alerts.

    ☒ **C** is incorrect because announcing policy to the organization is likely to cause confusion unless the security leader first works with all individual departments to understand the potential impact of the new data classification policy.

58. An organization wants to implement an IPS that utilizes SSL inspection. What must first be implemented so that the IPS will function?

    A. A span port on the Internet switch must be configured.

    B. A new root certificate must be pushed to all user workstations.

C. Users must sign a consent for their personal traffic to be monitored.

D. All end-user private keys must be refreshed.

☑ **B.** Unless the organization creates a root certificate and pushes it to all end-user workstations, users' browsers will throw certificate errors.

☒ **A** is incorrect because an inline IPS does not use a span port, but rather is inline.

☒ **C** is incorrect because users are not usually required to sign a separate consent form. Generally, as a result of employment and through using company-provided information systems, employees are told that company information systems are provided for company business only and are subject to monitoring.

☒ **D** is incorrect because an IPS does not rely on any private keys used by end users.

59. In what manner does a PKI support whole disk encryption on end-user workstations?

A. PKI stores the bootup passwords used on each end-user workstation.

B. PKI detects unauthorized use of data on end-user workstations.

C. PKI stores decryption keys in the event an end-user forgets their bootup password.

D. PKI records encryption and decryption operations.

☑ **C.** While a PKI is not required to implement whole disk encryption on end-user workstations, a PKI can be used to store administrative keys that can be used to unlock a workstation in the event that the user has forgotten their bootup password.

☒ **A** is incorrect because a PKI does not store the bootup password used on end-user workstations.

☒ **B** is incorrect, as a PKI does not monitor file access on systems.

☒ **D** is incorrect because a PKI does not record encryption and decryption operations, but instead can store administrative keys that can be used to unlock a workstation.

60. A browser contacts a web server and requests a web page. The web server responds with a status code 200. What is the meaning of this status code?

A. The user has been redirected to another URL on the same domain.

B. The user has been redirected to another URL on a different domain.

C. The requested page requires prior authentication.

D. The request is valid and has been accepted.

☑ **D.** A response code 200 means the request is valid and has been responded to.

☒ **A** and **B** are incorrect because a code 200 is a successful transaction and not related to redirection.

☒ **C** is incorrect because a code 200 is a successful transaction and not related to authentication.

61. For what reason would an engineer choose to use a hosted hypervisor versus a bare-metal hypervisor?

A. There are insufficient resources available for a bare-metal hypervisor.

B. Features available only in a host operating system are required.

C. Guest OS monitoring is required.

D. The hypervisor is supporting a VDI environment.

☑ B. An engineer would select a hosted hypervisor (that is, a hypervisor that runs on an operating system like Windows, Linux, or macOS) because one or more features or functions found only on the operating system are required.

☒ A is incorrect because a bare-metal hypervisor actually consumes fewer resources than a full OS.

☒ C is incorrect because bare-metal hypervisors provide guest OS monitoring.

☒ D is incorrect as a bare-metal hypervisor is capable of supporting a VDI (virtual desktop infrastructure) environment.

62. The laboratory environment of a pharmaceutical research organization contains many scientific instruments that contain older versions of Windows and Linux operating systems that cannot be patched. What is the best remedy for this?

A. Isolate the scientific instruments on a separate, protected network.

B. Upgrade the OSs on the scientific instruments to current OS versions.

C. Disconnect the OSs from the network.

D. Audit user accounts on the OSs periodically.

☑ A. The presence of older and/or unpatchable OSs on scientific equipment is a common problem that is not easily solved. Most often, the best approach is to isolate those systems through network segmentation and security controls to ensure that all attempts to attack those systems will be automatically detected and blocked.

☒ B is incorrect because often the OSs on such equipment cannot be upgraded for various reasons (e.g., laboratory software will not run on newer OS versions, or there are insufficient resources such as memory to run newer OSs).

☒ C is incorrect because disconnecting those older OSs may impair their operation.

☒ D is incorrect because auditing user accounts does little to protect these older OSs from attack.

63. Which of the following is the best policy for a security awareness training course?

A. Users are not required to take competency quizzes.

B. Users are required to repeat modules when they fail competency quizzes.

C. Users are required to take competency quizzes only one time, regardless of score.

D. Users can skip training if they pass competency quizzes.

☑ **B.** When a user fails to achieve the minimum passing grade on a competency quiz, the user should be required to repeat the learning module and then take the quiz again.

☒ **A** is incorrect because users should be required to take competency quizzes to see how well they retained the learning content.

☒ **C** is incorrect because users should be required to repeat the learning module if they fail the competency quiz.

☒ **D** is incorrect because some learning content may not have accompanying quizzes.

64. Guessing that an intended victim has a particular online banking session open, an attacker attempts to trick the victim into clicking on a link that will attempt to execute a transaction on the online banking site. This type of an attack is known as:

   A. Cross-site scripting

   B. Cross-site request forgery

   C. Man in the middle

   D. Man in the browser

☑ **B.** A cross-site request forgery (CSRF) attack is one in which an attacker attempts to trick a victim into performing a transaction on another web site (for example, a banking transaction in which the victim transfers money to the attacker).

☒ **A** is incorrect because a cross-site scripting attack is one in which an attacker attempts to inject code into a web site, where the code is then executed later by others who visit the site (for example, placing code on a discussion forum).

☒ **C** is incorrect because a man-in-the-middle (MITM) attack is one in which an attacker attempts to subvert communications between two parties by intercepting and injecting forged content into the communications.

☒ **D** is incorrect because a man-in-the-browser (MITB) attack is one in which an attacker attempts to exploit a vulnerability in a user's browser by tricking the user into downloading malicious code that alters the browser's operation.

65. Which of the following tools is considered a search engine that can be used to list vulnerabilities in devices?

   A. OpenVAS

   B. Burp Suite

   C. Shodan

   D. John the Ripper

☑ **C.** Shodan is a search engine that scans the Internet using common protocols and catalogs the responses returned from devices. This is a useful tool for seeing what devices are visible from the Internet.

☒ **A** is incorrect because OpenVAS is a network vulnerability testing tool.

☒ **B** is incorrect because Burp Suite is a web site vulnerability testing tool.

☒ **D** is incorrect because John the Ripper is a password cracking tool.

66. All of the following tools are used to detect changes in static files *except:*

   A. Blacklight

   B. OSSEC

   C. Tripwire

   D. Firesheep

   ☑ **D.** Firesheep is not a file integrity monitoring (FIM) tool, but instead is a tool used to steal cookies from other user sessions in unprotected Wi-Fi networks.

   ☒ **A, B,** and **C** are incorrect because these are all examples of file integrity monitoring (FIM) tools.

67. Which of the following correctly describes the correct sequence for computer security incident response?

   A. Protect, detect, respond, recover

   B. Identify, protect, detect, respond, recover

   C. Evaluate, detect, eradicate, contain, recover, closure

   D. Detect, initiate, evaluate, contain, eradicate, recover, remediate

   ☑ **D.** The correct sequence for organizing computer security incident response is detect, initiate, evaluate, contain, eradicate, recover, and remediate. This is often followed by a post-incident review.

   ☒ **A** is incorrect because protect, detect, respond, recover are not the correct steps in computer security incident response.

   ☒ **B** is incorrect, as identify, protect, detect, respond, and recover are the pillars of the NIST CSF framework.

   ☒ **C** is incorrect because these are not the correct steps. Namely, evaluate and detect are out of sequence: an incident is first detected and then it is evaluated.

68. Which of the following devices is needed for the creation of a forensically identical hard disk drive?

   A. Diode

   B. Bit locker

   C. Read blocker

   D. Write blocker

   ☑ **D.** A write blocker is a device used to read data from a hard drive whose contents are being evaluated. The write blocker makes it impossible for data to be written to the hard drive.

☒ **A** is incorrect because a diode is an electronic component.

☒ **B** is incorrect because bit locker (properly, BitLocker) is the name of a hard drive encryption program from Microsoft.

☒ **C** is incorrect because there is no such device as a read blocker.

69. Which of the following statements about NIST CSF is true?

   A. NIST CSF is a security controls framework.

   B. NIST CSF is a policy framework for cybersecurity.

   C. NIST CSF is a computer security incident response framework.

   D. NIST CSF is a software development framework.

   ☑ **B.** NIST CSF is a policy framework for cybersecurity that provides guidance for organizations that want to improve their cybersecurity capabilities.

   ☒ **A** is incorrect because NIST CSF is not a controls framework.

   ☒ **C** is incorrect because NIST CSF is not an incident response framework.

   ☒ **D** is incorrect because NIST CSF is not a software development framework.

70. The "right to be forgotten" was first implemented by:

   A. GDPR

   B. Google

   C. NYDFS

   D. Facebook

   ☑ **A.** The "right to be forgotten" is a concept that has been codified in the European General Data Protection Regulation (GDPR). A European citizen can make requests of online service providers and ask that records associated with them be anonymized or expunged.

   ☒ **B, C,** and **D** are incorrect because Google, NYDFS, and Facebook did not first implement the "right to be forgotten."

71. The term "tailgating" most often refers to:

   A. Personnel who prop or shim doors so that others can enter a protected facility without authentication

   B. Personnel who permit others to follow them into a protected facility without authentication

   C. Personnel who follow others into a protected facility without authentication

   D. Personnel who loan their keycards to others to enter a protected facility

   ☑ **C.** Tailgating refers to people who follow others into a protected facility without themselves authenticating with their keycard or other device.

⊠ **A** is incorrect because tailgating does not refer to propping doors open (which is also a potentially serious security violation).

⊠ **B** is incorrect because tailgating is the act of following others in to a protected facility.

⊠ **D** is incorrect because tailgating is not the act of loaning a keycard to another person (which is potentially a serious security violation).

72. A security manager in a large organization has found that the IT department has no central management of privileged user accounts. What kind of a tool should the security manager introduce to remedy this practice?

    A. FAM tools

    B. FIM tools

    C. PAM tools

    D. SIEM tools

    ☑ **C.** Privileged Access Management (PAM) tools are used to centrally control the use of privileged accounts, both for administrative personnel and for service accounts.

    ⊠ **A** is incorrect because file activity monitoring (FAM) tools are not a proper remedy.

    ⊠ **B** is incorrect because file integrity monitoring (FIM) tools are not a proper remedy.

    ⊠ **D** is incorrect, as security information and event management (SIEM) tools are not a proper remedy.

73. A security analyst has determined that some of the OS configuration file alterations have taken place without proper authorization. Which tool did the security analyst use to determine this?

    A. FAM

    B. FIM

    C. PAM

    D. SIEM

    ☑ **B.** The security analyst's use of file integrity monitoring (FIM) tools revealed that files were being changed without authorization. FIM tools do not reveal the subject(s) who altered the files; other means are needed, such as examining login logs.

    ⊠ **A** is incorrect because file activity monitoring (FAM) tools record accesses to files, but not alterations to files.

    ⊠ **C** is incorrect because Privileged Access Management (PAM) tools do not all record administrator activities.

    ⊠ **D** is incorrect, as a security information and event management (SIEM) tool cannot by itself detect file changes, but only in conjunction with file integrity monitoring (FIM) tools.

74. An employee notes that a company document is marked "Confidential." Is it acceptable for the employee to e-mail the document to a party outside the company?

A. Yes, but the document must be encrypted first.

B. Yes, the document can be e-mailed to an outside party in plaintext.

C. This cannot be determined without first consulting the data classification and handling policy.

D. No, the document cannot be e-mailed to any inside or outside party.

☑ **C.** A simple marking on a document such as "Confidential" does not by itself reveal what handling is permitted. An employee would need to consult a data classification and handling policy to see what actions are permitted.

☒ **A, B,** and **D** are incorrect because the "Confidential" document marking does not itself reveal what handling is appropriate. An employee would need to read the data classification and handling policy to know what actions are permitted.

75. An auditor has completed an audit of an organization's use of a tool that generates SSL certificates for its external web sites. The auditor has determined that key management procedures are insufficient and that split custody of the key generation procedure is required. How might this be implemented?

A. Of two engineers, one creates the certificate and the other verifies its creation.

B. Of two engineers, each performs half of the procedure used to create a new certificate.

C. Of two engineers, each has one half of the password required to create a new certificate.

D. Of two engineers, one approves the creation of the certificate and the other creates the certificate.

☑ **C.** Split custody refers to the concept of splitting knowledge of a key task, such as two halves of a safe combination or two halves of a password. This requires that both parties cooperate to complete a sensitive task.

☒ **A** is incorrect because this activity is not a description of split custody, but instead the separation of duties.

☒ **B** is incorrect because this method is not a description of split custody, but instead the separation of duties.

☒ **D** is incorrect because this method is not a description of split custody, but instead the separation of duties.

76. An organization that issues digital certificates recently discovered that a digital certificate was issued to an unauthorized party. What is the appropriate response?

A. Create a CRLF entry.

B. Create a CRL entry.

C. Notify all certificate holders.

D. Call a press conference.

☑ **B.** Creating an entry in the certificate revocation list (CRL) is the appropriate response. In the future, when any party attempts to verify the integrity of the certificate, its presence in the CRL will render it invalid.

☒ **A** is incorrect because CRLF is shorthand for "carriage return, line feed," a character sequence found in text files.

☒ **C** is incorrect because notifying other certificate holders does not remedy the situation.

☒ **D** is incorrect because calling a press conference does not effectively remedy the situation.

77. Why is it important for a web session cookie to be encrypted?

A. Parties that can observe the communication will not be able to hijack the session.

B. Parties that observe the communication will not be able to view the user's password.

C. Third parties will not be able to push unsolicited advertising to the user.

D. The web site operator will not be able to record the user's session.

☑ **A.** When a user's session cookie is encrypted, another party that can observe the communication will not be able to hijack the user's session. The Firesheep tool is a proof-of-concept tool that was developed to demonstrate this technique.

☒ **B** is incorrect because encrypting a session cookie does not imply that the remainder of the communications is also encrypted.

☒ **C** is incorrect because encrypting a session cookie does not prevent advertising.

☒ **D** is incorrect because encrypting a session cookie does not prevent the web site operator from recording the user's session.

78. Why would a hypervisor conceal its existence from a guest OS?

A. To prevent the guest OS from breaking out of the container.

B. To improve the performance of the guest OS.

C. To avoid letting an intruder know that the OS is part of a virtualized environment.

D. To let an intruder know that the OS is part of a virtualized environment.

☑ **C.** Concealing the existence of the virtualized environment may lead an intruder to believe that the OS is running on bare metal. This is a security-by-obscurity tactic that does not prevent an intruder from attempting to break into the hypervisor.

☒ **A** is incorrect because this does not prevent an intruder from breaking out of the guest environment.

☒ **B** is incorrect because this has no effect on guest OS performance.

☒ **D** is incorrect because concealing this does not reveal it to an intruder.

79. How can an organization prevent employees from connecting to the corporate Exchange e-mail environment with personally owned mobile devices?

    A. Implement multifactor authentication.

    B. Permit only Outlook clients to connect to the Exchange server.

    C. Encrypt OWA traffic.

    D. Put the OWA server behind the firewall and VPN switch.

    ☑ **D.** By putting the OWA server behind the firewall and the VPN switch, the organization prevents personally owned mobile devices from reaching the OWA server—provided the VPN switch is configured to permit only company-managed devices to connect.

    ☒ **A** is incorrect because implementing MFA does nothing to prevent personally owned mobile devices from connecting to the Exchange server.

    ☒ **B** is incorrect because there is not a reliable way of preventing non-Outlook clients from connecting to the Exchange server.

    ☒ **C** is incorrect because encrypting OWA traffic does nothing to prevent personally owned mobile devices from connecting to the Exchange server.

80. What is the purpose of the Firesheep tool?

    A. It demonstrates the dangers of non-encrypted web sessions.

    B. It is used as an alternative browser to Firefox to illustrate security concepts.

    C. It is used to analyze firewall rules.

    D. It is used to back up firewall rules.

    ☑ **A.** Firesheep is a proof-of-concept tool used to demonstrate how easy it is to hijack unencrypted user sessions on a Wi-Fi network.

    ☒ **B** is incorrect because Firesheep is not a browser.

    ☒ **C** and **D** are incorrect because Firesheep is not a tool used to manage firewalls.

81. An organization is implementing a new SIEM. How must engineers get log data from systems and devices to the SIEM?

    A. Install agents on all systems and devices.

    B. Send them via Windows events.

    C. Send them via syslog.

    D. Send them via syslog and Windows events.

    ☑ **D.** Any SIEM can accept log entries sent via syslog and Windows events.

    ☒ **A** is incorrect because agents, while they may provide additional functionality, are not required to get basic log data from systems and devices.

    ☒ **B** is incorrect because syslog can also be used to send log data to a SIEM.

    ☒ **C** is incorrect because Windows events can also be used to send log data to a SIEM.

82. What is the appropriate consequence of SOC operators declaring incidents that turn out to be false positives?

   A. Additional training to improve their incident-handling skills.

   B. Termination of employment.

   C. Removal of incident declaration privileges.

   D. No consequence, as false positives are a part of business as usual.

   ☑ A. If SOC operators chronically declare incidents where none exist, this suggest that they need additional training to better recognize and distinguish real incidents from false positives. A false positive now and then should not be a big deal.

   ☒ B is incorrect because termination of employment is an unreasonably harsh consequence.

   ☒ C is incorrect because removal of incident declaration privileges is too harsh.

   ☒ D is incorrect because the number of false positives is high.

About the Online Content

This book comes complete with TotalTester Online customizable practice exam software with 150 practice exam questions.

System Requirements

The current and previous major versions of the following desktop browsers are recommended and supported: Chrome, Microsoft Edge, Firefox, and Safari. These browsers update frequently, and sometimes an update may cause compatibility issues with the TotalTester Online or other content hosted on the Training Hub. If you run into a problem using one of these browsers, please try using another until the problem is resolved.

Your Total Seminars Training Hub Account

To get access to the online content, you will need to create an account on the Total Seminars Training Hub. Registration is free, and you will be able to track all your online content using your account. You may also opt in if you wish to receive marketing information from McGraw-Hill Education or Total Seminars, but this is not required for you to gain access to the online content.

Privacy Notice

McGraw-Hill Education values your privacy. Please be sure to read the Privacy Notice available during registration to see how the information you have provided will be used. You may view our Corporate Customer Privacy Policy by visiting the McGraw-Hill Education Privacy Center. Visit the **mheducation.com** site and click **Privacy** at the bottom of the page.

Single User License Terms and Conditions

Online access to the digital content included with this book is governed by the McGraw-Hill Education License Agreement outlined next. By using this digital content, you agree to the terms of that license.

Access To register and activate your Total Seminars Training Hub account, simply follow these easy steps.

1. Go to this URL: **hub.totalsem.com/mheclaim**

2. To register and create a new Training Hub account, enter your e-mail address, name, and password on the **Register** tab. No further personal information (such as credit card number) is required to create an account.

   If you already have a Total Seminars Training Hub account, enter your e-mail address and password on the **Log in** tab.

3. Enter your Product Key: `vkfd-tptw-wt37`

4. Click to accept the user license terms.

5. For new users, click the **Register and Claim** button to create your account. For existing users, click the **Log in and Claim** button.

   You will be taken to the Training Hub and have access to the content for this book.

Duration of License Access to your online content through the Total Seminars Training Hub will expire one year from the date the publisher declares the book out of print.

Your purchase of this McGraw-Hill Education product, including its access code, through a retail store is subject to the refund policy of that store.

The Content is a copyrighted work of McGraw-Hill Education, and McGraw-Hill Education reserves all rights in and to the Content. The Work is © 2020 by McGraw Hill LLC.

Restrictions on Transfer The user is receiving only a limited right to use the Content for the user's own internal and personal use, dependent on purchase and continued ownership of this book. The user may not reproduce, forward, modify, create derivative works based upon, transmit, distribute, disseminate, sell, publish, or sublicense the Content or in any way commingle the Content with other third-party content without McGraw-Hill Education's consent.

Limited Warranty The McGraw-Hill Education Content is provided on an "as is" basis. Neither McGraw-Hill Education nor its licensors make any guarantees or warranties of any kind, either express or implied, including, but not limited to, implied warranties of merchantability or fitness for a particular purpose or use as to any McGraw-Hill Education Content or the information therein or any warranties as to the accuracy, completeness, correctness, or results to be obtained from, accessing or using the McGraw-Hill Education Content, or any material referenced in such Content or any information entered into licensee's product by users or other persons and/or any material available on or that can be accessed through the licensee's product (including via any hyperlink or otherwise) or as to non-infringement of third-party rights. Any warranties of any kind, whether express or implied, are disclaimed. Any material or data obtained through use of the McGraw-Hill Education Content is at your own discretion and risk and user understands that it will be solely responsible for any resulting damage to its computer system or loss of data.

Neither McGraw-Hill Education nor its licensors shall be liable to any subscriber or to any user or anyone else for any inaccuracy, delay, interruption in service, error or omission, regardless of cause, or for any damage resulting therefrom.

In no event will McGraw-Hill Education or its licensors be liable for any indirect, special or consequential damages, including but not limited to, lost time, lost money, lost profits or good will, whether in contract, tort, strict liability or otherwise, and whether or not such damages are foreseen or unforeseen with respect to any use of the McGraw-Hill Education Content.

TotalTester Online

TotalTester Online provides you with a simulation of the CISA exam. Exams can be taken in Practice Mode or Exam Mode. Practice Mode provides an assistance window with hints, references to the book, explanations of the correct and incorrect answers, and the option to check your answer as you take the test. Exam Mode provides a simulation of the actual exam. The number of questions, the types of questions, and the time allowed are intended to be an accurate representation of the exam environment. The option to customize your quiz allows you to create custom exams from selected domains or chapters, and you can further customize the number of questions and time allowed.

To take a test, follow the instructions provided in the previous section to register and activate your Total Seminars Training Hub account. When you register, you will be taken to the Total Seminars Training Hub. From the Training Hub Home page, select **CISA Practice Exams TotalTester** from the Study drop-down menu at the top of the page, or from the list of Your Topics on the Home page. You can then select the option to customize your quiz and begin testing yourself in Practice Mode or Exam Mode. All exams provide an overall grade and a grade broken down by domain.

Technical Support

For questions regarding the TotalTester or operation of the Training Hub, visit **www.totalsem .com** or e-mail **support@totalsem.com**.

For questions regarding book content, visit **www.mheducation.com/customerservice**.

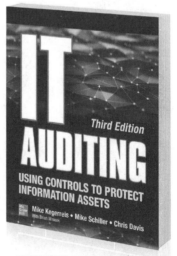